# THE TOUGHEST SHOW ON EARTH

# THE TOUGHEST SHOW ON EARTH

## MY RISE AND REIGN
### AT THE
## METROPOLITAN OPERA

### JOSEPH VOLPE

WITH

### CHARLES MICHENER

 ALFRED A. KNOPF · NEW YORK · 2006

THIS IS A BORZOI BOOK PUBLISHED BY ALFRED A. KNOPF

Copyright © 2006 by Joseph Volpe

www.aaknopf.com

Grateful acknowledgment is made to the following for permission to reprint previously published material.
Weidenfeld & Nicolson: Excerpt from Zeffirelli: An Autobiography by Franco Zeffirelli.
Reprinted by permission of Weidenfeld & Nicolson, an imprint of The Orion Publishing Group.

Library of Congress Cataloging-in-Publication Data
Volpe, Joseph.
The toughest show on earth : my rise and reign at the Metropolitan Opera / by Joseph
Volpe with Charles Michener.—1st ed.
p.   cm.
Includes bibliographical references and index.
ISBN 0-307-26285-5
1. Volpe, Joseph.   2. Opera producers and directors—United States—Biography.
3. Metropolitan Opera (New York, N.Y.)   I. Michener, Charles.   II. Title.
ML429.V65A3 2006
792.5092—dc22
[B]      2005057932

Manufactured in the United States of America

FIRST EDITION

*For Jean*

# CONTENTS

## PREFACE AND ACKNOWLEDGMENTS

This account of my early life and my forty-two years at the Metropolitan Opera is based on my memory, jogged by letters, notes, weekly appointment diaries, news clippings and articles, and the recollections of family members, friends, and colleagues. Re-creating past conversations was easier than anticipated because I retain vivid recollections of the exchanges described herein. I have done my best to convey their flavor and substance as accurately as possible.

My thanks to my collaborator, Charles Michener, go without saying. The book would not have been possible without his narrative organization, his research, and his knowledge of the Met. After an introductory first chapter, part 1 proceeds more or less chronologically. In part 2, I decided not to chronicle my stewardship of the Met season by season, but to view that sixteen-year period prismatically—devoting each chapter to a different aspect of the house or to people who played a significant role in the ongoing drama.

I would like to thank the following people for their invaluable assistance: my sisters, Joan and Anita; my uncle Michael Cavallaro and my aunts Angela D'Amico and Ellen Cavallaro; my son Michael; my son and backstage buddy, Philip; and my colleagues Joe Clark and Stewart Pearce.

In addition, I wish to express my thanks to Bruce Crawford, Jonathan Friend, Steve Diaz, Jr., Sandor Balint, Sylvia Danburg, Michael Parloff, Gloria Watson, and Rob Maher.

Robert Tuggle, the director of The Met's archives, provided much useful historical information. The photographer Nancy Ellison generously allowed me to borrow photographs taken for her splendid album of Met productions during the 2004–2005 season. Entitled *In Grand Style*, this sumptuous book was published by Rizzoli just a few months before *The Toughest Show on Earth*.

My assistant, Mary Pat Fortier, deserves special thanks for her tireless work in gathering information and collating the various drafts and corrections for each chapter. My editor, Shelley Wanger, at Knopf proved to be an ideal reader as I got down to the wire. And of course, I might never have maintained my cheerfulness throughout the whole process without the good humor and understanding of my family, particularly my youngest daughter, Anna, and, of course, my wife Jean.

PART ONE

# THE APPRENTICE

# 1

## "BE PATIENT"

My maternal grandmother, Marianna Cavallaro, spoke no English, and whenever she came to babysit for me and my sisters while our parents were out, she'd go over to a shelf in the living room, take down a record album, and say to me in Italian, "Joey, put this on."

I was only five or six, and carrying the bulky volume of 78s over to the Victrola wasn't easy. But I liked climbing up on a stool, removing a shiny black disc from its sleeve, hearing it plop into place, and then positioning the needle in the groove. My grandmother always sat in the same place—an armchair with a straight back that made it impossible to slouch. She wanted me to sit nearby on the sofa, perfectly still. But I hated sitting still. Once the music started and my grandmother closed her eyes, I slid down to the floor, leaned against the sofa, and imagined myself somewhere else.

The music was always the same—Mascagni's one-act opera *Cavalleria Rusticana*, which is set in a Sicilian village like the one from which my grandmother had come to America, not long after the opera was written, at the turn of the century. Nobody told me that this was "opera." Even if anyone had, I wouldn't have paid attention. This music belonged to my grandmother. It made her happy. She always insisted on listening to the whole album—there were perhaps eight or ten discs—and she never fell asleep. I guess she picked that particular chair so she wouldn't miss a note.

I couldn't fall asleep either. Before I knew it, the needle had reached the center of the disc, the loud, scratchy voices had stopped, and my grandmother was saying quietly in Italian, "Change the record, Joey."

Looking back, I find it interesting that my grandmother never asked my older sister, Joan, to participate in those musical séances—this was a job only for me. Was she sending me a message? Was this how it all began?

The thought that I could one day run the Metropolitan Opera first crossed my mind when Rudolf Bing retired as general manager in 1972. At the time, I was still only master carpenter, in charge of the seventy or eighty men who set up and dismantled the Met's stage for every performance. I'd wrestled with budgets. I'd demonstrated a knack for learning quickly on the job. I was good at solving problems and handling emergencies. I felt I knew better than anyone how the Met worked, mechanically and logistically.

The Met is the biggest performing arts institution in the world. Every year it presents some 240 performances of thirty or so different operas, each with an international cast and elaborate sets. It employs more than two thousand people and has annual operating expenses of more than $220 million. To keep it going requires not just the muscle and the know-how of carpenters, stagehands, painters, designers, electricians, and prop men, but also the skills of musicians, singers, vocal coaches, dancers, ballet masters, stage directors, conductors, artistic administrators, marketing and publicity people, and the efforts of the Met's board of directors, which raises the funds to pay for what the box office doesn't. In 1972, I didn't really understand how many of those jobs were done. Nor did I have the slightest idea how Rudolf Bing had managed to coordinate everyone during the two decades he'd been in charge.

Still, I thought that the top job at the Met—which means the top job in the opera world—was not out of reach. I felt that in some mysterious sense I'd been chosen by Rudolf Bing himself. Not that he ever hinted as much. He was too much the aristocrat, out of a Viennese operetta. But on more than one occasion, he'd taken me aside to offer advice in a way that suggested he had bigger things in mind for me.

One of our earliest encounters took place at the end of my first season as master carpenter. In those days, the Met went on an eight-week tour every spring. Boston, Cleveland, Atlanta, Memphis, Dallas, Minneapolis, Detroit—for years the company had been playing to packed houses beyond the Hudson River. That year, we opened with *La Gioconda* in Atlanta. The stars were the soprano Renata Tebaldi and the tenor Franco Corelli. After the performance, Mr. Bing came backstage and said, "Mr. Volpe, I'd like to see you in the morning."

The next morning, he led me into one of the principals' dressing rooms and closed the door. "Mr. Volpe," he said, "I think you're doing a wonderful job. I'm going to give you a raise of fifty dollars a week." That came as a huge relief, but then he said, "So how did Mr. Corelli do last night?"

"Excuse me?" I said.

"How was his behavior backstage?"

Before a performance, Franco Corelli was always a wreck, complaining that his girdle was too tight or fighting with his wife, Loretta, who never left his side until he was able to summon the courage to make his entrance. "You didn't notice?" Mr. Bing went on. "Franco Corelli, one of the most important tenors in the world, and you didn't *notice?*"

"I guess I was too busy with the scenery."

"Well," Mr. Bing said, "the next time I ask you about Mr. Corelli's behavior, you will have noticed!"

Rudolf Bing had his finger on the pulse of the Met. His retirement, after the 1971–1972 season, gave way to twenty years of turbulence. First came the death of his successor, Goeran Gentele, in a car crash in Sardinia. This was followed by a brief, rudderless period under Gentele's assistant, Schuyler Chapin. Next came the stormy triumvirate of John Dexter, the brilliant head of production; James Levine, the boy-wonder music director; and Anthony Bliss, a patrician estate lawyer who ran the Met out of a sense of family duty. Those years were marred by backstage intrigue, financial instability, and bitter fights with the Met's seventeen unions, culminating in the cancellation of the 1980 fall season—a labor lockout ordered by the Met's imperious board. The brief reign of Levine as artistic director and of

Bruce Crawford, a smooth, opera-loving advertising executive, as general manager, began in 1985. Bruce became something of a godfather to me. I admired his velvet manner, but it wasn't a style I would emulate.

Along the way, I'd been promoted from master carpenter to technical director to operations director (responsible for backstage budgets and labor negotiations) to assistant manager (in charge of everything except artistic matters and fund-raising). None of these advancements came without an objection from someone higher up; in each case, I had to swallow my pride. But I had been at the center of everything—watching, learning, and not keeping my mouth shut. In 1988, Crawford decided to return to Madison Avenue. I felt that I was his logical successor. Instead, the Met's board chose an arts bureaucrat named Hugh Southern whose only qualifications for running the company seemed to be that he'd never seen the front office of a great opera house—but he sported an English accent, courtesy of Cambridge University. Those qualifications turned out to be not quite enough. Southern was dismissed after seven months.

In the summer of 1990, Crawford, who was now the chairman of the Met's executive committee, came into my office to tell me that I was being promoted to "general director." For a moment I was speechless. Then I snapped, "Why not 'general manager'?"

Bruce explained that the board had decided to reinstate the triumvirate model of management. I would run the house internally. Jimmy Levine would remain artistic director. Marilyn Shapiro, who had been in charge of marketing and development, was now executive director for external affairs. We would all report to the president of the board, Louise Humphrey, a Cleveland heiress who had a plantation in Florida, a horse farm in Kentucky, and a summer compound in Maine. Hugh Southern had gone quail shooting at Louise's Florida spread. I'd never shot a quail in my life.

"Maybe I shouldn't accept it," I said.

"Joe," Bruce said, "it will all come to you in the end."

"Who gets the room at the end of the hall?" I asked, referring to the office from where Rudolf Bing had reigned.

Bruce said, "You'll stay where you are. The general manager's office will become a conference room."

"That's ridiculous," I said. "It works perfectly well as a conference room right now—with a real general manager behind the desk. It's like being asked to run the Met with one hand tied behind my back!"

"Trust me, Joe," Bruce said. "It will all work out. Be patient."

I knew that my blunt manner had ruffled a few feathers on the Met's board. After one board meeting, Bruce had taken me aside and said, "Joe, what you have to say is right. But it's the way you say it . . ."

During the search that coughed up Southern, I'd also heard that various board members were raising other objections about me. Would Volpe, the ex-carpenter, be able to talk to the singers? Would Volpe be able to "represent" the Met at gala fund-raising functions? Did Volpe have the right stuff . . . socially? Although my grandparents had come to America from the country where opera was born, I had never studied music. I didn't have a degree in arts management. I'd barely graduated from high school.

Everything I knew about running an opera house I had figured out for myself, starting by using my hands. I'd stayed at the Met for twenty-five years because I'd come to love opera. The Met had been my undergraduate education, my graduate school, my Ph.D. program. I considered the Met "family." Now I was supposed to take Bruce's advice: "Be patient."

For someone like me, that wasn't going to be easy.

## 2

# ALWAYS ON THE GO

In the den of my apartment in New York is a photograph of my parents' wedding reception. The date is September 8, 1935. The setting is Trommer's banquet hall at 1632 Bushwick Avenue, in Brooklyn. There are several hundred people in the high-ceilinged main dining room—the women with corsages, the men with slicked-down hair and dressed in double-breasted suits. At the head table are twenty-two people—the bride and groom and their immediate families. My parents—my mother in white satin, my father in white tie and tails—look happy and proud. There isn't a blonde in sight.

And there isn't an empty place. A thousand people were invited, and when some of them didn't show up, my grandfather went outside and brought in strangers off the street. He wanted a full house. I would have done the same thing.

Basilio Cavallaro was born in 1881 in the mountain village of Cesarò, in Sicily. At the age of twenty-six he came to America, arriving at Ellis Island on March 17, 1907. Soon, he met and married my grandmother, Marianna Cerami, who had arrived the previous year from a similar Sicilian village, Petralia Soprana. They settled in Lower Manhattan, where my grandfather started a little storefront business that made men's clothing. Another family photograph shows the shop as it was in 1914. B. CAVALLARO TAILORING CO. the letters read, and in front of the store is my mother astride a pony—one with a Sicilian pedigree, no doubt. My grandfather worked hard, enlarged his business, and in 1925 founded the Italian Coat Contractors Association, which eventually became the Greater Clothing Contractors Association, representing the interests of all the men's clothing manufacturers in New York.

*My mother at three in front of her father's shop, 1914*

My grandfather had highly placed friends among the police and politicians, especially Mayor Fiorello LaGuardia, who was a frequent guest at the family's three-story brick house in Jamaica, Queens. The only memento I have of my grandfather is his Colt revolver. I grew up with stories about how it had come in handy when mobsters tried to muscle in on the men's clothing business.

My grandfather's house had a big front porch, two stone lions on guard, a dark walnut stairway, and a dining room that seemed to stretch for miles. At Sunday dinners, my grandfather stood at the head of the table and surveyed his family, which included more aunts

*My maternal grandparents, Basilio and Marianna, 1920s*

*My parents, standing at rear, at their wedding reception,*
*Trommer's, Brooklyn, 1935*

than I could count. Among his eleven children was my mother, who was born on July 16, 1911. She was baptized Fortunata Angela Carmela Cavallaro. There were always at least twenty people seated around big bowls of pasta under stuffed pheasants mounted above the sideboard. My grandfather was an avid hunter, and his favorite hunting companion was his Irish setter, Red. When Red was accidentally shot and killed by another hunter, the wailing around that table went on for hours.

As a little girl, my mother—like her mother—spoke no English. When she started going to school she was made to sit in the corner and wear a dunce cap. She eventually went to Hunter College, where she earned a master's degree that enabled her to become a first-grade schoolteacher. Later, she taught in a predominantly black school in Glen Cove, Long Island, where she was known as a stickler for proper English. After my older sister was born, Mom wanted only English spoken in the house. No one could stop my father from speaking Italian. But Dad made it clear that none of his three children would learn Italian. After all, we were American.

My father's parents were immigrants from Avellino, a town outside Naples. I was named after my paternal grandfather, Joseph Michael Volpe, who was as quiet and reserved as my grandfather Basilio was outgoing and gregarious. For most of his life he had a tailor's shop in Red Bank, New Jersey. I remember very little about him or about my grandmother Nunziata, except that she was a great one for complaining about her health.

My father—his given names were Michael Joseph—was the oldest of five children. At a young age, he started Associated Clothing, which made men's suits and overcoats. Before long, he had a small factory at 142–144 West Fourteenth Street, which had several hundred employees. (The building is now occupied by the Pratt Institute.) A few years later, he opened another factory in Atlantic City. My father did so well that he was able to pay the law school tuition of his favorite younger brother.

My uncle Joe went on to become an important Washington lawyer. He was the general counsel of the Tennessee Valley Authority and, later, the general counsel for the Atomic Energy Commission. In the latter job, he became a close adviser to J. Robert Oppenheimer, who led the team that built the first atomic bomb at Los Alamos. After the war, Uncle Joe was counsel to "Oppie" during the House Un-American Activities Committee hearings, at which the physicist was questioned about his prewar associations with the Communist Party. When Oppenheimer, who had a quick tongue, said something during a congressional hearing on atomic energy that made one of the commissioners, Lewis Strauss, look foolish, my uncle—a very judicious man—cautioned him to watch his mouth. When I grew older, Uncle Joe would have given me the same advice. Like Oppie, I probably wouldn't have taken it.

My father ran his business in a tailored suit, white shirt, and tie. (I dress the same way at the Met.) Be-

*My father, back row, second from right;*
*Uncle Joe, second from left*

*My parents during their courtship*

hind his dapper appearance he was as tough as they come. He had gone to an Irish parochial school, where his one friend was the only other Italian kid in his class, Constantine Stigliano. Every time there was a discipline problem, my father or Connie got blamed because they were Italian. One day, a nun rapped my father on the knuckles for something he hadn't done. He punched her in the nose. After that, the Irish kids were really after him, and I grew up hearing tales about how he and Connie had to fight their way out of the schoolyard. Later, like his father-in-law, my father carried a revolver. He had to, he said, because he walked around with so much business cash.

But he also had a softer side. I have the letters that he and my mother wrote to each other when he was courting her. At the time, he belonged to his prospective father-in-law's clothing association, in whose offices my mother had a summer job as a switchboard operator. There was something forbidden about their romance: the letters refer to "stolen kisses" and fears that someone will catch them "embracing." Or maybe they'd just seen too many movies. In one letter, my father writes that he's worried he might not be "good enough" for his prospective mother-in-law. In another, he begs "my Fortunata" to steal away from her family for a Sunday outing on a "bicycle built for two."

I was born in Madison Park Hospital, in Brooklyn, on July 2, 1940. I was the second of three children. (My older sister, Joan, was born in 1939; my younger sister, Anita, in 1945.) On my birth certificate are two baby footprints; each measures two and a half inches. I don't know whether the size of my feet had anything to do with it, but when I was a kid I was always on the go. My father loved cameras, and our family outings are all documented in photographs and home movies—weekends in Atlantic City; spring vacations in St. Petersburg, Florida; summers at my grandparents' place in Bayville, Long Island, where my uncles dug for clams in the shallow water during the day and in the evening everyone sat around a big bonfire on the beach.

The houses I grew up in had one feature in common—an enormous dining room. Every Sunday, the entire Cavallaro clan and their friends—sometimes as many as forty, in all—gathered for Italian meals in the dining room off the kitchen at the rear of my grandfather's house in Bayville. They all talked at the top of their lungs. My father liked to say that my aunt Irene and my aunt Cecelia could carry on two different conversations at the same time with at least four people—"a Cavallaro trait," he said. It's a trait that has served me well at the Met.

Looking at the home movies and family photographs, I'm struck by how little evidence there is of me. Perhaps it's because I was always somewhere else, busy with my projects, which generally involved taking something apart, putting it back together, and getting into trouble. One day, in the first house that I can remember—a two-bedroom apartment in Elmhurst, Queens—I found a screwdriver in my father's toolbox (which he never opened), removed the lock from the apartment's front door, dismantled it, and put all the pieces on the floor. I was four years old. My mother almost never raised her voice, but when she saw what I had done, she hollered, "Joey, you put that back the way it was!" I waited until she returned to the kitchen, since I didn't want to be seen obeying orders. Then I reinstalled the lock. The incident was never spoken of again. But when my mother saw the lock back in place, the look on her face was clear: she was proud that I'd been able to fix a problem that I shouldn't have created in the first place.

That summer, my grandfather bought a big black Packard. I decided that it needed to be a different color. I found a can of paint and painted one of the doors white, transfixed by the difference it made. When my grandfather arrived, while I was still at work, he just stood there and watched. Then my father turned up and blew his stack. My grandfather grabbed him and said, "Don't touch the boy!" He must have thought I was the next Michelangelo.

When I was five, my father bought an old, four-bedroom brick house in Bayside, Queens. Before we could move in, though, the house needed certain alterations, starting with a new dining room that could accommodate a dining table big enough for the Cavallaros. Whenever my father went over to the new house to see how the work was going, he'd take me along. I loved picking up the carpenters' tools and enjoyed the heavy feel of them in my hand. My father and I usually stopped off in Corona, Queens to buy fresh mozzarella and anchovies. Another addition was a closet for storing Italian olives.

The furnace room in the new house became my secret laboratory for bending glass and making all sorts of mechanical devices. In my bedroom on the third floor, I laid out an electric train, installed locks on the drawers, and set traps to stop anyone from entering uninvited. I caught hell from my father when a pan of water I'd set over the door came crashing down on Aunt Irene, who always wanted to see what I was up to.

The radio in the living room was usually on, and I liked adding to the mischief of *Amos 'n' Andy* by collecting dead birds and mice in the backyard and putting them in the oven. Then I'd wait for my mother to open the oven door and scream. She couldn't be sure that I was responsible for the mice, but there was no other explanation for the birds.

I hated school. One Indian summer day in October of 1950, I sat in the fifth-grade classroom at Bayside P.S. 31 thinking about how to get out of there. While the rest of the kids were busy with their work, I went up to the teacher and told her that I felt sick. Chicken pox was going around, so the teacher sent me to the school nurse. The nurse touched my forehead and sent me home. I felt fine.

The next morning, my sister Joan and I walked to school. I lingered near the back of the schoolyard. As the other kids were filing in, I ran around the side of the building. Across the street was a field with grass as tall as I was. For the rest of the morning I hid there, wondering what to do. Finally, I started walking and soon I came to a street where a row of new houses was going up. The air was filled with the noise of hammering. I sat down under a tree. I forgot about lunch. The men no sooner got the flooring and the framing done on one house than they were on to the next one, where they did exactly the same thing. I had spent hours in my father's clothing shop, but this was different. There, the workers sat in one place doing the same boring thing over and over again. These men were constantly on the move, transforming piles of wood into houses.

When I got home, my mother, as usual, asked how my day had gone. "Fine," I said. I hung around to see if

*With my father in Atlantic City, 1948*

someone at school had called about my absence, but nobody had. I guess I hadn't been missed.

The next morning, I returned to the construction site. For the next two and a half weeks, I sat under the tree and watched the carpenters at work. One morning, a watchman came over and asked me why I wasn't in school. I told him I had the measles, and he didn't bother me again. Then, a few days later, a cop appeared and asked me my name and where I lived. This time, I couldn't lie. He grabbed me by the elbow and marched me home.

My father had always been tough on me. Whenever he discovered something broken or out of place, I got the blame—never my sisters. My mother, on the other hand, was my patron saint. In her eyes, I could do no wrong. When I told her that I'd been playing hooky, she said, "You'll have to tell it to the authorities, Joey."

The next day, I had my story ready for the assistant principal. I hadn't been coming to school, I said, because the air in the classroom was unhealthy. The assistant principal clearly didn't believe a word of it. The day was warm, and a fan was blowing on his desk. I decided to embellish my story: "And the class doesn't even have a fan," I said. The assistant principal clearly couldn't believe what he was hearing. "Dismissed" was all he could say.

I must have been punished for missing seventeen straight days of school, but I can't remember how. I've blanked out everything about that year except the days I spent under the tree, watching the houses go up.

When I was eleven, we moved to a bigger house in Glen Cove, on Long Island's north shore. There I built my first seafaring vessel—a ten-foot plywood skiff that immediately sank to the bottom of the Sound. My father bought a rowboat, and I loved taking it out to a spot where the only noise was that of the gulls. I'd pull up the oars, stretch out, look at the sky, and drift. Our house abutted much larger properties, including the Whitney estate. One day I found a sailboat on the Whitney property. It was up on pilings—forty feet long and all wood. I admired its lines and imagined how it would look with the sails up, and with me at the tiller. Mrs. Whitney came down from the big house and said, "You like that boat, don't you?" I said I sure did. "Well," she said, "you can have it, then. It's yours."

I raced home to tell my father what a wonderful project this would be for me. He said, "What, do you have a screw loose?"

I convinced him that Mrs. Whitney meant what she'd said, but he shook his head. "You can't have that boat, Joey," he said. "How are you going to take care of it?"

The boat stayed where it was, unused, until I was out of high school. Then it vanished. Mrs. Whitney had died. The big house was torn down. The estate was being divided up into a development called Whitney Circle. I asked a man who was building one of the new houses about the boat. He said that it had been chopped up and buried in the sand. I never went down to that part of the beach again.

At Glen Cove High, I excelled at making a spectacle of myself. I was always coming to school in a crazy outfit that I'd had specially made at my father's shop—for example, a blue-and-white-striped jacket that hung to my knees and bright red trousers with a bright red shirt. These outfits infuriated my science teacher. The less he liked how I looked, the more I liked it.

The population of Glen Cove was made up of wealthy white families who lived, as we did, on the "gold coast," far less affluent black families who lived in shacks in an area called Cottage Row, and several other ethnic groups. Most of my friends lived on Cottage Row. They appreciated my fashion sense, as well as my expertise with stink bombs—a concoction of sulfur and magnesium that sent everyone running to open a window after I'd poured the mixture into the science teacher's inkwell.

When the school organized a variety show, I formed a doo-wop group with my three best black buddies, Laurie Weng, "Junebug" Buchanan, and Ralphie Woodbury. I sang bass—I was good at carrying a tune—and we developed a repertoire of three songs: "Sincerely," "Work with Me, Annie," and "Annie Had a Baby (Can't Work No More)." I was in my red-on-red period, and we had all the moves down. Our first performance went so well that we decided to stage a second one in the lobby of the Glen Cove movie house. We hadn't gotten very far into "Sincerely" when the manager showed up and threw us out, thus putting an end to my singing career.

When my father caught me acting like a big shot, he'd say, "Joey, you may have a little more money than other kids, but that doesn't make you better. You're no different from anybody else." After he sold his clothing business, my father ran the Glen Cove Housing Authority. I have a picture of him handing out Christmas presents to the black kids who lived in a low-income apartment complex.

I was the only white kid who got invited to the black "socials." (If you were white, you went to a "party.") I attracted some strange looks, but those events were great. I loved the laughter and the kidding around. I liked walking home from school with a black girl named Zola Moses, a star on the track team whose skin was the color of charcoal. When my lighter-skinned buddy Laurie spotted us from across the street, he'd yell out, "Hey, Zola, you better get your black butt out of the sun, 'cause you're getting darker and darker!" I felt a great bond with them.

In high school, I became something of an activist. Glen Cove High had what they called the "sacred lawn"—a patch of green between the building's two wings where nobody was allowed to set foot. I set foot on it and got caught. Instead of accepting the punishment, I organized a protest. I got the support of the class officers, and the lawn was desanctified.

I finished my freshman year near the bottom of the class and was summoned to a meeting with Mr. Clark, the school's golf coach and guidance counselor. He pulled out my record and said, "Joe, when you came to this school, you had a brain. I look at these results, and they're really very disappointing. You don't work. You're in trouble more often than not. What are we going to do about it?" I said, "Mr.

Clark, you've just put your finger on something. If I came in with a good brain and you failed to develop it, is that my fault?" He said, "You know, Joe. You're a wise guy. And you're going to be a gold-bricker all your life. You'll never amount to anything." I said, "I hear you're a great golf coach, Mr. Clark, but you should get out of the counseling business." For that remark I was given a week's detention.

My parents decided to send me off to boarding school—Stony Brook Prep, an hour away. The school had been founded in 1922 with the motto "Character Before Career." Prayers were said before every meal. The teachers were great, and I completed my sophomore year with high honors. But I missed being at home. That year, my father developed phlebitis and had to stop working. I wanted to be with him and my mother, even if it meant returning to Glen Cove High. At least my black buddies were glad to see me back.

In fact, I was a goldbricker, but only in school. I liked working and earning a wage, even if it was just pocket money. When I was twelve, I got a job at my father's clothing factory on West Fourteenth Street. I operated a contraption that put buttonholes in men's suits and overcoats. Sweatshop would accurately describe the place. More than a hundred people worked from eight o'clock in the morning until five in the afternoon, bent over noisy machines in temperatures that approached a hundred degrees on a good day. I was bored stiff by the buttonholes, but I liked being part of a process that involved so many different jobs—from the unloading of fabric off the freight elevator to the cutting, sewing, making of collars and lapels, sleeve fitting, and pressing.

And I loved watching my father at work. He occupied an office at the center of the floor, from where he could see everything. He had an aura of strength and fairness about him that made everyone feel secure, and he issued orders with a polite formality that made every-one want to do his or her best. When someone fell down on the job, my father would call that person into his office for a face-to-face meeting, during which his commanding voice carried throughout the shop. Only two people in the shop had names that didn't end in a vowel. One was my father's right-hand man, the foreman Charlie Porter. Charlie had two responsibilities: supervising the flow of goods and keeping me out of trouble. I was especially taken with a very cool black fellow whom I knew only as James. He maintained my father's

Cadillac, did odd jobs, and organized the evenings at our house in Glen Cove when my father entertained his business associates. Later, when my father's phlebitis forced him to sell the business, James opened a storefront church in Harlem. Everyone knew that James was a real operator, but no one had known that he was a man of the cloth.

When I turned fourteen, I got a summer job framing pictures at a shop in Glen Cove for the minimum wage of sixty-five cents an hour. The next summer, I cut grass for $1.50. For two summers I worked at the Maserati Corporation of America. I started on a milling machine and then became an apprentice in the automobile division. The manager, Jerry Titus, liked my enthusiasm. I never came in late or left early, and I needed to be told only once how to do something. Jerry was my first mentor. He was a great mechanic who later became a top troubleshooter at General Motors. He took me along on his rounds of the racetracks in the tristate area, where we tuned up Maseratis and other high-speed cars. It was exhilarating to be in the pit during a big race, poised to change a tire or refuel an engine in a matter of seconds.

Before I left for Stony Brook Prep, I went with two friends to a junkyard and bought my first car, a Plymouth two-seater. My share of the purchase price was fifteen dollars. Since none of us was old enough for a driver's license, we hid the car in a grove at the beach. I hadn't been at my new school for very long when my mother called. "Joey?" she said. "Do you have a car? The police found an old Plymouth down at the beach." Back it went to the junkyard. As soon as I turned sixteen, I got my driver's license and bought a 1949 Ford sedan for $450 and fixed it up. I next owned a 1953 Oldsmobile and a 1936 Nash. They both needed a lot of work, but I had no interest in a new car.

During my junior year, I got a job pumping gas at a Shell station for a dollar an hour. My boss was a man named Mo Klein. Mo taught me a lesson about negotiating that was to come in handy many years later when I handled labor issues at the Met. Mo's station was at the bottom of a little hill, and one day a guy rolled in, motor off. Mo and I looked at the engine of his car and told him what was wrong.

"How much is it going to cost?" the man asked.

Mo said, "You want one price or ten?"

The guy said, "What do you mean? One price!"

Mo gave him a price, and the guy said, "You crazy? I can get it fixed for fifty dollars less someplace else."

Mo said, "Go ahead."

"What do you mean?"

"Take your car out of here and get someone else to fix it."

"I can't."

"I forgot to tell you," Mo said, "the one-day storage fee is fifty dollars."

The negotiation was over. We fixed the car.

Mo was also a slum landlord. He owned many of the shacks on Cottage Row, and his properties were always getting violations for broken windows. One day he said to me, "How would you like to make some extra money repairing windows?" I said, "Sure, but not for a dollar an hour." We agreed on a fee of $4.50 a window. There were so many violations that I hired a crew. Before long, we were doing house painting. Then evictions. We'd go over to the poor family's place and put their stuff out in the street. I felt terrible, so I bought an old Dodge pickup and made a deal to cart the stuff off to a friend of the evicted family. Going to school became an afterthought—my favorite teacher was a slum landlord.

At seventeen, I started my own business—an Amoco station and auto repair shop in a vacated garage a hundred yards from Mo's station. My uncle Mike Cavallaro, who was an accountant, helped me set up a corporation; my father arranged a bank loan; and a hotshot local lawyer named Nate Zausmer did the paperwork. The place opened in January of 1958. Winter is a good time for gas stations, and I got a lot of action. To get even more, I started a gas war, cutting the price of gasoline to three cents less than what Mo was charging. Mo and the other station owners fought back. One morning, when I got to work, I discovered that my gas and water hoses had been cut. But I refused to raise my prices. Eventually, I joined the local association of gas station owners, and peace was restored.

When I graduated from high school, my father wanted me to go to college. He said, "Joey, you're not like me. You could be a professional man, like your uncle Joe. Look at the success he's made in Washington."

I said, "But Dad, I am like you. I already have my own business. I don't have time for college."

He persisted, so I applied to St. John's University, in Queens.

Maybe they were having a bad year, but I got in. I lasted a week and then came home. "I just can't do it," I said to my father. This time, he didn't push it.

I went back to my Amoco station. I worked every day—seven in the morning until ten at night, Monday through Saturday, and eight to three on Sunday. It was a hard life, but it was mine.

In those days, everyone paid in cash, and it was satisfying to go to the bank every two days to make a deposit. I also liked knowing that my pumps were shared by everyone in Glen Cove, from the Gold Coast to Cottage Row. I had two skilled, hard-working mechanics working for me, and in 1960 I was named the most successful young businessman in Nassau County. I was on top of the world.

*At my Amoco station, at eighteen with my dad*

A sharp-looking young woman came in one day for gas. Her name was Mary Ann Maher. She was bright, a nurse at the Glen Cove hospital, and she had a great Irish sense of humor. We dated for a year, and then I proposed. I was twenty and Mary Ann was twenty-one when we got married. In March of 1961, our son Michael—the first of our five children—was born. As I'd told my father, I had to get on with things.

One Sunday afternoon, a gas leak started a fire in the repair shop. It wasn't until the volunteer fire department had the blaze under control that I remembered that my 1936 Nash was inside the shop. There was too much smoke for the firemen to go in after it, so they took axes to the building and salvaged the Nash. The next day, I called Nate Zausmer for advice on how to deal with the insurance company. As usual, Nate raced up in his big Buick and slammed on the brakes, missing the gas pump by inches.

"Joe," he said, "you blew it. Your first mistake was to call the fire department. You should have gone out to lunch and let the whole place burn to the ground. Then, when the insurance people showed up, there would be no discussion."

I reopened the shop, at 50 percent capacity, and installed temporary plywood doors. When Nate roared up again, he asked who had paid for the wood. I told him that I had. He said, "That's your second mistake. You have to learn how to get things without spending your own money."

Nate was right. The insurance company and I fought over everything. I was going to be left with very little. It was time to get on with something else.

# 3

## KING FAROUK

The person who may have taught me more than any-one about how to run an opera house never, as far as I know, set foot in one. Eddie Lapidus was the head electrician at the Booth Theatre and the Astor movie house in Times Square. Orson Welles–like in size and personality, Eddie missed his true calling: he should have made his living on the stage instead of behind it. He weighed over three hundred pounds and he would have looked naked without the big cigar he was always either chewing on or waving around. His nickname was "King Farouk" or just "Frook."

I met Eddie in October of 1961, a few weeks after I got a job as a stagehand, moving scenery around at the Morosco Theatre, on West Forty-fifth Street. My father-in-law, John Maher, who had been a Broadway stagehand for years, had asked me to help him unload the sets for a new show that was opening at the Morosco—*Blood, Sweat and Stanley Poole*, by James and William Goldman, starring Peter Fonda. I had been about to take a new job helping a friend of my father's in Parsippany, New Jersey, operate a mini-conglomerate of batting ranges, miniature golf courses, and a shop that manufactured baseball-throwing machines. But my heart wasn't in it. My wife had her nursing job in Glen Cove, and New Jersey seemed like Mars. Unloading theatrical sets off a truck and putting them in a grimy backstage area wouldn't be everyone's idea of how to spend their Sunday, but for me it opened up a strange, wonderful new world. I took to it at once.

Working with theatrical scenery is like solving an enormous three-dimensional puzzle. I loved unloading the different pieces and figuring out how they all fit together to create someone's living room, a garden, a street—all in a matter of hours. I discovered that I had a knack for looking at stage plans and knowing immediately where everything should go. Before long, I graduated to the "flies"—the grid above the proscenium. The old Morosco was a "hemp house"—in reference to the ropes the "fly men" pulled to raise and lower the curtain and scenic drops, just like on an old sailing ship. In those days, you pulled hemp, not nylon. Some of the fly men wore gloves, but I didn't because two grizzled veterans of the trade advised me to toughen up my hands. Over the next couple of years, I learned the ropes on, among other shows, Arthur Kopit's *Oh, Dad, Poor Dad, Mamma's Hung You in the Closet and I'm Feelin' So Sad;* Peter Shaffer's *The Private Ear* and *The Public Eye;* Lee Strasberg's production of Chekhov's *Three Sisters;* and, over at the Schubert, Harold Rome's musical about the garment district, *I Can Get It for You Wholesale,* starring a tough waif from Brooklyn named Barbra Streisand. Everyone in New York was going crazy over her star-is-born performance in that show, but I was more interested in what was going on behind the curtain. I didn't want to be like Henry Fonda's son; I wanted to be like Eddie Lapidus.

*Eddie Lapidus, my "rabbi"*

One day, Eddie came over to the Morosco to light Samuel Taylor's *First Love.* From then on, he became my rabbi. Eddie was a very smart man. He'd gone to Yale and become a chemical engineer at Pfizer. During World War II, he served in the army as a supply sergeant. After the war, he discovered that he could make more money as a union stagehand than as a Pfizer chemist.

Calling Eddie an electrician was like saying that James Bond was in the import/export business. Eddie was a natural politician, an expert in union contracts, and a born entrepreneur. He always had a million sidelines going, and he always needed somebody to help out. "Are you interested in some extra dough?" he'd say, and I'd run over to the Astor to help his company, Broadway Premieres, set up a searchlight or lay down a red carpet for the movie premiere that night. There was never any problem about permits with Eddie. Everything went like clockwork—the traffic lanes were closed, the crowd was controlled. Eddie had "friends in the City," especially in the police department. They'd all been taken care of. If the movie screen at the old Paramount needed replacing, Eddie would tell the manager, "I have just the guy for you"—me. Eddie got me a job at Feller Scenic Studios, in the Bronx, where I helped to build sets on days when there was no matinee at the Morosco. After all, I had a family to raise.

Through Eddie's brother-in-law, the night man at the Astor, I got a job changing movie titles on the marquee at the Astor, the Victoria, and the Paramount. My income rose to the point where I was able to make a down payment on a four-bedroom ranch house near my parents' place in Glen Cove. Changing a marquee took four to five hours. Before you put up the new titles, you had to open the marquee's panels, replace burned-out bulbs, and wash acres of glass. I did this with another stagehand on quiet nights and stormy nights, hot nights and freezing nights. It was surreal being out in Times Square at two in the morning when our only companions were the drunks who would have knocked us down if we hadn't fortified the ladders with garbage cans. We usually didn't finish until four-thirty or five in the morning. I spent more nights in a flophouse around the corner, too tired to worry about the cockroaches, than I did in my new bedroom in Glen Cove.

Eddie's favorite restaurants were the Great Wall, a Chinese place with a menu as long as its namesake, and the Piccadilly Hotel, for its smorgasbord. After Saturday matinees, Eddie and I would head to the Piccadilly, where he'd pile up his plate with shrimp because, at home, his wife was a strict observer of the Jewish dietary law against eating shellfish. He was always pontificating between mouthfuls of shrimp about how I could improve myself. He'd say, "You know what your biggest problem is, Joe? What's in here" (he'd point to his forehead) "is *here*" (he'd point to his lips). "You don't know how to keep your mouth shut." I once ran into some stagehands on the train to Glen Cove. They were trashing Eddie, and I almost threw a punch in his defense. When I told Eddie about the incident, he said. "Are you stupid? Next time agree with them. Tell them I *am* a sonuvabitch. That way you'll find out where they're coming from."

One day, Eddie was confronting a stagehand who had just lit a cigar. He waved me over for a tutorial: "Murray," he said, "there's only one guy at this theater with a cigar, and that's me. You want to work here? Get rid of the cigar and work with both hands." You did what Eddie told you to do. I once heard him say to a stage manager, "I don't care what the actors or the director says, that curtain has to come down at ten twenty, not ten thirty, so I can make my train to Baldwin Harbor." The curtain came down at 10:20.

Baldwin Harbor, on Long Island, was where Eddie lived with his wife and their two daughters. I was the "son" he looked after in the city. We were having spareribs at the Great Wall when he said to me, "You know, Joe, you could be doing better than this. You should be in the union." In those days, Local One of the International Alliance of Theatrical Stage Employees was harder to get into than the exclusive Piping Rock Club, in Locust Valley. A member's son or nephew filled any vacancy that came up.

In 1963, however, Local One decided to loosen its admissions policy. The union announced a test aimed at filling four hundred openings for apprenticeships in the various stagecrafts. Of course, the test wasn't open to everyone—you had to be sponsored by a Local One man. Eddie heard about the test and said he'd sponsor me. "You start studying, Joe," he said. "Now."

Studying? I hadn't cracked a book since Stony Brook Prep. But I did what Eddie said. He told me that the test, which was being given at New York University, would last three hours and address general intelligence, as well as an aptitude for math, mechanical reasoning, and spatial relations. The format would be multiple-choice. I went to the library in Glen Cove and pored over whatever books I thought would be helpful. I went to the New York State Unemployment Office and took sample tests to get the hang of the multiple-choice format. I read a book that gave tips about preparing for an exam. ("Arrive early." "Study for an hour." "Clear your head for an hour." "If you don't know the answer, skip it and keep going.") Between curtain cues at the Morosco, I did my homework up in the flies.

On the day of the exam, a thousand applicants showed up. I found the test surprisingly easy, and I answered all the questions. A few weeks later, I was on the fly floor when Eddie came onstage and called up, "Jooooe! I've got the results: ninety-nine in mechanical reasoning; ninety-nine in spatial relations; ninety-nine in math. Only ninety-four in general intelligence. You're not as smart as you think you are."

"How did the others do?" I asked.

"You came out on top," Eddie said. "Number one."

With a sweep of his cigar, Eddie announced to everyone that he was taking "the genius" to the Piccadilly to celebrate. Over the shrimp, he asked me what kind of apprenticeship appealed to me.

"I'd like to learn how to build scenery," I said.

Eddie said, "You want to build the best and biggest sets in the world? You don't do that on Broadway, where you've got the same show every night. You do that at the Metropolitan Opera."

4

# A BOX AT THE METROPOLITAN

The Metropolitan Opera was founded on a woman's dress. According to the nineteenth-century German diva Lilli Lehmann, who was an early star with the company, "As on a particular evening, one of the beautiful millionairesses did not receive a box in which she intended to shine because another beautiful woman had anticipated her, the husband of the former took prompt action and caused the Metropolitan Opera to arise, wherein his beloved wife might dazzle."

The year was 1880, and at issue was a red-and-gold box at the Academy of Music, which had been putting on grand opera in New York since 1854. It seems that a socially ambitious New York matron—the wife of William H. Vanderbilt, a son of Commodore Cornelius Vanderbilt—had been denied this badge of acceptance into the New York upper crust, and her husband wasn't a man to take the insult lying down. Although William H's wealth was more than respectable, it had been too recently acquired to qualify him for one of the Academy's eighteen boxes. Members of the city's Knickerbocker gentry, who had made their pile before the Civil War and who looked on people like the Vanderbilts as upstarts, had long ago snapped up those perches. In an article entitled "New York Society on Parade," Ralph Pulitzer (who had married a Vanderbilt girl) got to the heart of the matter: "Exclusive society, to have any reason to exist, must exclude. . . . The reunion in the midst of its foes gives an esprit de corps, a solidarity never secured or maintained by uninterrupted aloofness. If not for the many called, the few chosen would not experience any peculiar gratification."

The upstarts fought back. Vanderbilt's lawyer, George Henry Warren, organized a meeting of other boxed-out swells, who included some of the most powerful names in American finance—among them were J. P. Morgan and Jay Gould. They decided to build their own opera house, where their wives could be seen in full regalia. When Colonel James Henry Mapleson, the impresario at the Academy, got wind of this, he proposed adding twenty-six boxes to head off the competition. But since the new boxes would be regarded as socially inferior to the old ones, Vanderbilt and his pals turned down the offer.

Fifteen years after the end of the Civil War and thirty-three years before the establishment of the income tax, New York was awash in new money. In *The Saga of American Society*, Dixon Wecter described the people who were beginning to dominate the city in the 1880s:

> This was the day of Coal Barons, Merchant Princes, Tin-Plate Kings, and Monarchs of Finance. Bigness was synonymous with greatness, and expensiveness with worth. Although dynasties were often short—"three generations from shirtsleeves to shirtsleeves," as Oliver Wendell Holmes remarked—they sought to be as gloriously baroque as the brief reign of Heliogabalus. A chateau by Hunt, a box at the Metropolitan and a pair of opera glasses made by Lemaire [at a cost of $75,000], a C-spring carriage and a pair of sparkling bays to drive through Central Park, and a yacht with rosewood paneling and marble pilasters in the saloon were the dream of every young accountant and bond salesman. To own them was to belong to Society.

Within a few months, Vanderbilt's opera project had attracted seventy subscribers, many of whom were also stockholders in the Academy. They agreed to purchase boxes for fifteen thousand dollars each, providing an equity base of just over $1 million. The estimated combined wealth of the Met's founding patrons was colossal: $540 million, which in today's terms would probably be over $100 billion.

The initial site of the proposed theater was on Vanderbilt Avenue, across the street from Grand Central Station. That plan was abandoned when it turned out that two churches, which had covenants on the land, weren't thrilled about having a place of entertainment on their soil, no matter how grand the clientele. Only a few years earlier, *Rigoletto* had been banned in Boston and *La Traviata* in Brooklyn, because it was believed they stirred up improper emotions. Another site was found—the block between Seventh Avenue and Broadway and West Thirty-ninth and Fortieth streets. In keeping with an iron law of New York real estate, the estimated cost of the new house climbed from $430,000 to nearly $1.8 million, and the cost of a box went up to $17,500.

The architect of the Met's first house, Josiah Cleaveland Cady, had recently completed the American Museum of Natural History. For this showplace of a more evolved species, he got most of his ideas from the Palais Garnier in Paris and the Royal Opera House in Covent Garden. In an article for *The American Architect,* Cady cited three purposes for an American opera house—musical, dramatic, and social. In Europe, he noted, the government subsidized opera. In America, "where the Government is not 'paternal,'" financial support had to come from "the wealthy fashionable classes, who, even if not caring especially for, nor appreciating deeply the music, find it a peculiar and valuable social feature. . . . The social feature is so important in a financial way that it naturally is the foundation of any enterprise of this kind, and in no small degree determines the size and character of the house."

The building designed by Cady and his partner, Louis de Coppet Bergh, was the biggest opera house in the world. Its auditorium had a capacity of 3,045 seats, 732 of which were in boxes, and a stage slightly smaller than the one at the Paris Opera and the Imperial Opera in St. Petersburg. The facade, in mustard-colored brick, was Italian Renaissance in style; the interior was even more elaborate. Before construction began, Cady explained the rise in costs:

> Each part of the building is so varied and so complex, and the whole such a large structure, that plans and specifications involved an immense amount of labor and thought. . . . Take the iron work, for instance. It is estimated that there are nearly three

*A view of the first parterre—The Diamond Horseshoe—at the old Met, 1895*

million pounds of iron in the building, or over one hundred thousand separate pieces . . . excluding bolts, plates, brackets, etc. about 16,000 beams, channels, rods or other constructional pieces. The greater part of these had to be thought over and designed separately for their respective work and positions.

Today, it would take a couple of decades to pull this off. But on October 22, 1883, less than three years after the meeting in Warren's office, the new Metropolitan Opera House gave its first performance—Gounod's *Faust*. The Brooklyn Bridge had opened a few months earlier; the Statue of Liberty was still going up.

The man who organized opening night was Henry E. Abbey, a theatrical impresario who had seven productions on Broadway that season and whose only musical background was playing cornet in his high school band in Akron. The performance featured the celebrated Swedish soprano Christine Nilsson as Marguerite, costumes made in Venice, and four intermissions, which gave the box holders plenty of time to compare diamonds.

The evening was a hit, but the new house wasn't universally liked. The ivory-and-gold interior and the enormous scale of the auditorium—104 feet from the stage to the back wall, 80 feet from floor to

*"The New Yellow Brewery" at Thirty-ninth and Broadway, circa 1900*

ceiling—made a great impression. But because of the hall's immense depth and the abundance of boxes, the acoustics were uneven and the sight lines in much of the house were poor. (One third of the seats had only a partial view of the stage.) Colonel Mapleson, whose Academy went out of business a few years later, dismissed the upstart with an epithet that stuck: "The New Yellow Brewery on Broadway."

In 1892, the hall was reduced to a smoldering ruin when a scene painter dropped a cigarette into a can of paint thinner. Fortunately, reconstruction started while the box holders were still flush. If the fire had happened a few months later, the Met would probably not have survived the Wall Street Panic of 1893. The house emerged looking better than ever thanks to the installation of electric lights. Their glow on the front of the parterre boxes gave the auditorium an enduring nickname—the Diamond Horseshoe.

The building outlasted most of 1880s New York, and what really kept it alive for eighty-three years—it was demolished in 1967—was not the Social Register, but the Met's stature as the world's most prestigious opera house for singers: Lilli Lehmann, Marcella Sembrich, Nellie Melba, Jean de Reszke, Olive Fremstad, Antonio Scotti, Enrico Caruso, Geraldine Farrar, Rosa Ponselle, Feodor Chaliapin, Giovanni Martinelli, Beniamino Gigli, Maria Jeritza, Ezio Pinza, Elisabeth Rethberg, Lawrence Tibbett, Kirsten Flagstad, Lauritz Melchior, Lily Pons, Jussi Björling, Bidu Sayao, Eleanor Steber, Risë Stevens, Zinka Milanov, Robert Merrill, Richard Tucker, Leonard Warren, Maria Callas, Franco Corelli, Birgit Nilsson, Renata Tebaldi, Leontyne Price . . .

They all came to the Met, and their descendants still do.

. . .

Rudolf Bing arrived in New York as an observer in the fall of 1949 and took over as general manager the following season. In his memoir 5000 *Nights at the Opera*, the man who did more than anyone else to shape the Met as it is today describes his first impressions of the old house:

> The more I learned about the technical resources of the Metro-
> politan, the more alarmed I became. The auditorium was of
> course one of the glories of the world—that deep Diamond
> Horseshoe that gave the box holders, who had once owned the
> house, an opportunity to look at each other unrivaled in any
> other opera house anywhere. . . . Behind the proscenium and its
> golden curtain, however, the theater had nothing at all to rec-
> ommend it. Everything backstage was cramped and dirty and
> poor. There were neither side stages nor a rear stage: every
> change of scene had to be done from scratch on the main stage
> itself, which meant that if an act had two scenes, the audience
> had just to sit and wait, wondering what the banging noises
> behind the curtain might mean. The lighting grid was decades
> behind European standards, and there was no revolving stage.
> Cecil Smith, then editor of *Musical America*, gave a concise
> description of what was wrong backstage not long after my
> arrival: "It is exceedingly cramped. . . . The settings for each
> opera must be carted to and from the warehouse for each per-
> formance. Often they lie for several hours, half covered with
> tarpaulins and at the mercy of rain or snow, on the sidewalk of
> Seventh Avenue at the back of the house. One of the pastimes
> of those who stroll down Seventh Avenue is to look for the sten-
> ciled stamp on these pieces of scenery (*Figaro* or *Forza* or *Tristan*)
> to see which opera is being exposed to the elements this time.
> The principal singers complain about their dressing rooms,
> which amount to a rabbit warren, with worse plumbing than
> most rabbits are willing to tolerate. Chorus, ballet and orchestra
> are herded into crowded, poorly ventilated common rooms . . ."

Things were even shabbier when I arrived fourteen years later. Although I didn't know it at the time, the Met's assistant manager for operations, Herman Krawitz, had opened the door for me when he overheard a stagehand talking about some kid who'd aced the Local One test. Krawitz called the union. Eddie Lapidus got word of the job opening. And in December of 1963, I reported to The Yellow Brewery as an apprentice carpenter.

When I arrived at the stage entrance, next door to Bleeck's, the famous newspapermen's hangout on West Fortieth Street, I could have been back at my father's suit factory: same freight elevator, same grimy windows, same walls that hadn't been painted in fifty years. But I looked past all this. Here was a new adventure. I was given a locker in the world's smallest locker room. Every space was so pinched that I wondered how they got the scenery in and out.

The first thing I was asked to do was go out and get coffee. I refused. The shop foreman, Charlie Perin, looked at me in disbelief.

"I didn't come here to be a gofer," I told him. "I came here to learn how to build scenery."

Charlie threw his hands up. "What do you mean?" he said. "Every apprentice gets coffee."

"I don't," I said.

Charlie said, "C'mon, kid, let's go see Tex."

Warren "Tex" Lawrence was the head of the carpenter shop, the man in charge of all the Met's scenic work. He was a tall straight-arrow type and the sort of guy you could imagine handling a fifty-five-caliber machine gun on the bow of John F. Kennedy's PT-109. When Charlie told Tex that I refused to be a gofer, Tex smiled and said, "Ask the porter." The porter, who liked being outdoors and collecting tips, went for coffee. I went to work.

My first job was Charlie's way of letting me know that he hadn't forgotten about the coffee. The shop was working on a new production of Lucia di Lammermoor. (Donizetti's opera, whose heroine goes mad, has plagued me ever since.) My task was to cut 2,400 feet of pine dowels, four inches around, in eight-foot lengths so that they could be attached to the thirty or so octagonal "stone" columns that would add to the Scottish gloom of Lammermoor Castle. Charlie showed me how to get started. First, I had to construct a box that supported the dowels at a proper angle. I had to make sure to keep the dowels absolutely straight so that the saw blade wouldn't bind and make a terrible whine. Eight hours a day, for a week, I cut dowels. There were twenty-five carpenters in the shop doing similar work. There was no ventilation. No one wore a face mask. You couldn't cover your mouth to keep the dust out because you needed both hands to manage the saw. But I got the work done to Charlie's satisfaction.

Tex, who liked my spirit, took me under his wing. He taught me how to construct scenery in pieces so that it could be assembled, disassembled, and reassembled quickly, stored efficiently, and carried out of the miserable backstage exits and entrances to be loaded on trucks that transported everything to and from a warehouse in Harlem. The scenic designer would give Tex a drawing that indicated the different elements in a cathedral, a prison, or a castle. Tex showed me how to lay it all out so that each piece completed the puzzle. Before long, I was Tex's right-hand man.

Many of the operas required two complete sets. One was for New York; the other was for the Met's spring tour—a scaled-down version that could be loaded on trains and squeezed onto the smaller stages in Boston, Cleveland, Atlanta, Memphis, Dallas, Minneapolis, and Detroit. One day, I was stapling pieces of one-eighth-inch plywood onto columns for the road version of *Samson and Dalilah* when I missed the target. Charlie came over and held the column. "Aim here," he said, placing a finger on the right place. I fired a staple into his finger. Charlie howled. "Well," I said, "you told me that's where you wanted it." I don't know how Charlie put up with me.

*My first set:* Lucia di Lammermoor, *1963*

· · ·

The Met tolerated moonlighting because what it paid its stage-hands was hardly a living wage. (I was making seventy-four dollars a week.) Charlie was also the head carpenter at the Billy Rose Theater, next door, and through him I got a Sunday job, unloading and putting together scenery for Edward Albee's *Tiny Alice.* I became the curtain man at the Billy Rose, working nights after putting in a full day at the Met. I even worked the Wednesday matinees. I'd vanish from the carpenter shop a few minutes before two, scoot down the fire escape, and raise the curtain at the Billy Rose; then I'd scoot back up the fire escape. An hour later, I'd scoot back down the fire escape to lower the curtain for intermission, then raise it after the intermission. Back to the Met, then back to the Billy Rose to bring the curtain down at the end of the show. All that exercise earned me three hundred dollars a week. It also irritated older carpenters, who didn't like to see an apprentice making so much extra cash.

I also moonlighted as a curtain man at the Morosco. One day, Hymie Gates, the theater's longtime property manager, complained that I'd arrived late. "You're supposed to be here forty minutes before the show," he said. "I said, "Hymie, the contract says half an hour, not forty minutes." Hymie went to Eddie Lapidus. "Eddie," he said, "you hire this guy, he becomes an apprentice at the Met, and now he's telling me he knows the union contract. Pretty soon, he'll come in here with a machine gun and mow us all down."

The carpenter shop at the old Met may have been bad for the lungs, but it was a better place to be than the stage itself. The Met made its own paints for painting the scenic drops, which hung on a big frame over the stage. What held the paint together was glue made from cooked horse bones and hides. The muck simmered all day in a propane-heated cauldron bigger than the one in *Macbeth.* When you came onstage, the first thing that hit you was the stench from that bucket of glue—that and the odor of mildewed scenery that had been hauled down from the Met's warehouse on West 129th Street. The "old Met smell."

I was only peripherally aware of how all my work paid off in front of the golden curtain. This place put on bigger shows than any theater I'd ever worked in, but to me they were just shows. One day, I was onstage repairing a set during a closed rehearsal of *Turandot.* The cast and orchestra had just started the trial scene in Act 2, during which the Chinese princess reveals her terrible secret ("In questa reggia").

On this occasion, the Chinese princess was a soprano named Birgit Nilsson.

I was hammering away when Charlie came over and said, "Hey, Joe, you're making too much noise!"

I said, "No one's going to hear me with that woman singing."

But then I started tapping a little more softly and began to listen. When "In questa reggia" is sung well—and who ever sang it better than Nilsson?—it weaves a spell that puts everyone onstage under the princess's power, including her suitor, Calaf, who was being sung by a tenor named Franco Corelli.

*Franco Corelli and Birgit Nilsson in* Turandot, *1960-1961*

I couldn't see them, but I could hear them, and I found myself so drawn to their voices that I called over to Charlie, "Is it okay if I go out and listen?"

"Sure," he said. "I'll come with you."

The house lights were off, and except for the director and his assistants, the conductor, the orchestra, and the hundred or so people onstage, the auditorium was empty. Charlie and I took seats about ten rows back.

The music coming out of the orchestra pit reminded me of colored smoke, but it was nothing compared to what Nilsson and Corelli were producing with their vocal cords.

"Where are the loudspeakers?" I whispered to Charlie.

Charlie said, "This is the Metropolitan Opera, Joe. We don't use speakers."

I said, "There's more to this opera stuff than building scenery."

Charlie nodded.

5

## TOO MANY CLOUDS

T he Met's directors had been talking about finding a
new home since the 1920s. Thanks to a rising tax
bill, the box holders who funded the Metropolitan
Opera Real Estate Company, which owned the property at Thirty-
ninth Street and Broadway, were not getting much of a return on their
investment. In 1922, the president of the Met's board, the financier
Otto Kahn, floated a proposal for a city arts center that would include
a new opera house. He felt that the Met had more than established
itself as one of the world's great opera companies, not just for the box
holders but also for the thousands of ordinary music lovers who were
turned away whenever a Caruso or a Ponselle was singing. He
thought the city of New York should be more than willing to donate a
piece of land farther uptown for the new complex. This fantasy,
which anticipated the creation of Lincoln Center by forty years, went
nowhere.

In 1925, Kahn acquired two-fifths of the block between West Fifty-
sixth and West Fifty-seventh streets and Eighth and Ninth avenues
with the idea of building a new house that would have better back-

stage facilities and more seats with an unobstructed view of the stage. The box holders rejected the location as too drab for an institution that, as one of them put it, "should be monumental and an ornament to the city." (The Parc Vendome apartments now occupy the site.)

In 1928, the Rockefeller brothers proposed making a new opera house the showpiece of their new Rockefeller Center. (What is now the skating rink would have been "Metropolitan Square.") the Met's directors found the offer too costly, especially after the stock market crashed. The Rockefellers, who were having trouble renting space in their midtown development, suggested that the Met camp out in a new "Center Theater" until times got better. Since the temporary house promised to be worse than the old one, the Met's board declined. Years later, Herman Krawitz, who supervised planning for the new house at Lincoln Center, pointed out that the Rockefeller architects had forgotten to include a box office in their design.

One of the most influential board members in the Met's history was Charles M. Spofford, a lawyer and an amateur musician who was close to Mayor Fiorello LaGuardia. According to Spofford, LaGuardia wanted to leave New York two legacies, "an airfield and a music center." He lived to see the first dream realized, but the second one, which Spofford and the mayor envisioned for a spot just inside Central Park at Columbus Circle, did not come true until nearly twenty years after the death of the "Little Flower."

During the Depression and World War II, the dream of building a new Met was set aside. But postwar optimism revived talk of a new opera house within the context of one of the fashionable schemes of the day—"urban renewal." By then, the Met had become so popular that the demand for opera exceeded the supply of tickets. Robert Moses, the city's redevelopment czar, proposed a site one block south of Washington Square. The Met's board, after taking a poll of opera patrons, rejected the location as "too remote." Moses then offered Columbus Circle—this time, in a spot opposite Central Park. The Met raised nearly a million dollars for the new house, but Moses reneged. An ugly building for trade shows, the Coliseum, went up instead.

The old Met had been born out of a social crisis. The new Met was hatched out of a cultural crisis when a developer named Louis Gluckman bought Carnegie Hall with the aim of tearing down America's premier concert hall and replacing it with an office building. (Civic activists mounted an unprecedented preservation campaign, led by the violinist Isaac Stern; eventually, in 1960, the hall was saved.)

The Rockefellers' favorite architect, Wallace K. Harrison, who had been doodling designs for a new opera house since the building of Rockefeller Center, suggested that Carnegie's chief tenant, the New York Philharmonic, avoid homelessness by joining forces with the Met. For financial help, Spofford and the Philharmonic chairman, Arthur Houghton, approached John D. Rockefeller III, whose foundation had recently decided to make support for the performing arts a top priority. Rockefeller gave the seed money toward the formation of a new arts center, and Harrison pulled out his old doodles. In 1956, an exploratory committee became Lincoln Center, Inc.

Moses proposed a new site, located just north of Columbus Circle, at the intersection of Broadway and Columbus Avenue. The area was home to one of the city's worst slums, many of whose residents were recent arrivals from Puerto Rico. When Spofford rode the subway to West Sixty-fifth Street to show the land to Harrison's partner, Max Abramowitz, the architect took one look at the surrounding area and said, "What a hell of a neighborhood!"

It turned out to be a hell of a project. In addition to negotiating with dozens of slum landlords, Lincoln Center had to deal with Joseph P. Kennedy, the future president's father and an enemy of the Rockefellers. Kennedy delayed demolition for nearly two years because he objected to the condemnation of the largest building on the site, a warehouse he leased to General Motors for storing Cadillacs. As usual with such projects, the initial cost estimate (from the usual consultants) was absurdly low: $55 million. (The ultimate cost of the entire complex was $190 million.) The cost of the new Met more than doubled—from $23.6 million to over $50 million. Eventually, the state was asked to help out, and this led to the construction of the New York State Theater. Tailored to the needs of the New York City Ballet, whose head, Lincoln Kirstein, was an early proponent of Lincoln Center, the State Theater also became home to the New York City Opera. From the beginning, the city's number-two opera company, which was devoted to promoting young artists and a new repertoire, resented its stepchild status in a house designed to muffle the sound of dancers' feet without doing anything for singers' voices.

*The new Met, which was under construction for three years,
seen from the back of the house, 1964*

Rudolf Bing viewed City Opera as a troublemaker—though not, as
it turned out, for the right reason. What he was right about was his
insistence that the Met and the New York Philharmonic not be put
under the same roof. In a memo to the president of the Met's board,
Anthony Bliss, he wrote:

> My first reaction is one of dismay at the inevitable lowering of
> artistic standards. . . . I understood from the earliest days of the
> Lincoln Center planning that the basic concept was no other
> opera company should be permitted at Lincoln Center without
> the Metropolitan's approval. . . . Does it seem fair that a gun
> should now be pointed at the Metropolitan's head just because
> new political developments may put money at the disposal of
> Lincoln Center for the building of a house which in fact is not
> wanted?

Not surprisingly, the Met's new quarters took longer to open than the
others. It was by far the most complex building on the campus—the
biggest, most technically advanced opera house in the world. The
manufacturing of costumes (which had previously been made by out-

side contractors) and scenery (some of which had also been farmed out) would now be done entirely at the Met. The lighting of productions, the raising and lowering of stages, the mechanical movement of scenery were all state of the art—or as Joe Clark, the Met's assistant manager for technical affairs, approvingly calls the backstage machinery, "nineteen-fifties ocean-liner technology." What that means is, if something's broke we can fix it.

The auditorium was configured so that each of the 3,800 seats would have an unblocked view of the stage, as well as acoustical intimacy with the singers. Leg room in the auditorium and parking slots in the garage were ample. There would be generous space for lobbies, gift shops, restaurants, bars, and the Metropolitan Opera Club, a private opera fraternity that had installed itself in the undamaged assembly rooms of the old Met when the auditorium caught fire in 1892. The decor of the new house would be "modernist plush"—with acres of red velvet—but sleeker and less ornate than at the old Met. The crowning touch was the hanging of thirty-two chandeliers, shaped like bursting stars, which would ascend to the gold-leaf ceiling as the house lights dimmed.

I got my first look at the new Met in the spring of 1966. One afternoon, Tex Lawrence said, "Put your jacket on, Joe. We're going somewhere." We took the subway up to West Sixty-fifth Street and Broadway—a new part of town for me. I couldn't believe my eyes when we emerged into the sunlight. The State Theater and Philharmonic Hall (as Avery Fisher was then called) had already opened, but they were dwarfed by the building in between, which was obscured by scaffolding. The plaza swarmed with workers and gawkers.

Tex led me around to Sixty-second Street, where we entered the new Met by a side door. We went through a maze of corridors until we finally found ourselves in the auditorium. No seats had been installed, and dozens of painters on scaffolding were applying gold leaf to the ceiling. Tex mentioned that a few days earlier, one of them had missed his footing and fallen to his death—a drop of ninety feet. Though no one could have known it at the time, the accident was a forewarning. (Since then, there have been four more fatal falls in the house.) We went onstage, and I was astonished at the scale of the stage house—150 feet to the back wall and 220 feet from side wall to side wall.

We took an elevator to the fifth floor, where Tex entered a little office and told me to wait outside. This was when I first heard the booming voice of Herman Krawitz, who wanted to know why Tex hadn't already set up the carpenter shop. Opening night was only a few months away, and four new productions were waiting to be built. What the hell was going on? Tex came out looking chastened, and we went down to the fourth floor and into an enormous empty room. "We have to build racks to store the lumber," he said.

My first job at the new Met was to help set up the carpenter shop. For weeks, I built lumber racks, benches on which to cut the lumber into pieces, mobile storage trucks, and tables on which to lay out drawings for new productions. I installed a wood lathe, a table saw, and a band saw. My handprints are still there. After the shop was organized, Tex and the other carpenters and I began work on the scenic elements for the opening-night opera: the world premiere of *Antony and Cleopatra*, by Samuel Barber. The director, Franco Zeffirelli, had designed and directed his first new production in the old house— a staging of Verdi's *Falstaff* that featured the largest sets built at the Met up to that time. Until then, most of the Met's sets had been

*Franco Zeffirelli, Thomas Schippers, and Samuel Barber: the trio for* Antony and Cleopatra, *1966*

painted drops. Zeffirelli's *Falstaff* introduced a new era of three-dimensional scenery that took months to design, build, and paint and required many hands to put up and take down. For the Nile epic, Zeffirelli had outdone himself.

There were forty of us in the new shop—and the same number in the shop at the old Met. We started work at eight in the morning, took a half hour off for lunch, and worked until ten or eleven in the evening. I once spent three consecutive days and nights in the shop. By the time I got on the Glen Cove train, I wasn't sure that my wife and my three children, Michael, Beth, and Tara, would be able to recognize me. A fourth child, my son Philip, was due to be born any minute.

One of the opening new productions was *La Traviata*, staged by Cecil Beaton. I had my first experience on the big stage when Tex told me to go down and help the stage crew put the Act 3 units together. The old Met had lacked side stages, or "wagons," where scenery can be assembled before moving it into place on the main stage. As a result, all the work had to be done on the main stage. At the new Met, I encountered a veteran stagehand who was busy putting units of *Traviata* together on the main stage, a job that could have been done more easily on one of the side stages. I said, "You don't need to go to all that trouble. Put it together on the wagon." The old-timer glared at me with a look that said, "Who the hell do you think you are?" I explained that I was just doing what I was told to do, and he grudgingly took my suggestion. I'd become friendly with a guy on the night stage crew, Steve Diaz, who told me that another veteran, Henny Hardecker, had muttered about me, "See that kid over there? He walks around like he's going to run the place."

A few days later, one of the old-timers came over during a break and said, "You play chess?"

"Not really," I said. "I've only played a couple of times."

"C'mon," he persisted, "I'll take you on."

"Okay."

We set up the board. The other guys crowded around, looking for blood. I soon realized that my only hope of beating this guy was to take as much time as possible between moves. I took so long that my opponent got bored and lost his concentration. Finally, I had him cornered. "Another game?" he said. We set up the board again. This time he finished me off in less than a minute. I congratulated him, but he wouldn't shake my hand.

. . .

For me, the new Met was paradise. In the carpenter shop were manuals for every piece of equipment in the building—the seven stage elevators, the pipe systems, the cycloramas. These manuals became my weekend reading. During lunch hours, I explored every nook and cranny backstage to familiarize myself with the location and layout of each department. I couldn't believe the immensity of the place—and today, forty years later, I still can't quite believe it.

The architects who designed the house conceived of it as an entirely self-sufficient factory for producing musical theater on the grandest possible scale—a place that could accommodate an entire season's efforts, from honing voices to making shoes. The Met's imposing facade doesn't begin to suggest all that goes on behind it. Patrons get their first sense of a magic kingdom when they enter the auditorium and are confronted by that huge gold curtain, which drapes a proscenium arch fifty-four feet wide and forty feet high. The present curtain is the fourth one to be hung since the house opened in 1966. (The first curtain had to be rehung so that its back side faced the audience, because the gold pattern was too bright.) The new curtain, which was installed in 2005, consists of 1,200 yards of silk damask and 48 yards of fringe. It was woven by elves at Scalamandre, at a cost of $250,000.

The Met's productions vary considerably in their use of the visible stage, but even those that consume the most space give no sense of how large the whole area is. The main stage is 100 feet wide and 80 feet deep. Each of the two side wagons is 60 feet wide. One is 48 feet deep; the other, 40 feet deep. A rear stage, which opens onto a loading dock, is 48 feet wide and 60 feet deep. It also moves, and houses a turntable 58 feet in diameter. The overall height of the entire playing field, from the deepest below-stage C level to the top of the flies (the galleries above the proscenium arch from which drops are unfurled), is 150 feet—about as high as a fifteen-story building.

The stage and surrounding storage areas can accommodate the sets of five or six productions at any given time, each waiting to be hauled onto the main stage and assembled for rehearsals and performances, then taken apart and hauled back to its waiting position. Virtually everything moves hydraulically or on wheels. There are two cycloramas—one white, one blue. Each consists of a single piece of heavy canvas big enough to wrap around the main stage. (They measure 180 feet long and 105 feet high.) They are rolled into place on tracks by a winding-cone mechanism that would make Leonardo proud. A few years ago, we replaced one with a cyclorama shipped from Germany. It was so big that we had to shut down three blocks of Amsterdam Avenue to get it into the back door.

The Met's stage elevators—good 1960s, heavy-duty hydraulics— were built to last, and they're still going strong. There are seven of them, sixty feet wide and eight feet deep. Joe Clark, who runs every-thing backstage, tells me that the city's elevator inspectors always look startled when they learn that each elevator has a lifting capacity of twenty thousand pounds.

Behind, above, below, and around the stage is a labyrinth of rehearsal spaces and workshops from which all aspects of the Met's productions emerge. On C level, three floors below the main stage, is another large stage on which the soloists and chorus rehearse for weeks before ascending to the main stage. On the upper floors—there are five above the main stage—the orchestra rehearses in a room with acoustics that match those of the auditorium. The chorus rehearses in List Hall, which doubles during performance time as a holding pen for patrons who arrive too late to be admitted to the auditorium. The dancers go through their paces in a big ballet rehearsal room. There are several other sizable rehearsal spaces, plus dozens of practice rooms in which the Met's musical staff coaches singers on proper lan-guage and musical style. Every rehearsal room comes equipped with a Yamaha piano. There are forty-two pianos throughout the building, ranging from grands to uprights.

In the midst of all this are hundreds of people making hairpieces in a wig shop, making shoes and cutting and sewing costumes in the men's and women's wardrobe shops, building sets in three carpenter shops, and working on electrical props in the electric shop. Since the 1980s, the productions have grown so big that additional carpentry is done in two auxilliary shops up in the Bronx. The backstage corridors are long and cluttered. The walls are painted institutional gray. The floors are scarred from forty years of constant traffic, much of it heavy. But everyone is too busy trying to perfect his or her piece of the enor-mous puzzle—an eighteenth-century ball gown, a Gothic castle, a high C—to care about the decor.

Add offices for the department heads and their assistants, fourteen dressing rooms for the principal singers, changing rooms for choristers and dancers, locker rooms, shower rooms, lounges, and a full-service cafeteria open all day and evening, and you have a world of its own. The other evening, I overheard one member of the chorus say to another as they left the Met after a long day and came out onto Sixty-fifth street, "Sometimes I'm surprised that the city is still here."

The pressure of trying to assemble *Antony and Cleopatra*, with its sixteen elaborate scene changes, in an untested new house was enormous. To make matters worse, Bing had also planned to open three more new productions during the first week—the Beaton *Traviata*, Ponchielli's *La Gioconda*, and the New York premiere of Strauss's *Die Frau ohne Schatten* ("The Woman Without a Shadow").

Three weeks before opening night, the most spectacular stage element of *Antony*—an enormous turntable that could spin and travel at the same time—collapsed. It was supposed to bring a revolving Sphinx onstage in Act 2, around which three hundred Egyptians would march as the beast rolled forward. The turntable had been built to support fifty pounds per square foot. But the engineers had been thinking of scenery, not people. At the first onstage rehearsal, three hundred Egyptians took up their positions around the Sphinx. Someone hit the switch. Nothing moved. The extra weight had caused the supporting frame to buckle, and there was no time to fix it. Someone suggested that the Sphinx enter on roller skates. Nobody laughed.

One night, I had arrived home early—at 11:30—when the phone rang. It was one of Krawitz's assistants, who told me that I was wanted back at the Met immediately. I pulled on my clothes and got to the Met at 1:30 in the morning. A dozen stagehands were standing around gazing at a hundred long, luminous tubes, painted like clouds, and wondering why some of them weren't moving across the Egyptian night. The cause of the traffic jam was obvious: there were too many clouds. I'd been called in because nobody wanted to take responsibility for doing something about it. They knew that I didn't have enough sense to keep my mouth shut.

"There are too many clouds," I said.

We began taking down clouds to ease the flow of traffic. We'd been at it for an hour or so when I heard a sharp voice speaking very precise English with an Italian accent: "Excuse me, what do you think you are doing?"

The speaker was a young guy dressed in a crewneck sweater. He

*Zeffirelli's set of a cloud-filled sky for* Antony and Cleopatra

didn't look like anybody I needed to pay attention to. In any case, I'd had it with the clouds.

"Some wacko designer put up too much scenery," I said. "I'm trying to make it work."

The Italian preppie stared at me coldly, then turned and muttered something to his entourage.

I recalled one of my moonlighting gigs—the all-night changeover at Radio City Music Hall. We were hanging a new show when a stranger walked in. Freddie Brausseau, the master carpenter, went over to him and said, "Excuse me, you don't belong here." The visitor announced that he was from "management." For good measure, he added that he was a "Rockefeller." Freddie said, "I don't care who you are. This is my stage. Get off." When the Rockefeller didn't move, Freddie ordered us to bring some pipes down from the flies and a couple of dust rags. "Do you want to watch us dust the pipes?" he said. The Rockefeller left.

Remembering Freddie, I barked, "Get off the stage."

The Italian visitor left.

The next morning, I was still onstage when one of Rudolf Bing's assistants appeared: I was wanted in Mr. Bing's office. At once.

*Zeffirelli getting involved with some fabric for*
Antony and Cleopatra *in the costume shop*

Although I'd been an apprentice at the Met for more than two years, this was my first encounter with the Met's general manager. I'd glimpsed him many times. Rudolf Bing had an uncanny habit of turning up whenever a problem or the rumor of a problem arose. A straight-backed, slender figure in a double-breasted English suit, white shirt, and dark tie, he always looked as though he'd just stepped out of a dressing room. The only time I'd ever heard him speak was to say "Good morning" to someone as he flashed by. The only thing I'd ever heard anyone say to him was "Good morning, Mr. Bing," without looking him in the eye.

There was another man in Rudolf Bing's office—the Italian preppie. He took a long pull on a cigarette and glanced at me with narrowed eyes.

Rudolf Bing said, "Good morning, Mr. Volpe. I want to introduce you to Franco Zeffirelli, our director and designer."

We shook hands. Then I heard that voice again, speaking in precise English with an Italian accent: "Did you get those clouds to move?"

I grinned and said, "I sure did."

"Good."

"Thank you, Mr. Volpe," said Rudolf Bing. "I'm sure you have other things to do."

# 6

## "CAN YOU HANDLE THE JOB?"

On September 16, 1966, *Antony and Cleopatra* opened at the new Met with fewer clouds over Alexandria and a new Sphinx big enough to conceal the stagehands pushing it onstage. Two days later, the master carpenter, Lou Edson, quit. Lou had been with the Met for sixteen years. In the old house he'd known more than anyone about how to get the scenery in place and taken down so that rehearsals and performances started and finished on time without anyone getting killed by a falling pyramid or breaking a leg on the way to the guillotine. With all the confusion in the new house, rehearsals had been starting later and later. Tempers were at the breaking point. Lou wasn't impressed by the fact that the opening-night crowd, led by Lady Bird Johnson, was the cream of New York society—Rudolf Bing greeted everyone personally at the front door—or that the event made news around the world. Nor was he particularly disappointed that Barber's opera got lousy reviews, despite raves for Leontyne Price's Cleopatra and Justino Diaz's Antony. Lou had had it. He wanted no part of the new house, with its fancy technology that didn't work. Tex Lawrence quit, too. "I'm out of here, Joe," he said. "I've got some sailing to do in the Caribbean."

I scarcely had time to thank Tex for everything he'd done for me when I was summoned to Herman Krawitz's office. "You know we're looking for a replacement for Lou Edson," Krawitz said. "Charlie Perin tells me you're the man for the job. Would you be interested?"

"Of course."

"Let's go down and see Mr. Bing."

Rudolf Bing stood up and shook my hand. Krawitz smiled, watching me carefully. Then we all sat down.

Mr. Bing said, "Good morning, Mr. Volpe. Herman tells me that Mr. Edson is leaving us."

"Yes, sir," I said.

"Do you think you can handle the job?"

"Yes, sir."

Rudolf Bing looked at Herman Krawitz. Krawitz looked at me.

Mr. Bing went on: "But of course there are members of the crew who would like the position—people who have been here many more years than you. The number-two man wants it. If he decides to leave, what will you do?"

"I'll replace him."

Mr. Bing nodded. "And there's a possibility that the leading fly man will leave. Then what will you do?"

"I've had a lot of experience as a fly man, and I know plenty of people who could do the job."

Krawitz smiled. One of Mr. Bing's eyebrows went up.

"You know, Mr. Volpe," he said, "this is a wonderful opportunity for you."

I said, "Yes, it is, and it's also a wonderful opportunity for the Met."

Both eyebrows went up. "Well," he said, "either you're very naive or you know what you're doing. But I'll take a chance on you."

"Thank you."

Mr. Bing leaned forward. "Mr. Volpe," he said, "how much are you earning now?"

"Right now I'm making about twelve hundred dollars a week."

Mr. Bing looked at Krawitz, who stopped smiling. Apparently, the assistant manager for operations hadn't told his boss about all the overtime the stagehands were making at the dysfunctional new Met.

"I see, Mr. Volpe. Well, as soon as you take on the new job you'll lose that overtime. I'm prepared to offer you four hundred dollars a week."

"Thank you, sir," I said. "I accept."

Mr. Bing said, "When are you prepared to start? We're opening *Die Frau ohne Schatten* on Sunday evening, four days from now. It's a very complicated show. You must be there, Mr. Volpe. It's *your* stage."

I said, "I'd like a few days off, but I'll be there."

"Fine, Mr. Volpe."

On my way back to the carpenter shop, I glanced at the bust of Caruso outside Mr. Bing's office. I nodded at the great tenor, and he nodded back. I took the elevator to stage level, where the crew was setting up the scenery for a rehearsal of Richard Strauss's *Die Frau ohne Schatten*.

The director and the designer, Nathaniel Merrill and Robert O'Hearn, were in a huddle. The conductor, Karl Böhm, was making his way into the pit. The singers—Leonie Rysanek, who was singing the Empress; James King, the Emperor; Walter Berry, the Dyer; and Christa Ludwig, the Dyer's Wife (and Berry's real-life wife)—were standing around in costume. I had noticed Christa Ludwig before and been struck by what a beautiful woman she was—strong yet feminine and with what I sensed was a wicked sense of humor. I wanted to go up to her and say, "I'm Joe Volpe, the new master carpenter. Don't worry, Miss Ludwig. You're in good hands." But she greeted my glance with a smile that could have been for the electrician. The orchestra was tuning up. The stagehands were putting the last bits of scenery in place. Most of them were in their thirties, forties, and fifties. I was twenty-six.

Charlie Rasmussen, a former carpenter in the old house, had been given Tex's job as head of the carpenter shop. He had always made it clear that I was still an apprentice as far as he was concerned. He didn't want me hanging around the office, as I had with Tex—he wanted me out in the shop building scenery. Apparently, Krawitz hadn't told Charlie my news yet, because he only grunted when he saw me. I grabbed a broom and started sweeping up wood shavings. The phone rang in the office. I steered the shavings toward a spot between Charlie and the phone. Charlie sidestepped them. I heard him say, "Are you kidding?" Then he came out and walked past me without a word.

*In the carpenter shop: from left, scenic designer Volodia Odinokov,
Charles Rasmussen, draftsman William Taylor, me, and
Charles Perin, with models of Zeffirelli's Sphinx and sand
dunes,* Antony and Cleopatra

The next day, Mary Ann and I flew to Puerto Rico, leaving the kids
with my parents. We checked into a nice hotel in San Juan, but I
never saw the pool. I had brought along the stage plans for *Die Frau,*
and instead of lying in the sun I committed them to memory—the cue
for every singer's entrance and exit, the cue for every change of lighting, every elevator move, and every curtain. *Die Frau* is Strauss's *Magic
Flute.* It takes place in two worlds—the fairy tale world of the
Emperor's island, and the Ralph Kramden world of the Dyer's hut. It
involves a lot of travel back and forth. As master carpenter, the person
in charge of everything that moved onstage and off, I had to make
sure that nobody broke an ankle getting on and off one of the fancy
new elevators.

Mary Ann and I flew back to New York on Saturday. The next day,
I was at the Met well before the curtain time of six in the evening. I
carried a walkie-talkie, and wore a black cape so that I wouldn't be
seen during the onstage scenery changes. Inwardly, I was a wreck.

Nobody broke an ankle. After the final curtain, Rudolf Bing came
backstage. He nodded his approval at me. Christa Ludwig swept past

us, and I caught her eye. This time, I swear she smiled only at me. I went down to the garage. My days on the midnight special to Glen Cove were over. I now had my own parking spot.

When I came in for a rehearsal of *Rigoletto* the next day, I discovered that my assistant master carpenter, Tom Curry, had called in sick. So had my fly man and his assistant. We couldn't get everything set up in time, and the rehearsal started fifteen minutes late. Several of the stagehands exchanged looks of satisfaction.

"Never again," I said to myself.

The Met lives in a state of near war: hundreds of people working on a dozen productions, current and future ones, each with a deadline that can't be missed. Wars require constant planning and replanning for today, tomorrow, the foreseeable future, and the unforeseeable future, which might arrive at any moment. The Met's artistic administrator, Jonathan Friend, who manages the incredibly complicated schedule of who's going to sing when, keeps a crystal ball on his desk. When you look into it, you see a message from the libretto of Mozart's *Idomeneo*. It reads "Qual nuovo disastro?" ("What new disaster?"). In terms of planning, the Met operates with double vision— nearsighted and farsighted. We all keep our fingers crossed.

Every day, singers, musicians, dancers, stagehands, electricians, scenery builders, wig makers, and costume makers pour in and out of the Met to meet a production schedule that begins at eight in the morning and ends at around midnight. Right now, I'm looking at a typical schedule for the week of November 2–12, 2005. The day begins with the crew setting up the main stage for a rehearsal of a new production of Gounod's *Roméo et Juliette;* the rehearsals for *Roméo,* as with all new productions and revivals, begin at 11:00 and end in the afternoon at 2:00 or 2:30. *Roméo's* opening night is November 14. At the same time, on the C-level rehearsal stage, singers are rehearsing for the world premiere of Tobias Picker's *An American Tragedy,* an adaptation of the Theodore Dreiser novel. *Tragedy* opens on December 2. Several of those rehearsals will last until 6:00 p.m. Meanwhile, during four of the five afternoons, the orchestra is rehearsing a revival of *La Bohème.*

As soon as the *Roméo* rehearsals are over, the scenery for that production will be taken down and the main stage will be reset for the week's performances: *Lucia di Lammermoor, The Marriage of Figaro, Aida,*

*Lucia* again, *Figaro* again, and on Saturday, *Bohème* in the afternoon and *Aida* in the evening. That's a lot of coming and going; a lot of putting up scenery for one show, taking it down to make room for the next one, putting up another show, taking it down, and so on. Many people at the Met work eighteen-hour days, Monday through Saturday (and sometimes Sunday). The whole process happens again the following week, with different productions and different singers, and it continues until the end of May.

As an apprentice carpenter, I had moved from small task to small task, only dimly aware that there must be a lot more going on than hammering plywood. When I became master carpenter, my understanding of the Met became a hundred times more complex. I was no longer just a cog; I was in charge of a crucial phase of the whole process—that of getting an opera up onstage before thousands of spectators, night after night. I had to make sure that the 150 or so stagehands under my command got all the stage elements perfectly in place, onstage and off.

The stagehands were still operating on the basis of long-established work habits. At the old Met, a night crew came in at the end of the show, dismantled the scenery, and took it in trucks to the warehouse on West 129th Street. Then they brought down the scenery for the next evening's performance and left it out on the street for the day crew to set up. In order to have everything in place for the eleven o'clock rehearsal, the day crew had been arriving at eight in the morning instead of the normal time of nine. For that extra hour, they were getting paid time and a half—thirty dollars above and beyond their normal weekly wage. Now that the Met had enough room to store everything under one roof, I saw no reason why the night crew couldn't set things up during their shift, so that the day crew wouldn't have to come in until nine—thus saving both time and money. When the night stagehands heard this, they screamed. The day crew screamed, too.

"Joe," Eddie Lapidus said over lunch at the Great Wall, "if you start out as Mr. Nice Guy, they'll kill you." Eddie also gave me another piece of advice: "Don't ever get into a discussion. Just say, 'This is what we're doing.' Period."

Herman Krawitz, Mr. Bing's efficiency expert, backed me up on the new work rules. (I also did away with dozens of other entrenched

*Rudolf Bing backstage during the stagehand strike*

habits.) As one rehearsal after another started on time, he took to call-ing me "the genius." In January, when my record for punctuality was broken by a delayed start for *Carmen*, Krawitz crowed, "The genius is late!"

One day Mr. Bing gave me a lesson in good management. We were setting the stage for Act 2 of *La Gioconda*, which takes place on the deck of a seventeenth-century Genovese ship. The ship was on the same wagon that had been cursed by Zeffirelli's Sphinx. When we tried to bring it onstage, the wagon wouldn't budge. We attached four lengths of rope to the ship, and I organized the crew into teams. I was about to give the order to "pull" when I noticed that Rudolf Bing had joined one of the teams. (His two assistants, I also noticed, were sit-ting offstage out of harm's way.) When I yelled, "Pull!" everyone pulled. One of the ropes came loose, and twenty stagehands fell to the floor—everyone but Mr. Bing, who stood there holding the rope.

"Shall we try it again, Mr. Volpe?" he said.

The old-timers continued to resent my new authority. Sure enough, their resentment came to a head during a revival of *Lucia di Lammermoor*, whose accursed columns I had built during my first week in the old Met. The platform for the main set had been made for the old house, and it was too wide to be moved hydraulically via one of the new side wagons. To get it offstage at the end of a performance required having the stage crew dismantle all the scenery so that the electricians could then raise the wagon and move the platform into the wings. Until the Christmas Eve performance of *Lucia*, the work had been done by the night crew, which arrived at the end of the show to take over from the day crew. As their Christmas present to me, the night crew balked. They had been testy ever since Krawitz had put out the word that some of them would be let go once things got better organized in the new house. When the night crew refused to strike the show, I said to the head of the day crew, Al Taylor, "You'll have to stay on for a few extra minutes and strike the platforms."

Taylor said, "We've never had to stay before, and we're not staying now." He turned his back on me and walked away.

I hollered, "Get your satchel out of your locker and get out!"

Taylor went to Local One, the stagehands' union, and complained that I had no right to fire him while he was engaged in "union business." Local One backed him up and charged me with violating my oath of union loyalty. I called Eddie Lapidus.

Eddie said, "Joe, you were just doing your job as a supervisor. They can't discipline you for making a management decision."

So now I was "management"?

The union put me on trial—a kangaroo court in a smoke-filled room at the Americana Hotel. I had Eddie at my side. After a lot of "witnesses" (friends of Al's) were paraded in, I was found guilty as charged and ordered to apologize to the union in writing. I had no intention of doing any such thing, and after the deadline passed I heard no more about it. Al Taylor returned to work, and he and one of his buddies, the shop steward, Ron Lynch, made it clear that I could expect no favors from them.

In the spring of 1967, I went on my first national Met tour. Until then, the company had traveled by rail. Now we were traveling by air, courtesy of the tour's sponsor, Eastern Airlines. The scenery, which had previously been transported by train, was being hauled overland on tractor trailers, directly to the regional venues. When we got to the Public Auditorium in Cleveland, we discovered that the driveway leading to the freight entrance was too narrow for the trailers. I ordered the stagehands to unload the scenery in a nearby alley; the local Teamsters protested because of the distance to the loading dock. They planted one of their men in the night crew, and he arrived for work drunk. I had him dismissed. Someone passed the word to me that the Teamster—encouraged by my pals Taylor and Lynch—was going to "get" me when I left the theater.

After work, I asked my one friend on the crew, Jimmy Harvey, to join me in the bar of the Auditorium Hotel for a nightcap. (My glorious room in that hotel was seven bucks a night.) Sure enough, the Teamster was at the bar, nursing shots of whiskey.

I went over to him and said, "I understand you have some beef with me."

He said, "Yeah, you had me fired."

I said, "You were drunk, and I can't allow someone in that condition to handle the Met's scenery. You put me in that position. You want to do something about it? I'm here."

He was pretty far gone, and after sizing up Jimmy and me, he caved. Before long, he was buying us drinks. After the tour, I told Al Taylor and Ron Lynch that, since I couldn't fire them, I was demoting them to grips. They quit.

But my stock was rising with the only man who counted—Rudolf Bing. Earlier that year, George Moore, the president of the Met's board (and the president of First National City Bank of New York) became alarmed by the rising cost of producing opera in the new house. Moore brought in the management consulting firm of Booz Allen Hamilton to come up with ways to decrease backstage operating expenses. Booz Allen had recently completed a study for First National that cut the bank's costs by improving the work habits of its tellers. A similar study reportedly saved a lot of money for Ocean Spray, the cranberry juice makers. From Moore's point of view, banking, cranberry juice, and opera were indistinguishable. The efficiency experts put their minds to work on the Met's stage operations, and the opera they chose to study was my old favorite, *Lucia*.

It didn't take long for them to come up with a brilliant idea: the Met could save significant money by reducing the number of stagehands used for scene changes. The consultants studied every scenic move in

*Lucia*—how many men and how long it took for them to get a set onstage, set it up, strike it, and carry it off. In particular, they focused on the scene change that precedes the heroine's mad scene. I thought *they* were nuts. In a memo to Rudolf Bing, I said that the whole exercise was a waste of time, and I added, "This isn't cranberry juice. This is an opera house."

The memo was forwarded to George Moore. A few days later, I was summoned to a meeting at First National City's headquarters—my boardroom debut. I sat outside while Moore and several other key Met trustees, Rudolf Bing, and the consultants spoke in hushed voices behind closed doors. Then I was called in.

"So, Mr. Volpe," Moore said, "I've read your memo, and you seem to have a difference of opinion with our consultants. Do you know what a work-time study is?"

"I do now," I said.

"I see," Moore went on, keeping his eyes on the papers in front of him. "Well, then, would you explain yourself?"

"Why don't the efficiency experts explain themselves first," I said.

Out came reams of paper with graphs and figures. Finally, the head consultant got to the mad scene. "Based on our calculations, it will take thirty-six stagehands to set the scene properly."

"What do you say to that, Mr. Volpe?" Moore said.

I thought for a minute. Then I said, "I'm sorry to say this, but your calculations are wrong. We now use twenty-eight stagehands to set that scene, and contrary to what your study says, they don't walk—they run. We don't need eight more stagehands."

No one said anything. Then Rudolf Bing spoke up: "Do you have anything further to say, Mr. Volpe?"

"No, sir," I said.

"Then you can wait outside."

This time, the voices in the boardroom were louder. Rudolf Bing emerged first. Gesturing to me as he headed for the elevator, he said, "We can leave now, Mr. Volpe." As the elevator doors closed behind us, he added, "That's the end of Booz Allen Hamilton. Their efficiency study has just been killed."

Recently, I received an unexpected testimonial about the efficiency of the Met's stagehands when I asked my guests in the general manager's box if they wanted to observe the scene change between *Cavalleria Rusticana* and *Pagliacci*, the Met's most popular double bill. One of the guests was an elegant New York woman who had never been backstage before. As she watched thirty sweaty men in jeans and T-shirts working silently and at top speed to dismantle Zeffirelli's massive picturesque Sicilian village with its crooked old houses and towering cathedral atop a long flight of steps, she said, "This is really erotic."

I felt nostalgic for my old job.

Contrary to my publicity, I'm not a natural screamer—I have too much Sicilian blood for that. When I've had it with someone, I become very quiet, because I've reached a point where the relationship is over. I also benefited from observing Rudolf Bing's approach to getting what he wanted. During the 1970–1971 season, our fragile Italian super-tenor, Franco Corelli, threw a fit during a rehearsal of Massenet's *Werther* because the set was blocking the view of one of his entrances. At such moments, Corelli, who was a very shy man behind his splendid appearance, never screamed because he was too worried about the condition of his vocal cords. Instead, he retired to his dressing room.

This prompted a call to the general manager, who arrived and said to the stage designer, Rudy Heinrich, "Mr. Heinrich, please move the walls a little bit so that the audience can see Mr. Corelli." Heinrich explained that the walls had been carefully positioned to create a certain "perspective." Mr. Bing smiled, nodded at me, and we moved the walls a couple of inches.

Corelli returned, took one look, and went right back to his dressing room.

"Mr. Heinrich," Rudolf Bing said, "please move the walls so that the *whole* audience can see Mr. Corelli."

Heinrich exploded: "You don't need a designer, you need a psychiatrist!"

Mr. Bing smiled and said, "I *am* a psychiatrist."

The walls were moved.

Unfortunately, I don't have Rudolf Bing's gift for a turn of phrase. But it didn't take me long to figure out that in order to be a successful leader in an opera house you sometimes have to behave operatically. One of nine new productions that first season in the new house was *Lohengrin*, staged by the composer's grandson Wieland Wagner. (He died before the rehearsals got under way.) Until then, I'd been careful to appear very much under control. During an orchestra rehearsal of *Lohengrin*, the crew was late in making a complicated scene change. I apologized to the conductor, Karl Böhm, and was trying to determine how to speed things up when one of Krawitz's assistants, Jay Rutherford, came over to see what the problem was. I heard him remark, "Volpe's just walking around as though nothing's happened. What's going on here?"

I went over to Rutherford and said, "I understand that you're upset because I'm not upset. If you want excitement, I'll give you excitement."

The next time Rutherford came onstage, I raised my voice at the crew for no good reason. They looked at me as though I were crazy. It was just an act, but it got results.

Presidents had been getting involved in the Met's labor problems since 1904, when the American Federation of Musicians appealed to Theodore Roosevelt to order the Met's management to stop hiring new players from abroad. It was an election year, and T.R. told immigration authorities to detain at the port of entry any musicians who arrived from Europe until the courts ruled on whether it was legal to allow them in. Management dropped the idea of an imported orchestra. In 1961, President John F. Kennedy saved the Met season when he ordered his secretary of labor, Arthur Goldberg, to arbitrate another dispute between the management and the musicians. Under the "Goldberg agreement," as the settlement came to be called, the musicians won a 14 percent increase over a three-year contract—far less than the 60 percent increase that they had asked for.

When the 1961 contracts ran out in 1964, all the Met's unions agreed to new terms (which included the sweetener of year-round employment) except the musicians, who played for two years without a contract. In 1966, while Zeffirelli was losing his hair over the turntable that wouldn't work, the musicians announced that, although they would play the opening-night performance of *Antony*, they would strike the next day if their demands weren't met. An agreement, highly favorable to the musicians, was finally reached during the third act, just as a servant was handing the Egyptian queen her poisonous asp. The stage was set for the most devastating labor conflict in the Met's history. At this moment in American history, however, Richard Nixon had his mind on the war in Vietnam.

In January of 1969, as negotiations for new union contracts were about to begin, the executive committee of the Met's board notified the other trustees: "We will not again be backed into a position where we are made to negotiate at gunpoint. Three years ago, we had to submit. The eyes of the world were upon us. The international press was gathered for the opening of the biggest and best-equipped opera house ever built. To fail to have opened would have created a national scandal."

This time, the unions were not going to be intimidated. The musicians sought a 50 percent increase in salary, spread out over two years, above and beyond their previous base pay of $260 a week, plus increased fringe benefits. The chorus asked for a greater increase—140 percent—over their previous salary range. The ballet asked for the biggest pay hike of all—200 percent. Dozens of other requests were also put on the table—among them, increases in per diem during tours, raises in pay for radio broadcasts, and (in the case of the choristers) compensation for time spent changing costumes.

To the Met's management, these requests were outrageous. Rudolf Bing said that if they were honored, the company's current deficit would increase by more than $2 million. The unions pointed out that that figure was too high since it failed to take into account projected annual contributions from the Met's donors. The union went on to argue that when those numbers were factored in, the house would break even. The unions were right. The Met's management had violated a principle of negotiations that I've followed ever since: don't fudge the truth.

As the expiration date of the old contracts, June 30, approached without any sign of an agreement, things got ugly. Rudolf Bing announced that the Met would not begin rehearsals for the 1969–1970 season until contracts had been signed with the major unions—Local 802 of the American Federation of Musicians, and the American Guild of Musical Artists (AGMA), which represented the soloists, choristers, and dancers. The unions' principal lawyer, Herman Gray, whom *Variety* described as a "tough hombre, rich in sarcasm and acid remark," responded, "If Mr. Bing finds himself unable to reach agreement with the entire staff of professional performers," he said, "he should resign and let somebody step in who has the capacity to do the job. His statement is a confession of his own ineptitude."

Although Rudolf Bing had run the Met for twenty years, he was a novice at labor negotiations—a task he'd always delegated to an assistant. "Negotiating" was not in his vocabulary. The deadline passed. The Met postponed rehearsals. State and city mediators were called in.

On August 26, the company announced that it was postponing the opening night performance, which had been scheduled for September 15. The Met's management explained that in the absence of any progress toward a settlement, the soloists were beginning to commit to engagements elsewhere. By then, contracts with some of the other unions had been agreed upon, but the musicians, soloists, choristers, and dancers were holding out. After one meeting in early September, the president of Local 802, Max Arons, described Rudolf Bing as behaving "like a waspish, irascible witch, straight out of some fourth-rate opera." Mr. Bing held his tongue, but not for long.

Opening night came and went. As postponement followed postponement, another issue was added to the demands—how much the Met would give in back pay to compensate for the mounting loss of wages. David Cole, a mediator appointed by Mayor John Lindsay, ordered a "cooling-off period." He added, "In all my years as a mediator, I have never seen anything so frozen. Each side does have valid points. Neither recognizes that the other has valid points."

Despite the lockout, I continued coming to work, since Local One had agreed that the heads of the stage departments could maintain equipment while the house was dark. I could have spent more time with my family, but my marriage had fallen apart. That summer, Mary Ann and I agreed to a divorce, and I moved out of our house in Glen Cove and into a small apartment near Lincoln Center. Fortunately, my kids had the stability of their grandparents, next door. My workload was light, and though I didn't take part in any of the negotiations, I occasionally popped into meetings with Local 802 and AGMA.

I was surprised at the level of anger. The musicians were all talented, highly educated professionals for whom keeping up their skills was an ongoing personal expense, and yet they felt like hired help. They especially resented the condescending manner of the board president, George Moore. During one meeting, a member of the ballet said to the banker, "No doubt you spend more on your French poodle, Mr. Moore, than you're willing to spend on a dancer at the Met."

In early December, the musicians settled on a new three-year con-

*President of the board William Rockefeller and the bearded me*

tract. This was followed by agreements with both the chorus and the ballet. Rehearsals started at once. On December 29, the truncated season opened with *Aïda*. But the issue of back pay remained unresolved. As one union member summed up the situation for *The New York Times*, "The bitterness will last." Just how bitter things had become is conveyed in this exchange between Rudolf Bing and Herman Gray during one of the many meetings that went nowhere:

Gray: "There you go again, Mr. Bing, showing your contempt for me."

Bing: "On the contrary, Mr. Gray. I'm trying to hide it."

When the season resumed, I marked my newly single life by growing a beard. It was doing nicely until Rudolf Bing noticed it and summoned me to his office.

"Mr. Volpe," he said, "I don't approve of facial hair on one of my supervisors. It's not appropriate. I would ask that you shave it."

I said, "With all due respect, sir, this is a personal thing. I can't do that."

"Mr. Volpe, you have a very responsible position here. You must set an example."

"Yes, sir, but my beard has nothing to do with the Met."

"I see," Mr. Bing said. "Well, I would ask that you consider seriously what I've just suggested."

"I will, sir."

I was dating one of the Met's ballerinas, a dancer named Nancy Sklenar. Together, we had found an old broken-down lakeshore cottage in New Jersey on Lake Hopatcong. The price was right—seventeen thousand dollars—but I didn't have the down payment. I asked to see Mr. Bing. I told him about the breakup of my marriage and the cottage I wanted to buy. He nodded sympathetically. Then I asked if I could I get a month's advance on my salary for the down payment.

"I'll grant your request, Mr. Volpe," he said, "but on one condition."

"Yes, sir?"

"You must agree to shave off your beard."

"Of course," I said.

"Thank you, Mr. Volpe."

I shaved off the beard, the advance came through, and I bought the cottage. Then I started growing the beard again. Two weeks later, Mr. Bing came striding across the stage and beckoned me over behind one of the sets.

"Mr. Volpe," he said in a half-whisper, "I thought that we had an understanding. You were going to shave off that beard."

"I did shave it off," I said. "But I didn't promise to keep it off."

Rudolf Bing's eyes narrowed. "Mr. Volpe," he said, "this will be the last time that you get the better of me."

7

## A MAN OF THE THEATER

When Rudolf Bing announced that he would retire after the 1971–1972 season, the year he turned seventy, George Moore and many members of the board were not sorry to see him go. Mr. Bing and "the bankers" (as he contemptuously referred to the trustees) had long clashed over his insistence on expensive, high-powered new productions, which he regarded—rightly—as essential long-term investments in the Met's future. It was Rudolf Bing who established the Met principle that new productions were worth doing only if they were built to last. The trustees were delighted to see him take the fall for the lockout, especially since he had only been following their orders—after all, wasn't he really just the hired help, too? In *5000 Nights at the Opera*, Bing defends himself against the rap:

> I cannot help resenting somewhat the way my business management was put in a bad light in the last years. When I came to the Metropolitan, there were essentially no assets. Now there are sixty productions in good shape (which do not appear on

the books), profit-making real estate where the old house stood (which yields $600,000 a year as a rental, but is carried on the books as an asset of only $1.8 million); three warehouses that we own, not rent; more than $1 million worth of paintings and sculpture in the new theater; and an endowment of $6 million.

Artistically, Bing went out on some memorable high notes. His last seasons included two parts of a new *Ring* cycle, conceived and conducted by Herbert von Karajan; the sensational double threat of Joan Sutherland and Marilyn Horne in *Norma*; and Birgit Nilsson's chandelier-rattling Isolde and a *Tosca*, during which the Swedish force of nature sang "Vissi d'arte" while lying on the stage—as Maria Jeritza, the Met's great Floria Tosca of the 1920s, had done. The most astonishing feat of Bing's last season was the introduction of a husky young tenor named Luciano Pavarotti, who popped off nine perfect high Cs in Donizetti's *The Daughter of the Regiment*.

But the 1969 strike was devastating. The Met had to refund $2.3 million of the $2.8 million in unused subscription revenue. Simply processing the returns for twenty thousand subscribers in twenty different series cost the company $160,000. Ticket sales, which had been at 96 percent of the seating capacity in 1968–1969, dropped to 89 percent the year after the strike and did not return to their prestrike level until the season of 1977–1978. Over the next five years, the Met's deficits rose to $9 million despite strenuous micromanagement by Moore and "the bankers."

Rudolf Bing's successor, Goeran Gentele, was a Swedish theater and film director who had run the Royal Opera in Stockholm with flair. (He'd notoriously staged a production of *The Masked Ball* in which it was suggested—with historical accuracy—that the hero, King Gustav III, was gay.) Shortly after he arrived as an observer before the start of the 1971–1972 season, Gentele called me into his office. He was charming and soft-spoken, without any of Rudolf Bing's edges—and also, I sensed, without an appetite for making tough decisions. But it was clear that he was a real pro. We spent several hours while I took him through my Bible—the loose-leaf notebook of rehearsal schedules and scenery budgets that determined what we did every day and how we could pay for it. He immediately grasped the interlocking complexity of the Met, and as we parted, he said, "I'm counting on you to be very helpful to me, Mr. Volpe." Nine months later, in July of

1972, Gentele and two of his three children were killed in an automobile accident during a vacation in Sardinia.

Rudolf Bing and his wife, Nina, had no children; his whole life had been the Met. After Gentele's death, he let it be known that he would be delighted to be asked back. It was a fantasy that would never have worked. Bing's time was over. He knew it but couldn't accept it. He was hurt when Moore tapped Schuyler Chapin, who had no experience running an opera house, to fill the gap left by Gentele's death. (Before coming to the Met as an assistant manager under Gentele, Chapin had been a vice president for programming at Lincoln Center and a close associate of Leonard Bernstein's.) I had only a few brief contacts with Chapin and found him very likable. But it was immediately apparent that he wasn't a man of the theater.

Chapin had been general manager for a couple of years when he came into the carpenter shop one day with the new president of the board, William Rockefeller. (George Moore had left in 1974, frustrated by the deficits.) I had become tired of my duties as master carpenter—the late hours were making things tough at home with my new wife, Nancy, and the job held no new challenges for me. I had returned to the shop to supervise the building of scenery, taking a 30 percent pay cut. When one of the carpenters spotted the visitors, he came into my office and said, "There are a couple of strangers here who look like they're lost." I went over to say hello and was surprised to see that Rockefeller was wearing Knapp steel-toed work shoes, along with his custom-made suit. I guess he thought that that was what you were supposed to wear in a carpenter shop.

In the early spring of 1975, Rockefeller told Chapin that his contract as general manager would not be renewed. In Chapin's memoirs, he writes, "Before I became general manager of the Met, I had always been number-two to someone else. This was my first chance to be number-one, which is a very different thing from being number-two. It takes time to learn. I was learning; but they wouldn't give me time." I'm sympathetic to his point, but our learning curves couldn't have been more different.

Chapin's notable legacy to the Met was the English director John Dexter, whom he hired to stage Verdi's *I Vespri Siciliani* for the 1973–1974 season. Dexter was a real man of the theater. He'd been a leading light of the Royal Court Theatre and Britain's National The-

*Director John Dexter*

atre since the early 1960s, where he'd worked with John Osborne, Laurence Olivier, Joan Plowright, Arnold Wesker, Maggie Smith, Paul Scofield, Peter Shaffer, Richard Burton, and Anthony Hopkins. He had also directed at the adventurous Hamburg State Opera, run by Rolf Liebermann. After Dexter's success with *I Vespri* (and with Peter Shaffer's *Equus*, on Broadway), he joined the Met's management. He was named director of productions—one third of a troika that included Chapin at the top and the unstoppable young conductor James Levine as music director, another new title in the Met's hierarchy. Gentele had established the position for the conductor Rafael Kubelik, but when Kubelik didn't work out, the job went to Levine. Dexter not only broadened the Met's taste for modern works but revolutionized how we produced opera. He also changed my life.

When Dexter entered a room, he altered the atmosphere. Everything about him was dark—his gaze, his temper, a beard that came and went. Rudolf Bing would have disapproved of how Dexter dressed—in clothes that looked as though they'd been slept in, in bedroom slippers instead of shoes. But Bing would have loved John's passion for creating new worlds onstage. In *The Honourable Beast*, a collection of letters and diary and notebook jottings posthumously compiled into an autobiography by his longtime partner, Riggs O'Hara,

John writes, "Fury for perfection makes me difficult to work with. The pressure that people feel is merely the after-burn of the blast off. They have no right to stand too close unless they are insured against fire." I couldn't get close enough.

John worked from the ground up—a new production started with his rough sketches for the basic design. (Both his grandfather and father were amateur artists.) He immediately wanted to consult with the people who were going to do the actual work to see whether what he had in mind was technically and financially feasible. In a diary entry for February 1977, he writes, "When I arrived [at the Met], there wasn't anyone who could give you a detailed reading of a working drawing with a cost on it. We had to find someone who could do that, so that we didn't continue to soar automatically over budget."

John found me. One morning, during the spring of 1975, he burst into the carpenter shop, clutching sheets of paper. Although we'd barely met, he said, "Joe, I want to show you something. We're thinking of doing Le Prophète in 1977–1978. Here are my thoughts."

Meyerbeer's opera about a false German prophet in the sixteenth century dates from a time and place—mid-nineteenth-century Paris—when opera was staged on a scale that wouldn't be seen again until Hollywood started grinding out biblical epics in the 1920s. But the sketches that John showed me were not of turreted castles and half-timbered houses. They merely showed a series of wooden frames in the shape of a Gothic arch, set against simple black drops. I'd never seen a stage design like it before—medieval minimalism. Would this work conceptually, John wanted to know. "Of course," I said. How much would it cost? "A lot less than we would normally spend," I said.

John said, "The production is about the people, not the scenery." He added that the members of the chorus and the leading characters would be dressed "out of Brueghel." There were going to be a lot of people in this Brueghel. How much would it cost? "Well within our budget," I said.

"Good." He dashed out of my office.

For the next six seasons, I worked hand in hand with John on a run of revolutionary new productions: Britten's Billy Budd; Poulenc's The Dialogues of the Carmelites; Berg's Lulu; Kurt Weill's The Rise and Fall of the City of Mahagonny; Parade, three short French operas by Satie, Poulenc, and Ravel; and the Stravinsky Triple Bill, three short works by the Russian composer. The French and Russian triple-headers, which were designed by David Hockney, fulfilled John's dream of uniting opera, theater, art, and dance. All were written in the twentieth century—a break from the Met's usual nineteenth-century bread and butter. All still rank among the Met's most beautifully conceived and designed productions. One of them, *Mahagonny*, with one of the most electrifying singing actresses of my time, Teresa Stratas, remains my favorite Met production.

*The opening scene of Dexter's Carmelites, 1977: nuns on the floor*

John was a man with a mission. In response to a mandate from the trustees to keep the costs of new productions as low as possible, he sums up his philosophy in his diary:

> Economy is not a policy, it is a fact. Imagination/Simplicity is a policy. It is an approach to opera for the twentieth century. When the theatre began to remove elaborate "realistic" effects, it became free so that from Schiffbauerdam to Sloane Square, any physical and emotional demand a playwright could make was capable of fulfillment. Time and place could flow freely in the audience's imagination (which, according to Coleridge, is where the excitement lies).
>
> Only at the Metropolitan has time stood still. The curtain can still rise on a performance and the audience can be transported back to the nineteenth century and sit and wallow in an imaginary world. Unfortunately drama is reality given meaning and form. Opera and drama are not a drug for the feeble-minded, they are an essential enhancement of our lives from which we can enrich ourselves and from which we can learn.
>
> Only when the operatic stage can share the freedom of the dramatic stage can the medium exist in the twentieth century

*David Hockney's* Les Mamelles de Tiresias, Parade, *1981*

and maybe help us understand the world and ourselves, instead of remaining the morphine of the over-privileged.

Economy as a watchword is meaningless. Imagination costs more in the mind but less in the purse. But the imagination must swing out from the stage to embrace the audience and the audience must be trained to join in an act of imagination.

To hell with economy, spend imagination.

John was a wonderful collaborator. He was always asking people, "What do you think?" He wanted all the backstage department heads to be aware of what everyone else was doing. This was a big change from the old mind-set, whereby everyone did his own thing without really being aware of how a new production was evolving. Before John, the Met ran like a mom-and-pop store. There was nobody in charge to make sure that productions went through a logical, monitored process before arriving onstage. Things just happened. In the old days, the Met simply hired a director and a designer, and if the company could afford what those individuals brought in, that was it. A new production got modified only out of financial necessity or because somebody happened to discover—usually at the eleventh hour—that something didn't work.

With the move to the new house, production styles had changed. At the old Met, much of the scenery had been painted drops. At the new Met, most of the scenery was three-dimensional, and the productions were considerably more complex, especially those of Franco Zeffirelli. The Met's management was now obliged to get involved at the outset to make sure that a new production was affordable, artistically sound, and workable. John professionalized the process. One of his early administrative acts was to hire the Met's first thoroughly trained director of lighting, Gil Wechsler, so that a show's lighting design was integrated into the process from the beginning. With the arrival of Wechsler, the irascible, longtime head electrician and de facto lighting designer, Rudy Kuntner, quit.

I became John's facilitator—the guy he came to at every step of the way to make sure he could get what he wanted. It was John who brought me into the auditorium and taught me how to look at a new production and critique it on the basis of what each and every detail would mean to the audience. He hated any scenic excess ("stage constipation," he called it) that distracted from the only thing that mattered to him—the human drama. At John's insistence, eight television monitors with a view of the podium were installed behind the proscenium arch—four on each side—so that the singers could follow the conductor without appearing to look at him as they moved about the stage.

Sitting next to John during stage rehearsals, I quickly learned how to spot a scenic element that stopped the flow or sapped the dramatic tension. With John, I never hesitated to speak up. Invariably, he answered with a nod that said "Fix it." Until John came along, I hadn't realized how often people at the Met said no. With John, the answer was, "Yes—if we can figure out how to do it."

John was always on the offensive. He operated on a level of intensity the likes of which the Met had never seen. Rehearsals were sacred rituals, and he ran them like the abbot of a Trappist monastery. You were there to work, nonstop. When he noticed that someone from the front office had violated his rule of closed rehearsals and was taking notes, he'd yell out, "Haven't you got anything better to do?" If members of the chorus were idly chatting upstage while he was downstage working with one of the principal singers, he'd fix them with a look that could start a forest fire. "Silence!" he'd holler. "You're still in character!" He was particularly hard on the dancers, who—as dancers do when they aren't dancing—were always chatting, stretching their limbs, and shifting positions. During a rehearsal of *Parade*, he screamed at them, "Goddammit! Can't you stand still? That's the trouble with dancers! They can't stand still!" People feared him, detested him, and did their best for him. He never hollered at me.

One day, after we'd been working together for a few months, John invited me to have lunch with him at his restaurant of choice—Sardi's, next door to the theater where *Equus* was playing. He was attacking the cannelloni when he put his fork down and said, "Joe, I want you to take over the technical side of the house. I can't deal with Michael Bronson [the Met's technical and business administrator]. Every time I ask him a question, it takes weeks to get an answer—*if* I get an answer. I have to have someone who knows how to get things done, who won't put up with the old crap. I want you as my supervisor for scenery, lighting, costumes, props, and all the budgets for anything backstage. You don't have to tell me about yourself. I've done my homework."

I didn't need to be asked twice. "Of course," I said.

"Good. I'll go to Bliss."

John went to Anthony Bliss, a lawyer and former president of the Met, who had replaced Schuyler Chapin in the troika, with the title of executive director. But Bliss refused John's request. The reason, I later discovered from John, was that Bronson, who was desperate to keep his full title, came up with every reason he could as to why I should not be given half his job.

Things dragged on for a year and a half. "Bliss tells me it's a matter of 'evolution'—whatever in God's name that means," John said. Finally, just before the start of the 1977–1978 season, John told me that at a meeting with Bliss, Bronson fired his last and most desperate shot. "We believe Volpe's taking stage lumber for his personal use," he said. It was true—but it wasn't stealing. After every season, we'd lay down a temporary plywood stage floor for the visiting ballet companies, which the Met presented in July and August. Instead of throwing the wood away at the end of summer (it was pretty beaten up by then), I continued the practice of giving it to anyone who could use it. A few years earlier, I'd taken some of it to finish a dock I was building on Lake Hopatcong.

When Bronson finished his spiel, John exploded. "If you really believe what you're saying," he said, "call the police. Bring charges. Tomorrow!" That was the last word out of Bronson.

Bliss finally acquiesced to John, and proposed giving me the title of technical administrator.

"Oh, no," I said to John. "Tell Mr. Bliss that I'm to be named technical director, or it's no deal. I'm not a bureaucrat."

I got my deal, and that August, I became a member of the Met's management. Leaving Local One after fifteen years was not an easy decision. It wasn't a matter of losing my modest pension, which was vested. I was giving up a sense of security—the feeling that if things didn't work out, I had a union to back me up. Apart from John, I didn't have a single friend in the Met's management—and who knew how long he would last?

But this was a chance I had to take. When Anthony Bliss said, "You'll be moving into the office next to Michael Bronson's," I said, "That's perfectly fine. Thank you very much."

One of my new responsibilities was to report to the board on technical matters. I didn't look forward to it. I had no skills as a speaker—nobody had ever asked me to give a speech—and I was afraid of making a fool of myself. I enrolled in a Dale Carnegie training course in public speaking, in Saddle River, New Jersey. For twelve weeks, every evening after work, I practiced standing up and talking extemporaneously, with a halting delivery and sweaty palms, before forty other tongue-tied self-improvers. I soon learned the tricks of projecting self-confidence—how to control my breathing, how to look relaxed, how to make eye contact with my listeners. The showman in me came out. Before long, I was having such a good time that the instructor joked after one particularly enthusiastic monologue, "Maybe we should get the hook."

In the annals of the company's upper management, Tony Bliss was the last patrician—a direct descendant of the company's founders who had regarded the house as their private domain. His grandfather, Cornelius Bliss, was secretary of the interior under President McKinley and a treasurer of the Republican National Committee. His father, also Cornelius Bliss, was an associate of J. P. Morgan and a Met box holder by inheritance. Caruso had sung for his supper at the Bliss mansion on Long Island's North Shore. In 1940, Tony's father, as chairman of the board, had ensured the Met's survival by leading a fund drive that enabled the Met to transfer ownership of the old house from the original investors' real estate holding company, which

*Anthony Bliss, the last patrician*

was on the verge of liquidation, to the non-profit Metropolitan Opera Association. Saving the Met was a family tradition as deep as Tony Bliss's Groton and Harvard education.

In 1956, Bliss was elected president of the board. For ten years, he was part of the faction (whose leader was one of the Met's most generous benefactors, Mrs. August Belmont) that supported Rudolf Bing's efforts to attract the world's best singers and conductors with costly new productions. Relations between Bliss and Bing soured as the Met began its move into the new house—a project in which Bliss was intimately involved. Bing objected to Bliss's formation of the National Company, an effort (led by the Met's beloved Carmen, Risë Stevens) to broaden the appeal of grand opera by touring young singers in Met productions. From Bing's point of view, the money spent on that project, which folded after two seasons, would be better spent at home. Bing insisted that a proposed gift to the National Company of $1 million from Lila Acheson Wallace of *Reader's Digest* be diverted to the Met's general fund. The gift was withdrawn.

The breach between Bing and Bliss widened when Bliss not so discreetly began casting around for a possible successor to Bing, after Bing said that he missed the more genial music world of England, where he had run the Glyndebourne and Edinburgh festivals in the 1940s. Bing retaliated by alerting the board to Bliss's marital troubles with his second wife and the affair he had begun with a beautiful dancer in the Met's ballet troupe, Sally Brayley. (There was some hypocrisy here. Bing's eye for a pretty dancer was well known to everyone who traveled on the spring tours when he was away from his wife.) In 1967, Bliss was voted out as president.

I first encountered Tony Bliss in the spring of 1975, soon after he rode back into the Met to rescue the company from a $9 million deficit. One morning, the new executive director summoned everyone, from administrators to cleaners, to assemble in the auditorium. A tall, slender man in a plain gray suit, he didn't make much of an entrance. He introduced himself quietly, without smiling, and when he said his last name, I detected the hint of a lisp. Then he went on to say that his father had helped out the Met in bad times, and that the Met was in bad times again. He had looked long and hard at the situation, and there was only one solution: he was asking everyone to take a 10 percent reduction in salary. He thanked everyone for their devotion to the Met, and then left the stage. No questions.

I went back to my office, called Bliss's assistant, and asked for a meeting. Bliss was too busy to see me—and he remained too busy for several weeks. Finally, I got an appointment. To my surprise, the Met's new executive director was running the company out of a makeshift cubicle. He seemed perfectly at home. Last patricians don't need a splashy office. He motioned me to a chair.

"You don't know me," I said. "I'm Joseph Volpe, the head of the carpenter shop, and I work as efficiently as possible. I was at the meeting where you asked everyone to take a ten percent pay cut. Well, I won't take it. As a matter of fact, I'll fight it, because I can think of a hundred ways the Met can save that money just by doing something about all the waste around here."

He took off his glasses and started cleaning them. He turned slightly sideways, so that I found myself talking to his shoulder. Finally, he said, "Can you be more specific?"

I cited various unnecessary practices on the production side and extravagances in the costume shop. "I realize that the designers have to be given a certain license," I said, "but if you have peasants in more than one opera, why make new costumes? Peasants are peasants." When he didn't smile, I added, "And there's maybe a little flab on the administrative side, too."

"I see," he said, turning more of his shoulder to me. Off came the glasses again. Then he said, "Well, thank you for stopping by, Joe. I'll think about what you've told me." My days as "Mr. Volpe" were over.

A month later, I received a hand-delivered note from Bliss in an envelope marked CONFIDENTIAL. It said that I was "requested" to make an appointment with the executive director. The days when the head

*With Joe Clark, my right hand*

of the house suddenly materialized backstage and pulled you into the wings were also over. The meeting was brief: "I'd like you to write down all your ideas about reducing costs," Bliss said.

I went to work on my list, presented my suggestions at another meeting, and got no response, then or later—another sign of the new, Byzantine style of leadership.

B ut Tony Bliss, as John had said, believed in "evolution." As techni-cal director, I quickly shored up my position by hiring two bril-liant young assistants. One was Joe Clark, whom the designer Ming Cho Lee had recommended for an internship while Clark was still writing his Yale doctorate on *Tannhäuser*. When the director Otto Schenk overheard Joe speaking fluent German, he tried to lure him away. "Hands off," I said. "He's mine." Joe has been my indispensable right hand ever since. My other assistant technical director was Horst Zeiglitz, a technical whiz from the Hamburg State Opera. We'd first met when that company came for a brief run at the Met during the summer of 1967. We met again during one of my many trips to Euro-pean opera houses, where I was sent to prepare visiting companies and directors on backstage operations at the Met.

Since Dexter hated confronting European heavyweights such as

Schenk, August Everding, and Jean-Pierre Ponnelle about their con-
cepts for a new production, he'd dispatch me to bring them down to
earth by whatever cajolery and technical mumbo-jumbo I could come
up with. It was excellent training in director-speak—especially when
both parties are talking in a different language—and I could always
stop things from blowing up by saying, "Well, I'm only the messenger." In Salzburg, Hamburg, Vienna, Munich, London, Rome, and San
Francisco, I established relationships with directors that I've drawn on
ever since.

By 1979, the Met had wiped out its deficit, thanks to a big uptick in
fund-raising led by a sharp new director of development, Marilyn
Shapiro, who'd come over from the political arena. (The proposed,
horribly handled 10 percent pay cut went nowhere.) In August of that
year, a confidential note summoned me to Bliss's office—by then he'd
moved into the general manager's quarters. I was given another pro-
motion, this time to director of operations. Now I was to be in charge
of all the Met's nonadministrative and nonartistic functions, both
backstage and in the front of the house, where I would oversee ushers,
box office, house maintenance, and so on. My principal mandate was
damage control. Runaway budgets were my priority.

For John Dexter, the 1979–1980 season was a triumph. Two of his
new productions that fall—a sparkling period pastiche for
Mozart's *The Abduction from the Seraglio* and a bold updating of Brecht for
*Mahagonny*—were critical and box-office hits. But John was feeling
increasingly marginalized. James Levine, with whom he'd been arm in
arm as a fellow missionary for twentieth-century opera, had hired a
strong-minded artistic administrator, Joan Ingpen, who had been at
Covent Garden and with Rolf Liebermann at the Paris Opera. John
began to be excluded from discussions involving the choice of singers
and repertory. A period that he describes in his autobiography as "the
happiest of my life" was coming to an end. Just how painful this
became for him is reflected in the case of shingles he contracted that
winter. It continued to plague him for many months, keeping him, as
he wrote, "flat on my back in bed."

In opera, the potential for conflict between musical and dramatic
considerations is always there. John once said, "Conductors see only
with their ears." To which a conductor might reply, "Directors have
no ears." In the case of James Levine and John Dexter, the creative

tension was heightened by a polar difference in personality. Jimmy was all nonconfrontational sweetness on the surface; underneath, he was determined to achieve his musical goals without interference— and with the protection of the most powerful agent in the business, Ronald Wilford, the head of Columbia Artists. John, on the other hand, was incorrigibly up-front, also determined to get what he wanted, but easily wounded and inept at protecting his flanks.

Their relationship deteriorated. In the fall of 1980, John resigned as director of productions, but stayed on as a staging consultant and house director. By March of 1983, he was writing in his diary, "I could not work with JL in any creative way and I do not enjoy the 'political' atmosphere he creates and the relentless pursuit of popularity in which he drowns himself and the work like a child with a sweet trolley."

From Jimmy there wasn't a peep.

To John, I had also become a bad guy. In my new capacity as director of operations, I now had the authority to tell him what was or wasn't financially realistic. In one of John's most bitter diary entries, he writes, "This Hurt: My own discovery, someone I took from the floor and trained and promoted to an office position, betrayed me. JV chose money over loyalty."

My sense of loyalty to John was never in question, but I had a new job to do. In 1982, by which point he scarcely ever came into the house, John asked that the Met pay for a full-time assistant. In my zeal to trim company fat, I turned him down. The best we could do, I said, was to pay an assistant's salary for three days a week. After a flurry of memos to all concerned—John's issues with the Met were always accompanied by a flurry of memos—he came into my office. "This means war!" he said.

"What's the matter with you?" I said.

"You're a turncoat!"

"Wait a minute, John. . . ."

He fixed me with his best menacing stare. "I want you to know," he growled, "that I was in a real war with real live ammunition. For me, this is child's play."

"John," I said. "This is the way it is. Period."

He glared at me, turned his back, and never spoke to me again.

The next year, he submitted his designs for a new production of Verdi's *Simon Boccanegra*. For costly excess, they out-Zeffirellied Zeffirelli. I advised Tony Bliss that the production was much larger than it needed to be. The Dexter designs were rejected. They may have been John's way of telling the Met that he could do as lavish a production as anyone, especially since he'd been out of his element with *Aida* and *Rigoletto*. It was also his way of telling the Met that he'd had enough.

In November of 1985, John wrote in his diary (as later published in *The Honourable Beast*): "If a revolution fails there is no need for bloodshed as long as the first revolution is only the first and not the last. And anyway it's silly to go on playing Trotsky to Volpe's Stalin (if you follow my political and literary drift). So never send to know from whose hands the ice pick cometh, it comes for Thee baby, if you really want to know, and I prefer not to watch the end of the revolution."

John died five years later, in March 1990. We never reconciled, but I'm still using what he taught me.

# 8

## FROM THE WATER TO THE BRIDGE

Isadore Philip Sipser, senior partner of Sipser, Weinstock, Harper, and Dorn, was a classic of the Old Left. In 1953, Sipser—his old friends called him Izzy; his new friends called him Phil; his wife, Martha, called him Sipser—had refused to tell the House Un-American Activities Committee whether he was a Communist. Before he was thirty, he'd lost three political races on the American Labor Party ticket for the New York State legislature. In 1968, he'd managed the unsuccessful mayoral campaign of the city's leading champion of underdogs, Paul O'Dwyer.

Izzy Sipser grew up on Manhattan's Lower East Side, where he helped his father peddle tomatoes from a pushcart. Over the years, he'd represented all the little guys—longshoremen, ironworkers, brewery workers, social workers, film editors, and museum employees.

In 1967, he took up the cause of another group with a long history of employment grievances—orchestra musicians—when he was called upon to mediate a contract dispute at the New York Philharmonic. He became so good at it that *The New York Times* called him "the Moses who has led the symphony and opera musicians of this country to within sight of the promised land of milk and honey, after years of wandering the deserts of short seasons, low pay and no vacations." When I first encountered him at the negotiating table, I thought he was the most inflexible man I'd ever met. Within two months, we had developed a relationship of trust and respect.

In 1972, Sipser was hired as special counsel by the ninety-plus members of the Met Orchestra to represent them in their upcoming contract negotiations. Eight years later, in the spring of 1980, about nine months before the current contract was due to expire on July 31, he sat down with Tony Bliss. In a voice like Lee J. Cobb's, he said, "You've been to the well twice. Now it's our turn."

The well had been filling up nicely, thanks in part to the Met's previous two contracts with the musicians, who had accepted modest wage increases when the company was running deep deficits. Now it was a different story. The Met was operating in the black for the first time in years. The 1979–1980 season had shown a profit of $100,000. A drive to build up the Met's once-paltry endowment, led by the new board president Frank E. Taplin, had added $40 million to the savings account. This time around, the members of Local 802 were not inclined to roll over, especially after Taplin and Bliss announced that they expected the endowment to reach $100 million by the Met's centennial season of 1983–1984. It wasn't very smart to talk about pulling in that kind of money and not expect the people who work for you to want a piece of the action. But Bliss and Taplin, another blue-chip lawyer, hadn't gone to the same school as Izzy Sipser.

In that first meeting, Bliss, as I later learned from Sipser, made another mistake. Sipser told Bliss that, apart from wage and pension increases, what the orchestra musicians cared most about was a lighter workload. Currently, they were obligated to play five of the Met's seven performances each week. Now they wanted that obligation reduced to four performances a week. (After the 1965 contract, the musicians had gone from seven performances to five—an arrangement made possible by the Met's hiring of extra musicians at a lower wage level.)

Sipser pointed out that the request was in line with prevailing conditions at the major American symphony orchestras. Hiring extra musicians, he maintained, wouldn't strain the budget.

Bliss nodded favorably. At heart, he was more a lover of ballet than of opera. Whenever he ventured backstage, he had his eye out for the dancers, not the singers. For some time, he'd been toying with the idea of cutting costs by reducing the number of weekly performances from seven to four and filling the "dark" nights with the Joffrey Ballet, of which he'd been chairman during his years away from the Met. (His new wife, Sally, a former Met ballet dancer, was the founder of Joffrey II, the company's troupe for younger dancers.) The musicians' desire for a four-performance week seemed to fit right in with his plans. He looked Sipser in the eye and said that he didn't see any problem. Why *not* change the Met's weekly schedule of opera from seven to four performances?

Sipser was a man of his word, and he took Tony Bliss at his word. Thus, the die was cast for a battle that made the labor dispute of ten years earlier look like a tea party.

Contract negotiations began in the late spring of 1980, by which point Bliss, after realizing the budgetary implications of the musicians' proposal, had changed his mind. The specter of the old debt-ridden days was still in the air, and Bliss and the board wanted nothing to do with anything that would raise expenses, such as hiring additional players. Moreover, since the contract with Local 802 traditionally set the pattern for all Met contracts, the trustees were worried that acceding to the orchestra's demands for a reduced workload would inspire similar demands from the other unions. The board also feared that adding more substitute players might damage the Met artistically, even though the musicians had already consulted James Levine on the subject, and the Met's music director had assured them that it wouldn't.

For the musicians, the basic issue was quality of life. During the years since the move into the new house, their working lives had changed. In the old days, most of the musicians—and the stagehands, chorus members, and dancers—lived within walking distance or a short subway ride from the Met. Now, thanks to rising crime and rents in the city, they lived increasingly in the suburbs. For many, getting to and from the daily rehearsals and returning for an evening performance took hours, not minutes.

Life had also changed within the house. Under Levine, musical standards were higher. The Met's first music director was determined to build a world-class orchestra. His rigorous rehearsals often went into overtime. Bliss and Taplin seemed to be trying to turn back the clock when they took the position that the musicians' demand for parity with the leading symphony organizations was absurd. The two men argued that the Met Orchestra was by no means the principal attraction—only a cog in the mechanism. True. But neither Bliss nor Taplin (who happened to be a good amateur pianist) had ever been in the Met's pit for five hours of *Parsifal* or *Die Meistersinger.* In Wagner, if you're a string player, you never stop cranking. Nor is it likely that either man had ever looked at the score of one of Levine's favorite works, *Lulu,* which is like three operas in one. Considering the time that the musicians spent practicing at home to show up for work fully prepared, their request wasn't so outrageous.

But the Met's management was playing hardball. When the musicians offered to accept slightly less in wages to cover the cost of a shorter week, Bliss and Taplin turned them down. The Met's labor counsel, Edward Silver, said publicly that he couldn't understand why the musicians were so adamant about the four-performance issue. Apparently, Tony Bliss hadn't informed Silver about what he had in effect, promised Sipser.

With no agreement in sight, the Met's management canceled rehearsals. Two weeks later, Bliss announced that he was canceling the opening night's performance of *Turandot,* with Luciano Pavarotti and Montserrat Caballé. If the loss of any two opera stars for opening night was tantamount to a national emergency, it was the loss of those two.

Jimmy Carter called up Bliss and offered to step in. But there was no progress. When the lights stayed off, Bliss and Taplin followed the example of Rudolf Bing and George Moore. They locked the doors.

"Cancellation of the season is a decision we have made with great reluctance," Taplin announced, "but it is a decision we have been forced to make. There is no way we could accept the orchestra's demand for a four-performance week and expect the Met to survive."

For good measure, Bliss added, "There appears to be no speedy resolution in sight with our orchestra. Acceptance of their current proposals would return us to the dark ages—season after season burdened with overwhelming deficits. We have worked too hard in recent years to turn this company around both artistically and financially to see it destroyed by giving in to the orchestra's demands. The future of the Metropolitan Opera itself is at stake."

Sipser and the musicians had one answer for Bliss: "Resign." Then Sipser invoked the wrath of the Old Left. The Met, he declared, was a public trust. By locking out the employees, it was not living up to its fiduciary responsibilities. Unless the employees were allowed to go back to work, he would go to the attorney general and have the board removed.

There was nothing personal in Sipser's threat, but Bliss, who probably hadn't heard a lot of talk about the public trust at the family dinner table, took it personally. He retaliated by committing a third blunder that violated a cardinal rule of successful labor talks: don't negotiate in the press.

During the next few weeks, the New York papers gave more ink to the Met's lockout than they did to the war between Iran and Iraq. The *Daily News* reported that Bliss had taken to referring to the musicians as "lemmings," and the paper quoted him as saying, "If we weren't running in the black, they [the musicians] would probably be out selling ice cream."

Sandor Balint, a violinist and the chairman of the orchestra's negotiating committee, returned the compliment: "the Met was founded in the 1880s by robber barons as their plaything," he told a reporter. "The attitude has persisted that everybody who walks through the door is a servant."

The *Times* ran a front-page story that got to the heart of the matter—the headline read, "Class Distinctions Add to Discord Complicating Met Labor Problem." Missing in this and other articles was any mention of the most serious side effect of the class issue: a lot of the "little" donors whose support had become increasingly crucial to the Met's financial security were turned off by all the bloodletting. Opera is habit-forming, but once the habit is broken, it's easily kicked. The rank-and-file Met patrons started thinking about spending their Met dollars on a family vacation in the Caribbean or the Grand Tetons. It would be

*Met musicians during the 1980 lockout*

several seasons before those thousands of disillusioned opera lovers in the Met's huge national and international "family" were wooed back.

I hadn't taken part in any of the contract talks, and it was only after the cancellation of opening night that I understood how bad things had become. During a meeting called to determine which staff members should be kept on to maintain the house while it was dark, Tony Bliss said, "If we don't get this dispute settled in a week or two, we'll just close the place down and start another company from scratch."

I couldn't believe what I was hearing. Was Bliss seriously entertaining the idea of throwing eighteen hundred employees out of work and doing away with the Met as if it were nothing more than a broken train set? I said, "Tony, you can't do that. You don't have that right."

"What do you mean?" he said.

"What I mean is the Met doesn't belong to you and the board. It belongs to everyone who works here and the public who loves and pays for opera."

He frowned and began cleaning his glasses. "Well," he finally said, "what would *you* suggest?"

"Sit down and work out an agreement."

"All right," he said. "Carter is sending in a federal mediator. Why don't you talk to him and see what you can do."

A few days later, I was invited to meet the Met's labor attorney, Ed Silver, in Tony Bliss's office. Silver had recently represented Mayor Ed Koch's administration in the city's difficult but successful negotiations with municipal employees, and he was riding high. With me was Jane Hermann, the Met's savvy director of outside presentations (visiting ballet companies and the like). Despite her close friendship with Bliss, she wasn't shy about asking tough questions of her boss.

I asked Silver to go over his position on possible modifications to the orchestra's work rules. He spoke for ten minutes. He used three of those minutes to tell me why he wouldn't answer the question; four to give me the answer; and three to tell me to forget everything he'd just said.

I said, "Excuse me, what are you getting at?"

Silver peered at me over his glasses. "Mr. Volpe," he said, "we're not building scenery. I'll do the negotiations. You go back to cutting plywood."

I'd already done some homework on Silver. He'd grown up in Manhattan and summered in Brighton Beach. It was long way from Bliss territory on the North Shore. I retorted, "That's something I'd expect an attorney to say."

Shortly afterward, we met with I. Philip Sipser in the palatial conference room at Silver's law firm, Proskauer Rose, on Madison Avenue. The walls were paneled in walnut, the table was marble, and the carpet was softer than the sand had ever been on Brighton Beach. If a telephone rang, you wouldn't have heard it. So this was where the Met's money was going.

Silver wore a hundred-dollar haircut and a trim, custom-made suit. Sipser hadn't seen a barber in months, and his suit could have doubled as a poncho. Silver's smile looked like it hurt. Sipser didn't even bother to smile. As I shook his hand, I felt him studying me.

I began sitting in on negotiation meetings, and it became clear that Silver wasn't part of the solution; he was part of the problem. He didn't talk to the musicians; he talked over them. He gave speeches, not positions. His windy rationales for the Met's hard line always began with "Let me explain. . . ." It was as though he were talking to a bunch of morons. Gradually, I realized that he was trying to impress Tony Bliss. Silver, the smooth hotshot who grew up on the West Side, wasn't about to challenge an East Side WASP mind-set that viewed the musicians as spoiled kids who didn't know their place.

Meanwhile, Sipser just sat there, revealing nothing. Finally, in plain English that everyone could understand, he would say, in effect, "No dice." This was a guy you didn't want to go up against.

Now, in my first private meeting with the two of them, I began to sense that Sipser's stubbornness was based on something that wasn't on the table.

I made a private appointment to see him. I didn't tell Tony Bliss where I was going—if I had, I would have been fired. The firm of Sipser, Weinstock, Harper and Dorn was also on Madison Avenue, but in a building whose marble hadn't been cleaned since the Depression. Getting to Sipser's office was like going through a war zone. I threaded my way past cartons of files piled every which way and stacks of old newspapers. A dozen phones were ringing at once. Everyone was hollering over partitions. This wasn't too different from my father's old place on Fourteenth Street.

"Have a seat, Joe," Sipser said. "Call me Phil."

"So what's really going on?" I said. "This is killing everyone. Why won't the orchestra budge?"

"We were promised a four-performance week," he said.

This was news to me. "And what led you to that conclusion?" I said.

"Mr. Bliss," he began—and then proceeded to fill me in about their initial meeting.

I said, "Sounds like Mr. Bliss spoke before he knew all the facts."

Sipser smiled as though I'd just said that the moon was made of green cheese. "Well, let me tell you something, Joe," he said. "When you're dealing with people's lives, working people's lives, you don't make casual promises you have no intention of keeping. Not in my world."

I nodded.

He went on: "I'll tell you something else. We've done our projections on the cost of hiring new musicians, and the number is considerably lower than what Ed Silver is throwing around. He keeps talking about bringing in regular players at full pay and with full benefits. We're talking about bringing in extras at less pay and with no benefits. In that case, the Met can easily afford a four-performance week. Moreover, Mr. Levine has already assured us that there will be no loss of artistic quality. But if my old friend Ed Silver continues to pretend not to have heard any of this, the dispute will go on. Do the math."

I did. Sipser was right: the Met could easily absorb the cost of hiring extra players at reduced pay. But math alone would not bend Bliss and Taplin—they would lose too much face. I remembered something that Eddie Lapidus had once told me at the Great Wall, inspired no doubt by the spareribs: "It's called yin and yang, Joe. When someone asks you to give them something and you think it's tough to give it, ask for something in return."

I came up with the yin and the yang, and sat down with Tony Bliss. I pointed out that the Met was now paying the musicians an hourly rate for rehearsals. What if the orchestra, in return for a four-performance week, "gave" the Met four extra hours of rehearsal time?

"I'll take it up with Ed Silver," Bliss said.

The kiss of death, I thought, and sure enough, a few days later Bliss called me into his office and said, "Silver says it will never work."

I wasn't going to be brushed off that easily. When I persisted, Bliss finally agreed that I could raise the idea with Sipser.

"Alone?" I said.

"No," Bliss said. "With Silver and another member of management."

He suggested my old pal Michael Bronson, whom the musicians thoroughly distrusted. I chose Jane Hermann.

Silver opened the meeting sounding as though there was this ridiculous little business that had to be dispensed with before he and Sipser could get on with the real issues: "Volpe wants to say something."

I began, "Phil . . ."

Silver nearly jumped out of his chair. Where did I get off calling the enemy by his first name? I paid no attention and pitched my idea of four "free" hours of rehearsal in exchange for the four-performance week.

Sipser listened without taking his eyes off me, and then said quietly in a voice that would have stopped a train, "This is out of the question."

I took a deep breath. "Sipser," I said, pausing to let that sink in, "you'll never get an agreement because you're not flexible." I gave him the hint of a smile.

Silver turned scarlet.

Sipser didn't blink. "I'll get back to you," he said, looking at me, not Silver. He gave me the hint of a smile, too.

During the next two weeks, I became Tony Bliss's de facto chief negotiator in an airless suite of conference rooms at the Doral Inn on Lexington Avenue—a world away from the Met. Jimmy Carter's mediator, Wayne Horvitz, was an effective messenger between the two camps, and little by little, things loosened up. One night, as I was walking back to the hotel after dinner with Martin Oppenheimer, Silver's number two, I said, "Marty, you know we can get more out of this than just the rehearsal payback. How about asking the orchestra to give us a free Sunday concert—we'll call it a benefit for their pension fund."

Bliss was skeptical, but Marty passed the suggestion along to Horvitz, and the orchestra agreed. Bliss was impressed that in the middle of all this turmoil I'd been able to come up with another break for the Met. Since then, I've made it a practice to use an impasse as an opportunity to bring up fresh ideas. Joe Clark says that I approach a problem by "surrounding" it. Bombarding is more like it.

On October 27, eleven weeks after the Met closed its doors, the orchestra ratified a four-year contract during a meeting at the Roseland Ballroom. Among other things, the musicians got their four performances a week, and the Met got a cut in rehearsal costs. Getting an agreement with the choristers, who demanded parity with the musicians, took two more weeks after Taplin—with his usual tin ear and bad timing—crowed to the press prematurely about the deal with the orchestra.

When the smoke had cleared—the season finally opened on December 10, with James Levine conducting an orchestral concert of Mahler's Second Symphony, appropriately entitled *Resurrection*—Sipser called me up. "Joe," he said, quoting Bogie, "I think this is the beginning of a beautiful friendship. Let's have lunch."

One of the lessons learned from the lockout was that the lines of authority at the Met had to be clarified. In January, the board named Tony Bliss general manager—a return to the old Rudolf Bing days of top-down leadership—and retained Levine as music director. The board also established three new administrative positions just under Bliss: assistant manager for development (Marilyn Shapiro), assistant manager for artistic planning (Joan Ingpen), and assistant manager for operations (me).

My new responsibilities included the coordination of personnel and budgets for all aspects of the house except for fund-raising, choosing repertory, and casting. The job also came with a special mission: "Joe," Tony Bliss said, "I don't ever want to go through anything like this again. The musicians seem to trust you. I want you to be the company's liaison with the unions. You'll be working with Ed Silver."

"I'm sorry," I said, "but I can't take the job with Ed Silver."

Off came the glasses.

I went on, "He doesn't listen to anyone but himself. He doesn't understand the musicians, and the musicians don't understand him."

Bliss said, "But you have to work with an attorney."

"Okay, but not Silver."

In the end, we agreed that I'd work with another lawyer from Bliss's old firm of Milbank, Tweed, Hadley and McCloy—a nice, able guy named John Dean.

I was delighted with the assignment, though I still felt that my real home at the Met was backstage. After all, my personal life was only a more complicated version of what most of the Met's musicians, dancers, and choristers had to contend with. I commuted into the city every morning from my house in Sparta, New Jersey, and on weekends I'd head to Long Island for family dinners with my parents and my older kids.

The first thing I did in my new job was to invite Sipser to lunch, this time on me. Our Chinese restaurant of choice was Shun Lee on West Sixty-fifth Street. It was a step up from the Great Wall. During lunch, Sipser said, "One day, when my father and I were selling tomatoes on Delancey Street, he said to me, 'Sonny, you think you're pretty smart? You see that bridge there? Any man can jump from the bridge to the water, but only a great man can jump from the water to the bridge.'"

I said, "What are you talking about, Phil?"

He said, "We're going to jump from the water to the bridge. We'll start on the next contract eighteen months ahead of time. But we need a deadline."

I said, "How about the centennial gala? That's on October 23, 1983, nine months before the contracts expire. If we can get a deal by then, Tony Bliss can announce it from the stage. I'll make sure that you and your wife get seats in a parterre box—Tony Bliss's neighborhood."

"There's nothing wrong with New Rochelle," Sipser growled.

"And you can use the occasion as an excuse to buy your wife a new dress."

"Point taken."

Bliss was dubious about our working so far ahead of time, but during the next eighteen months, Sipser and I had regular discussions about the Met's needs and the musicians' needs. He was very tough, but he was also the kind of guy who could tell you to go to hell one minute and the next minute say, "What are you and your wife doing for dinner on Saturday night?"

A few days before the centennial gala, I told Bliss that we had a deal. At the gala, which was nationally televised and which featured virtually every great living opera star in the Met's past and present, Bliss stepped out in front of the curtain and hailed the early agreement with the musicians as a milestone in the company's history. In his thanks, he pointed me out in my seat on the main floor and—higher up in a parterre box—Phil Sipser and his wife, Martha. She was wearing a new dress.

. . .

*Lecturing with Phil Sipser at Wharton, circa 1985*

Phil Sipser became something of a paternal figure to me after my father died on New Year's Eve, 1984. Dad had long since sold the clothing business because his phlebitis had made it impossible for him to go to work. The drop in his income had been traumatic. But after selling the big house and moving into a smaller one, he'd had a wonderful twenty years getting involved in town politics and running the Glen Cove Housing Authority. He loved helping kids, particularly ones who, as he put it, "didn't have a chance." He was especially proud of the low-income housing development on Back Road Hill. Every Christmas, he went over there to hand out presents.

My mother, on the other hand, had become such a popular first-grade English teacher that she couldn't walk down Main Street without former pupils coming up and saying hello.

My father and I had a special relationship. It was not uncommon for us to get into an argument at the dinner table—usually over my insane belief that Muhammad Ali was a better fighter than Rocky Marciano. After one particularly heated exchange on the subject, I withdrew to the backyard for a cigarette. I was joined by one of my father's old friends. "Joey," he said, "it's disrespectful to speak to your father that way." I went back in and told my father that his friend had objected to the tone of our argument. "What argument?" my father said. "We were having a conversation."

On Easter Sunday of 1984, we were all down at my sister Joan's place in Fairfax, Virginia, when my father got up from the table and went into the bathroom. He couldn't keep his food down. I insisted he see a doctor immediately. He was diagnosed with stomach cancer. When it spread to his esophagus, he underwent surgery. The cancer continued to spread.

A week before Christmas, my father summoned the entire family to Glen Cove. On Christmas Day, he asked to see me alone in his bedroom. In a voice like Marlon Brando's whisper to Al Pacino toward the end of *The Godfather,* he went through everything that was on his mind. "I didn't want your mother to be taken advantage of at the funeral home," he began, "so I called Guy Minutoli [the funeral director] and chose a simple wooden box for the coffin. Why get a more expensive one? It's only going to go into the ground. The cemetery will require that you purchase a concrete box to hold the coffin. They'll also try to sell you a lead liner to preserve the coffin. Forgot about it. Preserve it for what?"

Then he said, "Your mother stays in the house. Your sisters will suggest that she move in with one of them. That would not be good for her. Make sure she stays here." He went on. "When does your contract expire?"

I told him.

He said, "Well, make sure you get everything that's coming to you. By the way, I have no use for your boss. [He and Tony Bliss had never met.] You're doing all the work, and he's taking all the credit."

"Right, Dad," I said.

"And one more thing," he said. "I checked the positions of the headstones in the family plot at Holy Rood [a cemetery in the neighboring town of Westbury]. They'll want to put the coffin in the ground so that my head is next to the headstone. Don't let them. I want my feet next to the headstone so that I'll be facing east. I want to see the sunrise."

A few days after Christmas, my mother asked everyone to come back for New Year's Eve. I said, "But we have plans for New Year's Eve." She said, "Hold on, I'll tell him." She returned to the phone and said, "He says, 'New Year's Eve.' "

We went out to Glen Cove on New Year's Eve and found my father in a new hospital bed that allowed him to sit up. He'd insisted that it be moved into the dining room. His voice was gone, but he wanted to be at the center of the action. At four in the afternoon, one of my uncles came over and said, "Joe, your father wants you."

I went into the dining room. My father gestured that he wanted to get out of bed. I lifted him into a chair and sat next to him with my arm around him. My mother came over and sat on his other side. We sat like that for a few minutes, not saying anything. Finally, he stopped breathing, and I realized that he hadn't wanted to die lying down.

Seventeen years later, on April 5, 2001, the *Times* ran an obituary under the headline, "I. Philip Sipser, an Advocate of Musicians, Is Dead at 82."

Izzy Sipser had not been directly involved in the most recent contract talks because some of the musicians felt that he and I—now the Met's general manager—had grown too close. It was true. We had become real pals, but we'd also remained the best of adversaries. One result of our relationship was that there had been no repeat of the 1980 battle with Local 802. Between the two of us, we'd settled every contract disagreement peacefully, far in advance of the expiration date. We had jumped from the water to the bridge.

# 9

## TEXAS GRIT

Franco Zeffirelli hadn't worked at the Met since 1971, when, during Rudolf Bing's last season, he staged an *Otello* whose ship in Act 1 was big enough for the entire Venetian navy. The Bliss regime's obsession with budgetary discipline, John Dexter's fondness for lean-and-mean productions, and Zeffirelli's ambition to become a famous international film director like his mentor, Luchino Visconti, had kept him away from the house for ten years. But at the end of the decade, he was welcomed back, thanks to a rich widow from the Texas Panhandle, Mrs. Donald D. Harrington, whose taste in opera made them a perfect match.

Sybil Harrington once told me that she'd been born in a house in Amarillo that had dirt floors. She was the granddaughter of one of the town's original families, the Buckinghams, and she grew up learning how to fish and shoot like a man. Her hair—snow white when I knew her—always looked as though she'd just been to the beauty parlor, and she wore jewelry from the window at Cartier and suits and outfits from the House of Dior. But she'd never lost her Texas grit. You could easily see her as the little woman standing with a shotgun in the door-way of her house on the prairie, warning a band of painted Indians, "I'll shoot the first one who moves."

She grew up loving dance and music, and she studied piano, organ, and ballet. She was a fan of the Met's Saturday matinee broadcasts from the moment they started in 1931. According to Panhandle lore, she was a pretty young thing who was crossing the main street in Amarillo when she spotted a dapper young man stepping out of a Stutz Bearcat. She is reported to have said to a girlfriend, "I'm going to marry that fellow. Watch me!" (I have a letter from Sybil that she wrote to my wife Jean, congratulating us on the birth of our daughter, Anna. Every sentence ends with an exclamation point.)

Sybil married the man with the Stutz. He was Donald Harrington, one of the richest oilmen in Texas, with a major interest in hundreds of oil and gas wells throughout the Panhandle. He was also one of the most generous. The Harrington Foundation supported everything in that part of the state, from the Boy Scouts to a cancer research insti-tute to a ballet company to a museum of Texas wildcatting. After the Harringtons' only child, Sally, died unexpectedly within a few months of her father's death in 1974, Sybil Harrington made a new family for herself at the Met.

She and her husband had been longtime contributors to the Met, and one day in 1978, when she was in New York to attend some operas, Sybil asked two board members, Mrs. Louis Douglas and Mrs. John Barry "Nin" Ryan, if there was something more she could do for the company. She was stunned when they suggested that she underwrite a new production of *Don Carlo*. She later told a reporter, "Like most everyone else, I thought the Met was this rich house that all these New Yorkers gave all this money to. But the Met doesn't have that much money. Opera is the most expensive of all the arts to produce."

It became a lot more expensive once Mrs. Harrington agreed to bankroll *Don Carlo*. When rehearsals began, she sat through all of them. "I was so excited," she recalled, "I didn't even know there was such a thing as a donor putting on a production." She later made it a practice not to interfere with the director, but she put her foot down when John Dexter, who was directing *Don Carlo*, tried to eliminate a white horse and Irish wolfhounds from the opening hunt scene. "If it's grand opera," she said, "it's got to be *grand*." The animals stayed, and

*Sybil Harrington, left, with Risë Stevens, the Met's great Carmen*

they're still there. She also hated the flat silver walls that Dexter and the designer, David Reppa, came up with, but she bided her time until after Dexter left the Met. Once he did, the scenery department, at her insistence, redid the walls with an elaborate pattern more in keeping with King Philip's—and her—taste.

Dexter's *Don Carlo* was not received with much enthusiasm, and the next new production that Sybil Harrington backed didn't fare much better. A staging of Verdi's *The Masked Ball*—which the director, Elijah Moshinsky, updated to colonial Boston during the Tea Party—got a mixed verdict when it opened in 1980. (Sybil was among the detractors.) A month later, the critics panned a dull, picture-postcard *Manon Lescaut*, directed by Gian Carlo Menotti, which Sybil had also paid for. A new Harrington-backed *Traviata*, directed by Colin Graham, was lackluster.

But Sybil Harrington had gumption, and she was determined to make a success with her new family. (I love what she told Joan Ingpen: "I have to do things in Texas, but there is a limit to what you can do in Texas.") In 1980, she promised $20 million for the Centennial Fund, a gift that prompted Tony Bliss to recommend rechristening the auditorium in her name. The following season, she hit her stride when the Met hired Franco Zeffirelli to replace the decrepit old *La Bohème* with a new one.

. . .

Zeffirelli's *Bohème*, which opened on December 14, 1981, is the most successful production in the Met's history. It has been performed 327 times during the past twenty-five years, appearing in all but two of the seasons; on average, it's filled 94 percent of the house. A few years ago, *La Bohème* became the most performed opera in the Met's history, replacing *Aida* as number one. (Number three is *Carmen*.) By my best estimate, the production has been seen by more than four million operagoers, and it's brought in over $140 million at the box office. Not a bad return on an initial investment of $823,900 ($2.5 million in today's money).

Zeffirelli had been staging *Bohème* for many years, and by the time it arrived at the Met, his latest version had already been done at La Scala and at the Vienna State Opera. But no one had ever seen a *Bohème* like this one—it was Metrified. To fill out the big proscenium, Zeffirelli added a second level to the garret scene in Act 1, so that Mimi and Rodolfo meet in an attic, beyond which are glimpses of the Paris skyline in the mid-nineteenth century. For the Café Momus scene in Act 2, he installed a dozen steps so that the audience could get the full impact of seeing 143 Parisian revelers, 24 street urchins, 19 soldiers, 14 vendors, a marching band of 12, 2 live animals, and a fake bear. Franco and Sybil really connected on animals.

There's always a method to Franco's madness. Some critics complained that Puccini's little story about starving artists got swamped by spectacle—to which Zeffirelli replied that he wanted to show "the fragility of the Bohemian group as against the large, grey French capital. While the garret is small and intimate, the public is treated to Parisian skies, roofs, chimneys and balconies. . . . I want to underline the helplessness and humanity of these nice young people lost in the large city." Critics, like the one in the *Times* who said that it was "a production for people who come *wanting* to applaud the scenery," missed the point. The "gasp effect" is an integral part of grand opera.

In fact, nobody could complain that the characters got lost because there was too much to look at. Franco is such a master of stage design—of color and architecture, perspective and movement—that no matter how opulent his productions become, they never look cluttered. In a Zeffirelli circus, you always know who's singing and what they're singing about.

In his memoir, Franco is absolutely right when he writes:

> What so intrigued the audience about my new *Bohème* was the way I treated the role of Mimi, the waif whose last love affair, as she dies of consumption, is the subject of the opera. Every production I had ever seen had had Mimi arrive at the artist's studio (where she meets the poet Rodolfo) as a beautiful, radiant young woman. Only later does she succumb to her illness. This seemed to me to make nonsense of the piece. Why, I asked, does she immediately faint in front of him? The problem in other productions has been that the average soprano is just too big and healthy to do what the libretto and the score demand, so the truth is usually fudged. But I had [Teresa] Stratas again [who had been the Violetta in Zeffirelli's landmark production and film of *La Traviata*] and, as no one else before, she could be both beautiful and waif-like. . . . Thus, when Stratas as Mimi entered the studio, she was already clearly dying: pallid, coughing and feverish, she fainted dead away, and only when Rodolfo has carried her to the fire and sings "Che viso da malata" does he see that beneath her pallor she is beautiful. It is then that false hope is raised, and because we had admitted the audience to the truth, they were able fully to experience the tragedy. Only the petite and haunting Teresa Stratas could have got away with it, and only José Carreras looked youthful enough to set beside her. It was an extraordinary and unique combination, and one I doubt I shall see bettered.

The cheering that followed the opening night performance was unlike any I'd ever heard. Leading the applause from one of the center parterre boxes was Sybil Harrington, who had found the director of her dreams.

Sybil wasn't hands-on during the course of putting together a new production, but she wasn't hands-off either. In 1984, at the instigation of James Levine, she backed a rarity—Riccardo Zandonai's *Francesca da Rimini*, a post-Puccini work with enough lurid twists and turns for six operas. The director, Piero Faggioni, was a first-timer at the Met. Joe Clark and I spent weeks with him in Rome, educating him about the scenic possibilities at the Met.

When Faggioni came to New York, we immediately ran into a problem: he wanted nothing to do with the Met's assigned lighting

designer, Gil Wechsler, who happened to be a favorite of Sybil Harrington's. "I do my own lighting," Faggioni announced—which didn't
leave Gil much to do except hang around and pout (which he was
good at). But Wechsler could not be dislodged as the credited lighting
designer, which drove Faggioni nuts. After the dress rehearsal, everyone gathered at Giordano's restaurant on West Thirty-ninth Street,
including Sybil. During the meal, Faggioni turned to Wechsler and
said, "You're nothing but a gofer. Why are you getting any credit?"
The smoke that came out of Sybil's ears was what you would have
seen after she shot the Indians. In a voice that brought the room to a
hush, she said to Faggioni, "Why don't you keep your mouth shut?"
He did.

The following season, the Met approached Faggioni for a new
*Tosca*. Again, Joe and I went to Rome to work on the stage design.
When we returned to New York, Bliss vetoed Faggioni. "Sybil won't
pay for it," he said. It was left to me to break the news to Faggioni. "I
know who's behind this," he said. He was right: the Met's new *Tosca*
was staged by Zeffirelli, whose every extravagance Sybil more than
indulged. In addition to *La Bohème* and *Tosca*, she paid for Zeffirelli's
spectacular *Turandot* (1984–1985) and *Don Giovanni* (1989–1990).
Although the cost of these productions was enormous—today, the
cost of mounting Zeffirelli's *Turandot* would be close to $4 million—
they all earned their money back, many times over.

A fter Sybil arrived in town for the opening of a new season, she
was at the Met every day. She always seemed to have more fun
watching what the stagehands and scenery painters and wig makers
were up to than she did having lunch with other board members—
this, after all, was a woman whose fifteen-thousand-square-foot house
in Amarillo was supported by Ionic columns that had been hauled
from Kansas City by mule train. By the time of her death, in September 1998, she had given the Met more than $30 million and sixteen
new productions (including Otto Schenk's *Die Fledermaus, Das Rheingold*,
and *Die Meistersinger*, and Elijah Moshinsky's *Otello*). Having discovered
the magic of the Met through radio, she also paid for thirteen *Metropolitan Opera Presents* national telecasts on PBS. Her aim, she said, was
to give the Met "things that they'll use for years to come." With very
few exceptions, that's what she did. Sybil was in it for the long haul.
During the years since her death, the Sybil B. Harrington Trust has

continued to support the refurbishment and revivals of not only her productions but also of other breadwinners. The Harrington legacy is unmatched by that of any other Met donor.

Sybil was on a first-name basis with everybody, and I wasn't surprised when, after overhearing one of the electricians complaining about the Met's antiquated lighting board, she immediately offered to pay for a new computerized one. Every house needs to change lightbulbs from time to time. For Sybil, this house was home.

# 10

# THE TURNAROUND MAN

Closet space is at a premium in New York, and no New York family needs more of it than the Met. Operas take place in every period and every historical setting, and the Met has by far the biggest standing repertory in the world—more than a hundred productions that can be mounted in any given season. Where do we keep all those mountains, clouds, forests, meadows, rocks, gardens, churches, prisons, tombs, skylines, village squares, mansions, huts, forts, gypsy camps, royal courts, ballrooms, gaming rooms, bedrooms, taverns, garrets, staircases, columns, terraces, statues, ships, and countless other bits of theatrical reality where they won't get ravaged by fire, mildew, or termites?

For years, the Met stored all its scenery at a thirty-five-thousand-square foot warehouse on West 129th Street. Night after night, trucks rumbled up to Harlem and back, loaded with the show that had just ended and the one that was playing the next night. The move to Lincoln Center enabled the company to keep half a dozen current productions backstage, reducing the frequency of those trips. But as the productions grew in number and size, the Met had to acquire more warehouses—one in Maspeth, Queens; one in Weehawken, New Jersey; and one up at East 186th Street, in the Bronx—for the thousands of wigs and costumes that turn singers into gods, goddesses, monsters, fairies, kings, queens, princes, princesses, dukes, duchesses, courtiers, priests, servants, barbers, gardeners, assassins, courtesans, doctors, lawyers, artists, writers, clowns, soldiers, sailors, peasants, shepherds, prisoners, and urchins.

For years, I'd been saying that we were getting killed by the cost of all that warehouse maintenance and all that hauling, which also didn't contribute to the scenery's longevity. The solution I proposed was to replace the warehouses with giant containers. One container could hold the equivalent of two or three truckloads. Moreover, a container required only one driver and a lot fewer hands to do the loading and unloading. Whenever I brought up the subject, Tony Bliss nodded vaguely and changed the subject. There must have been a lot of closet space in those Bliss mansions. With the arrival of Bruce Crawford as general manager in 1986, I finally prevailed.

Crawford was the first CEO to run the Met. He'd spent his life as an ad executive on Madison Avenue, where he was known for turning around BBDO's failing international division and building the company into the world's sixth largest ad agency. He was a real opera nut. As a kid in the Boston area, he'd been a fan of both the Red Sox and the Texaco Met broadcasts. When he was seventeen, he came to New York for a matinee of *Otello* at the old Met. As he was standing in line, a well-dressed woman came up to him and introduced herself as the personal secretary of Stella Roman, the Romanian Desdemona of that afternoon. She'd been sent by the diva to bestow one of her house seats on a needy fan. Bruce landed a place under the big chandelier. As his career went on to demonstrate, he was a guy with a knack for putting himself in the right place at the right time.

As Bruce rose in the world of corporate advertising, he became a regular at the Met. In 1976, he joined the Met's board of directors and became chairman of the media and television committee. In 1984, he became president, and when Tony Bliss announced his retirement that summer, the board turned again to one of its own. Memories of the Bing autocracy remained fresh, and the trustees were still in comfort mode.

Crawford, the turnaround man of Madison Avenue, had his work cut out for him. By the end of the centennial 1983–1984 season, the

Met was deeper in red ink than at any time in its history, with a deficit of $8 million (or $23 million in today's terms). Tony Bliss, who was not in good health, had not been minding the store. Although the Met had virtually broken even in the 1982–1983 season, the picture changed dramatically during the centennial. The culprits were uncontrolled expenses, a fall-off at the box office, and a huge diversion of donations to the endowment drive. Just as the board hadn't anticipated the negative impact the drive would have on the labor dispute of 1980–1981, so too were the trustees blind to the effect it would have on the annual giving that was essential to cover operating expenses. As Crawford later observed to a reporter, "Things go wrong very fast in an opera house."

Outside my office is a corridor about seventy feet long. I don't have a view of it. My furniture is arranged as it was during Rudolf Bing's time: the desk is parallel to windows that look out onto Damrosch Park and I face into the room, with a direct view of a television monitor that shows me everything that's taking place on the Met's stage, from morning to night. I can't see who's coming down the hall, and they can't see me. When Tony Bliss occupied the office, he faced the door and often looked up to see who was heading his way. Bruce Crawford sat where Tony sat. But Bruce wasn't looking at the door. He was looking at the big picture.

Whenever I came down the hall for a meeting with Crawford, I saw him gazing out the window. He'd be sitting in profile, head raised, chin supported by a thumb, elbow on the desk. He was deep in thought—strategizing. Or, as he might have put it, "orchestrating."

Crawford was as decisive as his predecessor had been wobbly. At BBDO, he'd been known as a surgical slasher who had no qualms about shutting down unprofitable offices and replacing tired employees with more energetic ones. His first act as CEO of the Met was to take an ax to one of the most cherished pieces of the company's big picture—the annual spring tour. From the beginning, the six- to eight-week tours had been regarded as essential to the company's fortunes. Touring had made the Met a national brand name. It had helped create an expanding base of opera lovers—an extended family with deep loyalty (and, in some cases, pockets); an audience for the Saturday afternoon broadcasts; and markets for the company's new ventures into telecasts, recordings, and home videos. Some of the most active board members had developed a lifelong attachment to the company because of the Met's annual visit to their hometown. Among them were Frank Taplin and Louise Humphrey, who succeeded Crawford as president. Both had grown up in Cleveland, which had been a Met stronghold since 1926.

Crawford, the ace marketer, recognized as well as anyone the value of this vital aspect of the Met's history. But the tour was becoming more a burden than a blessing. Dallas dropped out in 1984. In 1985, the sponsors in Detroit resigned as hosts. In 1986, Boston folded. Only Atlanta, Cleveland, and Minneapolis remained enthusiastic about the Met's visits. Crawford explained the situation in *Opera News:* "The amount of money it takes to bring the Met to a city is extraordinarily high. The fee to the Met, plus the local costs involved for the house and marketing, amounts to almost $200,000 a performance. Now there's no way you can price and sell a house and get $200,000 a performance in Detroit, Minneapolis or Boston. In fact, you can't really get $150,000, which leaves a tremendous amount of money to be raised locally by the sponsoring group." Crawford went on to note that American opera companies were springing up everywhere, thanks to the Met's years of trailblazing. In many cities, there was no longer enough underwriting to support both the regional company and the Met.

For some time, James Levine and I had also pointed out that maintaining the company's artistic standards on tour was becoming increasingly difficult. Many international stars were now heavily booked at the glamorous European festivals, and they no longer wanted to schlep around America like a rock act. The Met's productions of standard repertory had become so elaborate that hauling them from city to city and installing them in cut-down versions on inadequate stages was growing impossible. Not even the Ringling Brothers would have tried to take Zeffirelli's *Bohème* on the road.

I was going to miss that annual rite of spring. For the Met's working family, the tours had been a wonderful bonding experience and a real morale booster. They gave everybody a chance to get to know one another better offstage—sometimes a lot better. They got everyone out of the New York hothouse and away from the opera pack at Broadway and Sixty-fifth Street. Touring with the Met was like going back to the origins of musical theater—*Pagliacci* without the blood. But I had to admit that the tours had long since achieved their purpose.

Canceling the tour saved the Met a lot of money and headaches. It also created a new problem—what to do with all the musicians, singers, and dancers who now faced eight weeks of unemployment after the close of the regular season. A deal with Deutsche Grammophon to record the Met's new production of Wagner's *Ring Cycle* offered a partial solution. The project would give full post-season employment to the musicians and some principal singers, but very little work to the choristers, since *The Ring* calls for a chorus only briefly, in *Götterdämmerung*. And there was no employment for the Met's dancers.

As a result, in 1999–2000, we decided to extend our regular season from thirty to thirty-two weeks. Fortunately, the costs of a longer season were more than offset by the demand for tickets. Spring is a great time for opera. Since then, the Met's April and May performances have generally played to full or nearly full houses.

Bruce Crawford and I had an ideal working relationship. As assistant manager for operations, I was responsible for running the day-to-day activities of the house as efficiently as possible. As the keeper of the budget, I was involved with every aspect of the company, including casting, the choice of repertoire, and fund-raising. In other words, I not only kept track of how we spent the money we had, but I was also the person to see about anything that would cost the Met money it didn't have.

Bruce was a superb sounding board. As an ad man, he was good at kicking around ideas, and he generally supported my suggestions for new ways to cut costs or bring in extra revenue. He came to a decision after listening carefully to the relevant factors. He never went back on his word. He didn't micromanage—he was the kind of chief executive who trusts his number two to get the job done. And he was a Jack Webb, just-the-facts-ma'am kind of guy. "Don't confuse me with details," he'd say. "Give me the heart of the matter." He provided me with an excellent model for running such a complicated place, but I'm still addicted to the fine print.

Bruce took a longer view than his predecessors. When I suggested abandoning warehouses for containers, he understood that the initial cost of the conversion would more than pay off down the road. When the process began in 1988, we estimated that we'd need 550 containers. Today, the Met's scenery is kept in more than 1,000 containers at

*With Bruce Crawford and, behind, the bass Hans-Joachim Ketelsen*

a six-acre yard in New Jersey. If we hadn't containerized, we'd have had to acquire at least another three warehouses to store what we currently have in scenery.

The conversion not only saved the Met money, it also brought in cash. We kept the Bronx warehouse for costumes but sold the other two properties. I was particularly pleased with the deal I made to sell the Weehawken warehouse to the real estate developer Hartz Mountain, which bought the property as part of a scheme to build an office, hotel, and apartment complex in the area west of the Lincoln Tunnel.

We agreed on a figure of $4 million (netting us a profit of $2 million), $2 million of which would be given to the Met in cash. The other $2 million would be held as a mortgage by the Met, with an interest rate of 12.5 percent. Some of the trustees complained that we shouldn't settle for anything less than all cash, but I told them that we couldn't make the deal that way. For years, I'd been buying, fixing up, and selling houses, both to make some extra income and to satisfy my urge to build things. With my son P.J., I had spent a summer vacation restoring a Victorian cottage on the Jersey shore that had been washed into the bay during a hurricane in the 1930s. When it came to real estate, I knew a deal when I saw one.

The fact that I didn't take the trustees' complaint seriously rankled some of them. This was one of many occasions when I was seen to be overstepping my bounds. In the eyes of certain board members, I was nothing but a hired hand. But nobody complained about the Hartz Mountain deal after the stock market crashed a few months later. Interest rates plummeted, but the Met was left holding that nice fat rate of 12.5 percent.

Bruce was my buffer with the board. Although Louise Humphrey, his chosen president, was no pushover (she was also a wonderful hostess and a generous benefactor), he was still the real power. As one of "them," he knew which decisions he could make on his own and which ones he needed the board to approve. In most matters, he liked to keep everybody but himself out of the loop—another talent of his that I've tried to emulate. But when he needed the board's endorsement of a new initiative, he laid the groundwork so thoroughly that there was no chance of a surprise. Like Lyndon Johnson when he was the senate majority leader, Bruce lined everyone up in advance. The vote was a foregone conclusion, going exactly the way he wanted.

The press likes to portray me as "abrasive" and "tough," but a lot of that image stems from my habit of responding immediately to a problem. Although I can get a little emotional, I think most of the people who've worked with me will agree that my bark is worse than my bite. In any case, I don't worry a lot about whether my behavior fits the textbook model of a chief executive. Bruce, on the other hand, operated on a more calculated level. With his custom-tailored suits, perfectly groomed shock of blond hair, and his judicious manner, he liked being the picture of the perfect CEO.

After all, what sold Pepsi-Cola (one of BBDO's big accounts) was image as much as taste. Bruce was a master at selling "Bruce." At a reception that was held to mark Crawford's stepping down as general manager in the spring of 1989, the Met's chairman, James Marcus, was poised to cite Bruce's achievements when Bruce stood up and cited those achievements himself. And whenever he perused a magazine or newspaper article in which he figured, he'd fidget with his expensive tie, finish the article, and say happily, "No damage done."

Privately, Bruce was a thoughtful, in some ways shy, man with a good sense of humor. Publicly, he was inscrutable. He had a lot of theories about how to be a CEO, one of which was that if there's someone you want to fire, do it during your first year so that it reflects badly on your predecessor. If you do it later, it will reflect badly on you. He hadn't been general manager very long before he got rid of the Met's longtime finance director and replaced him with a honcho from Pepsi-Cola. The Met's office and financial staff weren't quite what the Pepsi guy was used to, and he didn't stick around very long. Around the Met, Bruce became known as "cut-'em-loose Bruce."

Joe Clark and I had our own nickname for him, inspired by a General Motors vice president, Chester Flynn, whose Ferrari I had serviced when I was a teenager working with Jerry Titus on the Tristate sports car racing circuit. Chester Flynn was the kind of guy who liked to stay in the middle of the pack, never going fast enough to win but always finishing the race in a good position. Jerry and I called him "Chester the Road Tester." After observing how Bruce glided untouchably through the daily chaos at the Met, I said to Joe Clark, "Bruce reminds me of Chester Flynn." From then on, Bruce was "Chester"—as in, "Joe, have you seen Chester?" "Yes. He's up in his office, where else?"

Although I learned a lot from Bruce, our approach to running an opera company was profoundly different. Whereas Bruce had the luxury of gazing out the window at the big picture, I was off in the house somewhere, getting my hands dirty. There are a dozen skirmishes a day at the Met and I was in the middle of all of them, whether it had to do with budgetary matters ("Do you really need that extra rehearsal time?"), onstage matters ("What are all those cancan dancers doing in Act 2?"), or competitive ego matters ("Okay, she won't stand in front of you during the duet"). Bruce hated to be the bearer of bad news. As a textbook CEO, he'd learned the value of messengers.

No one, least of all Bruce, wanted to tell the formidable Hungarian soprano Eva Marton that, despite what she'd been led to believe, she was not going to sing Brünnhilde in the Met's new recording of *The Ring*. The production, a fairy-tale staging of Wagner's epic by the Viennese director Otto Schenk and the German designer Günther Schneider-Siemssen, had been unveiled in 1986 with *Die Walküre*, featuring the German soprano Hildegard Behrens as the leader of the Valkyries. Deutsche Grammophon had already released a successful video of *Die Walküre* with Behrens. The people at DG insisted that she sing Brünnhilde on the recording, even though by the time the recording period rolled around, Marton was scheduled for the role.

Rudolf Bing would have considered it his duty to deliver the bad news himself, realizing that delegating that responsibility to an underling would have been insulting to a singer of Marton's stature. But Bruce preferred to remain immaculate. "I'm not going to tell her," he said. The other logical person to do the job—Jimmy Levine—was allergic to confrontations. "I'm not going to tell her," he said. They both said, "You tell her, Joe."

It was the spring of 1989, and Marton had arrived for eight performances in the title role of *Salome*. I knew that she was anxious about the production. A woman with a substantial figure, she wasn't used to slinking around the stage like a deranged nymphomaniac, and she didn't want to appear ridiculous as she dropped her seven veils. I decided to withhold the bad news about Brünnhilde until after opening night. During the rehearsals for *Salome*, I appointed myself Eva's babysitter. I was there to fix any little problem that came up. (I'd done the same for Teresa Stratas, whose hyperperfectionism drove everybody crazy during the *Bohème* rehearsals.) Eva delivered a great opening night. The next day I gave her the bad news.

There was no explosion, only a slow simmer of goulash. Eva performed the next six *Salome*s and then announced that she had to cancel the seventh one because of a "family problem" back in Budapest. the Met agreed, on the condition that she return for the eighth

performance. She left without buying a return ticket. From Budapest, she informed us that she was canceling not only the eighth *Salome*, but also all the *Andrea Cheniers* and *Girl of the Golden Wests*, which she'd signed on to do in future seasons. She punished the Met by staying away for eight years. Hungarian hardball.

In November of 1988, Bruce announced that he was resigning as general manager to become chairman and CEO of the Omnicom Group, the world's largest group of advertising and marketing services.

*Eva Marton as Salome*

During Bruce's two and a half years at the helm of the Met, he had achieved another turnaround: the company was back on solid financial footing. The opera world professed surprise at Crawford's decision, but I'd seen it coming. The Met may be the world's biggest performing arts institution, but it's not BBDO. Talent is what the Met is all about, and talent doesn't put the bottom line first. I always had the feeling that Bruce enjoyed knowing the artists from the general manager's box more than he enjoyed knowing the insecure people so many of them are when they aren't singing. For all his business savvy, he was still the kid who'd been touched by the magic wand of Stella Roman. I rarely saw him mixing it up with the singers, the dancers, or the crew when he was general manager. Since then, as a tremendously effective member of the Met's board, he's been much more visible backstage.

Bruce was bored. He told me as much during the Met's tour of Japan in the summer of 1988. Bruce dislikes being in a crowd, and one evening over drinks at our hotel in Tokyo, he complained about how much he hated standing around the endless receptions thrown by our Japanese sponsors. "Joe," he said, fidgeting with his tie, "Jimmy runs the artistic stuff, you run the house. I don't have enough to do."

Omnicom, the new global ad monster, was having trouble selling itself on Madison Avenue. Internally, the company was a mess. The chairman of the conglomerate, Allen Rosenshine, who engineered Bruce's return to the ad business, told a reporter, "I was dealing with massive problems of ego and turf, putting these agencies together." At the Met, Bruce had nothing to do. At Omnicom, he had another mess waiting for him to clean up.

Bruce's resignation as general manager hardly meant that he was saying good-bye to the Met. Pulling the strings at the world's biggest opera house was too important to "being Bruce." Since Bruce first got involved with the Met thirty years ago, he's had more titles and returns than General MacArthur: advisory director (1976–1977), managing director (1977–1978), vice president (1981–1982), president (1984–1986), general manager (1986–1989), chairman, Executive Committtee (1990–1991), president and chief executive officer (1991–1999), honorary chairman of the board (1999–2002), chairman emeritus of the board (2002–2005); chairman, executive committee (May 2005–). He's stopped fidgeting with his tie.

When Bruce announced that he was going back to Omnicom, I was able to talk to myself in a way that I hadn't been able to when Bing announced his retirement. Twenty years earlier, I had thought, "Someday, maybe I can run the Met." Now I thought, "I'm the only one who can run this madhouse."

The board thought otherwise.

R obert Tuggle, the Met's longtime keeper of the archives, recently showed me a remarkable set of interviews, résumés, and summaries. They constitute a confidential report to the board by the executive search firm of Heidrick and Struggles, which the board hired to comb the world for Crawford's successor. The American government hasn't searched that hard for Osama bin Laden. For eight months, Heidrick and Struggles looked at more than four hundred prospects for the position of general manager. The list included opera managers, businessmen, academics, music directors, museum directors, theater directors, ballet directors, TV executives, lawyers, agents, magazine editors, a baritone, a second violinist, and the president of Campbell Soup—everybody, as far as I could tell, but convicted felons.

My name is nowhere in the report. When members of the executive committee sounded me out on the kind of person I thought would be best for the job, I described myself. That was the last I heard from them. Although Bruce later told me that I had been the "other candidate" right down to the final selection, the reasons I was passed over aren't hard to figure out.

There was the James Levine factor. Although Jimmy and I had developed a good working relationship, there were times when, as the keeper of the purse and the schedules, I had to tell him that something he wanted, such as extra rehearsal time, wasn't in the cards. Jimmy wouldn't argue with a used-car dealer. He just wanted to be free to be Jimmy. He felt comfortable reporting to a hands-off executive like Bruce Crawford, but he didn't feel comfortable reporting to a hands-on longtime colleague.

There was the Marilyn Shapiro factor. Marilyn, the assistant manager in charge of development and marketing, had made it clear to various board members (especially to Sybil Harrington) that she also didn't want to report to me. She was held in high regard for her "creativity" at fund-raising, and she was equally creative at managing her own department. She was perpetually trying to add new people to her ever-growing staff, and she didn't like being questioned about why she needed thirty-three people when, in my opinion, thirty-one would have been more than enough. She also hadn't enjoyed my scrutiny of her expense reports for expensive lunches that had produced no donation in return. And she didn't take it kindly when I complained about her habit of extending the fiscal year deadline past July 31, so she could say that she'd met her fund-raising goals.

Marilyn told Sybil that she wanted to be general manager. I don't know exactly what she said about me, but I'm sure it was something along the lines of "But how can we take *him* to a fund-raiser? We need someone with more social status." According to what I later learned from Sybil, Marilyn said that if she couldn't have the job, I was the last person she wanted to have it.

Then there was the personality factor. Yes, I was often blunt when someone said something that I thought was a waste of time. I wasn't exactly known for speaking sotto voce. I'd had one particularly memorable exchange with Franco Zeffirelli while he was preparing his new production of *Turandot* in March of 1987. During an orchestra rehearsal, he came over to me and said, "Joe, I need you to open the hall on Sunday so I can have an extra lighting rehearsal."

"Franco," I said, "are you crazy? Do you know how much that will cost the Met?"

He shrugged.

"We'd have to pay a hundred stagehands double overtime," I said. "I'm sorry, but it's out of the question."

The orchestra and the chorus were going full tilt, but Franco had no trouble making himself heard over Puccini. "If I don't get the rehearsal," he screamed, "you can get another director!"

He turned and marched toward the exit. "Fine," I screamed. "I've already got one!"

A few aisles away, Paul Plishka, who was singing Timor in the production, stood up, raised a fist, and yelled, "Volpe for president!"

Franco didn't look back.

An hour or so later, I got a call from Zeffirelli's agent, Janet Roberts.

"Franco says he would like a discussion with you, but he doesn't want to talk to a volatile Italian," she said.

"He's calling me 'volatile'?" I said. "Who do you think started this?"

I called Franco.

"I'll find some extra time for you during the regular schedule," I reassured him. "Come home."

He did, and *Turandot* was lit with no overtime. It was a victory for me, but it came with a cost. Watching two Italians being volatile was Sybil Harrington, who wasn't pleased by how I'd yelled at her favorite director. And when Sybil spoke, the board listened.

After the board decided against me, an unnamed trustee told the *Times* that I was "N.O.C.D." I had to ask someone what that meant. The translation—"Not our class, dear"—didn't come as a surprise.

Hugh Southern, whom the board finally settled on, had the kind of pedigree the board was looking for—a bachelor's degree from Cambridge University, complete with an authentic (as opposed to Rudolf Bing's) English accent. There wasn't anything to suggest that he had a clue about running a place like the Met. Apart from a single year spent as a "management associate" (read:gofer) at the San Francisco Opera, his opera house experience was nil. He'd been a non-profit beach ball, bouncing from a job as treasurer of the Westport County Playhouse to an assistant director at the Repertory Theatre of Lincoln Center to executive director of the Theatre Development Fund to deputy chairman for programs at the National Endowment for the Arts. The Cambridge charm bounced with him.

Curiously, the language used by the sleuths at Heidrick and Struggles to recommend Southern pointed uncannily to the qualities the board found so lacking in me: "[Southern] has been described as a facilitator and one who fosters compromise, as opposed to a take charge/do-it-my-way manager," the report read. "He has the kind of refined style that will allow for favorable reception by major donors to the Met." The most vivid adjective about his management abilities was "calming." No one had ever said that about me.

As things turned out, "invisible" would have been a more accurate description of the Met's new general manager. During Southern's seven months in Rudolf Bing's old office, from November of 1989 until June of 1990, I think I laid eyes on the man twice. Joe Clark and Jimmy Levine probably saw him even less than that. He apparently had a lot of lunches. If he heard about the Met's daily crises, he didn't hear about them from me, because he never asked. After he moved into Mr. Bing's office, he hung a patchwork quilt on the wall. A quilt in an opera house?

Years later, after I had become general manager, Paul Montrone, who was then the president of the Met, invited me up to his country place on Lake Winnipesaukee. A car enthusiast like me, Paul collects beautiful old automobiles, and he suggested that I'd enjoy looking at a classic Jaguar he'd recently acquired. I went outside, and there, sitting in the Jaguar was a stranger. He introduced himself as Gerry Roche, a friend of Paul's and the chairman of Heidrick and Struggles.

"We owe you an apology for that Hugh Southern business," he said.

"Thanks very much," I said, "but you don't have to give me an apology. What you ought to do is give back that search fee to the Met."

I guess Paul had warned him that I'd probably say something like this, because he grinned and said, "You have a point." A few weeks later, the Met received an apology in the form of a check from Heidrick and Struggles for $250,000.

But the truth is that during Southern's time at the Met, I wasn't spending a lot of time thinking about how Heidrick and Struggles, or the board, had bungled the search. In June of 1988, I'd supervised the company's tour to Japan. In Tokyo, I'd fallen in love with Jean Anderson, a willowy, blond dancer in the Met's ballet corps. Jean is of solid midwestern stock. She's not only funny and elegant but also has no trouble standing up to me. In August, I married Jean. Two years later, our daughter, Anna, was born. I was making another family.

After Hugh Southern was dismissed in June of 1990, the executive committee, chaired by Bruce Crawford, held three meetings whose main order of business was to figure out how to give me the top job without giving me the top title. In virtually every other American opera house, the head of the company is called "general director." Since 1908, when Otto Kahn brought Giulio Gatti-Casazza, the intendant of La Scala, to New York to run the Met, the title of the top-salaried person in the house has been "general manager." Gatti (as he was called) held the title for an unmatched run of twenty-seven years. His successor, the Canadian tenor Edward Johnson, had the title for fifteen years. Rudolf Bing had it for twenty-two seasons. Even though the title disappeared from time to time during the relatively brief reigns of Chapin, Bliss, and Crawford, the board had had no trouble conferring it on a man with no experience in running an opera house and whose chief legacy to the Met was a deficit of more than $3 million.

When Bruce Crawford came into my office on July 6, 1990, he broached the subject of my elevation with a mixture of reassurance and evasiveness that should have alerted me to what was coming. "No candidate but you, Joe . . ." "Well, there's a *little* resistance on the board . . ." "You know, the usual talk of restructuring . . ." And, of course, "Don't worry, Joe, I'll handle it. . . . You'll be fine."

*Jean as a member of the Met's ballet corps*

Isn't that what they tell you before you go under the surgeon's knife?

Three days later, I went to Chicago for a meeting with Jimmy Levine, who was conducting at the Ravinia Festival, and Jimmy's right-hand man, Jonathan Friend. "Artistic planning for seasons down the road" was the alleged agenda. I was surprised to find a message from Bruce at my hotel, the Mayfair-Regent. He was there, too, and he wanted to meet me in his room. I couldn't imagine Bruce staying in anything other than the presidential suite, but his accommodations were as ordinary as mine.

"What? No suite, Bruce?" I said as I walked in.

He fingered his tie. "This is perfectly fine," he said quickly.

Fine for what? I thought. A beheading?

Bruce poured drinks and launched into forty-five minutes of small talk about everything except the business of my replacing Hugh Southern. The mindless joviality was suffocating, but I held my tongue. Later that evening, he and I (and Jean, who had accompanied me to Chicago with my son Jason) joined Jimmy and Jonathan for dinner in the hotel dining room. More joviality.

"Can we get together tomorrow morning, Joe?" Jimmy said as we were heading to the elevator.

"Sure," I said.

Jimmy outdid himself. "It's really great working with you, Joe," he said in about thirty different ways.

The artistic planning meeting went fine. Throughout, Jimmy smiled like the guy who administers Chinese water torture. Speaking of which, perhaps I should have paid more attention to the two fortune cookie messages I taped to the cover of my 1990 appointment book. "Avert misunderstanding by calm, poise, and balance." And: "Now is the time to resolve all unfinished business."

Back in New York, I called Sybil Harrington in Amarillo. "Sybil," I said, "I got passed over last time, and this time I want the job."

"I understand perfectly, Joe," she said sweetly. "Someone will get back to you."

Within minutes after I hung up, Bruce was in my office. "What the hell are you calling Sybil for?" he said. "You're going to louse everything up!"

"Louse what up?" I said. "What's going on, Bruce? I called Sybil because I wanted her to know it from me—I want the job."

"That's no way to go about it," he snapped. "You're a bull in a china shop!"

"Bruce," I said, "don't raise your voice to me."

"Okay, Joe," he said. "I apologize."

"I accept," I said.

"But from now on," he said, backing out the door, "leave everything to me. *I'll* orchestrate it."

Which he did. Toward the end of July, Bruce returned and laid out the terms of my new position. The board was offering me a five-year contract that would put me in charge of all aspects of the Met's business except two—artistic affairs (music, casting, and choice of repertoire), which would be supervised by James Levine, and external affairs (fund-raising and marketing), which would be handled by Marilyn Shapiro. The three of us would report to Louise Humphrey, the president. My title? General director.

"This is insulting!" I said. "Who do you think has been running this place?"

"Joe," Bruce said, "you're in control even though it doesn't say you're in control. You control the money. Trust me, it will all work out. Be patient."

PART TWO

# THE BOSS

# 11

## BREATHING WITH JIMMY

The first challenge I faced as general director was how to say no to the Met's artistic director, James Levine. Jimmy has conducted operas by just about every composer you can think of, but he has his preferences, and right at the top is Mozart. Others on his A list include Wagner (everything), Berlioz and Verdi (certain works), Berg (*Lulu* and *Wozzeck*), and Debussy (*Pelléas et Mélisande*). In 1978, he had conducted one of "his" operas, a production of *The Magic Flute* at Salzburg, staged by Jean-Pierre Ponnelle, a French director whom Jimmy greatly admired. Ponnelle came to the Met, where he staged six new productions during the next thirteen years—all conducted by Levine. Jimmy once said to an interviewer about Ponnelle, "He was the only director I worked with who directed from the full orchestral score. He knew the music, knew the text, and he understood the technical as well as the subliminal relationship between the two." Jimmy, who is as personally shy as he is musically self-assured, is all about subliminal relationships.

In 1988, Ponnelle agreed to restage *The Magic Flute* for the Met, but before he could begin work on it, he died of congestive heart failure, at the age of forty-eight. As a replacement, Jimmy suggested a director whose vision was about as far from Ponnelle's as you could get—Werner Herzog, the vanguard German film director. Herzog's best-known movie, *Fitzcarraldo*, was a nutty epic about a Caruso fanatic who builds an opera house in the Brazilian jungle. I loved it—how could I not, when I heard that Herzog and his crew had moved a 340-ton steamship over a mountain without using special effects? But I hadn't particularly loved Herzog's production of *Lohengrin*, which I'd seen at Bayreuth during the summer of 1991. The Germans gasped when the curtain rose on a stage full of water. Big deal. That was a puddle compared with the watery expanse the Met could conjure up. Everything else about the production struck me as generalized rather than fresh and specific.

I also didn't love the sketches for *The Magic Flute* that Herzog and his designer, Maurizo Balò, showed me when they came into my office two days after I'd started my new job. Although the drawings were rough, what they suggested was nothing that called to mind Mozart's Masonic fairy tale. A forest of giant Egyptian columns said *Aida*. A rugged ship suggested *The Flying Dutchman*. What was the rationale behind all this? I asked.

Herzog, an agreeable, noncombative man, was vague. "It needs development," he said. "Once you see where we're going with it, you'll love it." How many times have I heard that one?

"But the production is scheduled to open in January," I reminded him. "That's just six months away. All this should be in the shop by now."

Herzog assured me that he'd have finished drawings in a matter of days.

I wasn't convinced. Nor was I inclined to postpone the opening to give him more time. We had a terrific cast in place, led by Kathleen Battle as Pamina, Kurt Moll as Sarastro, Francisco Araiza as Tamino, and Manfred Hemm as Papageno. *The Magic Flute* was the perfect antidote to New York's after-Christmas gloom. Jimmy had seen the sketches earlier that summer in Europe and been enthusiastic. I wanted nothing to do with them.

Telling this to Herzog was easy. Telling it to Jimmy was another matter. There were two questions. The first was: did I have the authority to tell him? The second was: how to do it? The first one was easy, technically, I didn't have the authority, but by refusing to name me general manager, the Met's board had created a power vacuum. I felt no hesitation in filling it. The second issue was a tougher one: the last thing I wanted to do during my first days on the job was to alienate Jimmy Levine, whom everybody at the Met—me included—regarded as an indispensable treasure.

One of the board's major reservations about my becoming general manager had to do with what the trustees perceived as a lack of artistic know-how. How, several of them wondered aloud, would someone with my background be able to deal authoritatively with distinguished directors and designers and conductors? The answer was in my learning curve. For years I had been making trips to Europe to confer with directors about bringing existing productions to the Met or staging new ones. I had worked closely and become friendly with many of the leading European directors and designers, including Zeffirelli, Ponnelle, Otto Schenk, August Everding, Rudolf Heinrich, and Günther Schneider-Siemssen. I had studied countless design sketches and countless productions of every size and style in all the major opera houses, from Covent Garden to La Scala.

Along the way, I had developed a real distaste for what the Europeans call "regie opera"—productions in which a director transforms a work into something unrecognizable, according to some personal "vision." For me, most of these productions backfired because the director had rewritten the story for his own purposes, rather than attempting to translate it into terms the audience could understand. Forget about opera as spectacle, as entertainment, as *enjoyment*. These pedants, who were pretending to be innovators, were really doing commentaries about opera. I wasn't interested in going back to school.

Over the years, I'd also worked with and come to know many of the world's most revered conductors, including Thomas Schippers, who'd won his stripes along with the rest of us on *Antony and Cleopatra;* Zeffirelli's good buddy Leonard Bernstein; the elusive Carlos Kleiber; the lofty Karl Böhm; and, most memorably, Herbert von Karajan. Working around these musical geniuses all day, I'd long since lost any awe of them. As far as I was concerned, we were all in it together, just trying to get the show on.

I first met the lord of European music when Rudolf Bing sent me to Salzburg for the Easter Festival of 1966, at which Karajan was pre-

*Herbert von Karajan with James Levine*

senting *Das Rheingold*. He was to inaugurate a complete *Ring* Cycle at
the Met the following season, with *Die Walküre*. (The project was later
aborted midway, because of the 1980–1981 labor dispute.) I was in
Salzburg to see how the Karajan *Ring* worked.

As John Dexter liked to point out, most conductors—James Levine,
among them—see with their ears. Jimmy has said that he thinks opera
is 80 percent music and 20 percent stage work. I'd put the ratio at
60:40. But Karajan was not only a conductor, he was also a complete
man of the theater. This was *his Ring*—from the music to the acting,
stage design, costumes, and lighting. He worked with a full set of ears
*and* eyes. During one *Rheingold* rehearsal, a cavorting Rhine Maiden in
the opening scene managed to have her rear end in the air every time
Karajan glanced up from the score. Finally, he put down his baton and
said, "This is impossible. The audience will be in stitches. Fix that
woman's harness."

After a few adjustments, he began again. Up went the rear end.
"Stop!" he barked. He went onstage, told the Rhine Maiden to get out
of the harness, and said to the stagehands, "Strap me in." Up went the
maestro's rear end. "I see what the problem is," he said, stepping out of
the harness as gracefully as he undoubtedly stepped out of the cockpit
of one of his private jets. As he headed back to the podium, he threw
me a look that said, "See, I have to do everything!"

The rehearsal continued with Karajan cueing not only the musicians but also the lighting man, the singers, and the dancers—all seamlessly. Another Rhine Maiden, who was attached to something like a television boom and was always bobbing up at the wrong place at the wrong time, particularly bothered him. Karajan stopped and started, stopped and started, until he was more or less satisfied with the way things looked. After the rehearsal, he pulled me aside and said, "When this gets to New York, pay special attention to that Rhine Maiden."

The designer of the *Ring*, Günther Schneider-Siemssen, was allegedly the author of a famous Karajan joke: "Karajan asked me to build his tomb, and then said: 'But don't make it too expensive. I'll only be there for three days.'" But the Karajan I knew was approachable, open, and down-to-earth. We had become friendly after I saw him pulling up to rehearsal outside the Festspielehaus in Salzburg in a sporty little car. "Where did you get that Mini Cooper?" I said. "And is that a Climax engine inside?" He looked at me, astonished. "How did you know that?" he said. "I love cars," I said. He laughed and said, "Like me."

When Karajan came to the Met with the first two installments of the *Ring*, he took an immediate dislike to Rudy Kuntner, the longtime head electrician who was more of a diva than most divas. Karajan wouldn't address Rudy directly—possibly because he hated the way Rudy muttered to himself in bad German—so he addressed every problem to me. "Joe," he'd say, "we can fly to the moon, but we can't correct the noise from those fans. Get rid of them."

Sure enough, as Karajan had predicted, there was trouble with that Rhine Maiden on the boom. I was called onstage. When I entered through the stage door, there was Karajan standing in front of the contraption, arms folded. He glared at me. "I thought I said to pay special attention to this Rhine Maiden," he said. "Fix it."

"Yes, Maestro," I said.

The next year, I went to Salzburg to observe rehearsals for *Siegfried*, the third installment in the cycle. With me was my second wife, Nancy, the Met dancer whom I had just married. We strolled into the Festspielhaus and walked to the podium. When Karajan took a break, he said, "Joe, so good to see you."

"Maestro," I said, "good to see you. I want to introduce you to my wife."

Karajan studied Nancy carefully and—having recognized her as the dancer who'd been that troublesome Rhine Maiden on the boom—said, "You listened to me."

I knew that Jimmy Levine wouldn't listen to me about Herzog's sketches for *The Magic Flute* unless I kept my artistic opinions to myself. I've never challenged Jimmy on artistic issues, even after I eventually convinced him to relinquish the title of artistic director in favor of music director, a title that more accurately reflected what he was really concerned with. Ninety-nine percent of the time that we've worked together, we've had nothing to disagree about. The other 1 percent, he's bowed to my feelings, kept quiet about any discontent he might have, and gotten on with what's more important to him than eating or sleeping—making music. When it comes to giving public credit for a notable artistic success, I've always made it a point to say two words: "James Levine."

I also knew that if it were up to Jimmy to decide whether or not to go ahead with the Herzog production, the decision would never get made. As John Dexter once said, "Getting James Levine to make a decision would be like expecting Clytemnestra to fry you an egg."

Jimmy, as I've said, hates confrontations. When one is brewing, he wants to run out of the room and hide behind a score—the more notes in it, the better. As gently as possible, I told him my concerns—the strictly practical concerns—about Herzog's sketches. "We can't do it, Jimmy," I said.

"But, Joe," he said, "the production has real possibilities. And Werner Herzog is a world-famous director. How can you let him go?"

By the time I'd finished smiling sadly and saying, "I'll find a way," Jimmy had disappeared out the door.

I immediately called Bruce Crawford, who was now chairman of the executive committee. The board had to be informed that I wanted to cancel Herzog's *Flute*, and Bruce, in effect, *was* the board. I also knew that if Jimmy were to run to anyone, it would be Bruce. I needed to preempt him. "I want your backing, Bruce," I said.

He heard me out and said, "You're absolutely right, Joe."

I called Herzog and explained, as sensitively but as firmly as I could, that we simply couldn't get his *Flute* ready in the time available. When he said, "Give me another year," I pretended that I didn't register it—an easy thing to do with someone who has the disadvantage of not speaking in his native tongue. "I'm sorry," I said, "but that's the way it is."

Herzog took the news amicably. And I got my *Flute*—a wonderful confection of childlike sophistication that the painter David Hockney and the director John Cox had created fourteen years earlier for the Glyndebourne Festival, and later at the San Francisco Opera. Joe Clark and his people remade the costumes and the sets to fit the Met's specifications. The Hockney production had a successful life for the next fourteen years—and cost the Met half of what we would have spent on the Herzog production. I should also say that before I spoke with Bruce Crawford, I'd called Hockney. David, whom I'd known since the Dexter days, couldn't have been happier to oblige. I had my *Flute* in the bag.

The Met is a paradise for workaholics, and the number-one workaholic is James Levine. Since Jimmy made his debut in the house in 1971, conducting *Tosca* at the age of twenty-eight, he's conducted (before the start of the 2005–2006 season) more than 2,200 Met performances—or roughly 25 percent of the total repertoire. During those years, he has transformed the Met Orchestra into the world's best pit band and a major concert attraction in its own right, with a top ticket price at Carnegie Hall that just about matches what you'd pay to hear the Vienna or Berlin Philharmonic.

Since 1975, Jimmy has been instrumental in planning and casting the repertoire for each season. Musically, his tastes run to the challenging stuff that's necessary to keep the company's artistic profile high but is often costly in terms of the box office. (Schoenberg's *Moses und Aron*, which he championed as though his life depended on it, is a recent case in point.) Practically, he accepts the reality that the Met couldn't survive without the surefire warhorses—the *Aidas*, *Bohèmes*, and *Turandots* that he would just as soon have nothing to do with. He has never, however, said no when asked to step in and replace a conductor who's doing a lackluster job with one of the blockbusters.

Singers love to work with Jimmy because he has the patience of an elephant and because he knows everything there is to know about their craft. No conductor is better at enabling singers to do their best; Jimmy *breathes* with them. That's one reason the Met continues to attract all the top international artists, even at a time when the dollar

*Maestro Levine*

has gone to hell against the euro. Jimmy loves to coach as well as conduct, and I could name a dozen terrific young singers who wouldn't have the chops they have if it weren't for the hours he's spent with them, building their confidence and guiding them toward the correct way to sing a new role, dramatically and stylistically.

Despite the constant demand for his services elsewhere (and despite his new obligations as music director of the Boston Symphony Orchestra), Jimmy has committed himself to the Met 100 percent for roughly twenty-two weeks of each thirty-two-week season. He's been at it for more than forty years. The only conductor who had anything remotely like his impact on the company was Arturo Toscanini—and he was at the Met for just seven seasons, from 1908 to 1915.

One of the few things I'd never learned about the Met during my first twenty-six years at the house was that it's one of the biggest fishbowls in New York. The Met is the city's flagship performing arts institution, and its tensions and troubles, promotions and demotions are catnip to the tabloids and front-page news in the *Times*. The Met's penchant for drama in the wings and its lineup of operatic personalities make it the cultural equivalent of the Yankees. As with the Yankees' manager Joe Torre, my "personality" became larger than life.

The press wasted no time outfitting me with a character—or caricature. At the beginning, I was the "Phantom of the Opera," as the *New York Post* dubbed me, referring to my origins in the carpenter shop. Very quickly, however, I became the "Met's Maverick"; the "Met Man You Don't Mess With"; "A Boss as Tough as the Nails He Pounded"; the "Biggest, Baddest Wolf in Town"; "Mephistopheles"; and even, as the *Financial Times* put it, the "Theater Manager from Hell." I was "a blue collar among the blue bloods." I was said to provoke "hate and love, fear and respect." I threw "legendary tantrums." I "scowled." Personally, I think Franco Zeffirelli came closest to getting it right when he called me "gentle and powerful, loyal, compassionate and often horrendous."

Well, that's what sells newspapers. And though I wouldn't have stayed in my job for more than six months if anybody at the Met had really thought they were in hell, I have to admit that I did get into the character. When *Cigar Aficionado* magazine profiled me because of my fondness for Cohibas, the writer asked for my views on difficult singers. I said, "If they have a lack of confidence or are insecure, they are going to do some things you normally would not expect, like throw a chair or scream at someone." Then I laughed and added, "I do that all the time and I'm not insecure." Well, that's what sells opera.

For two years as general director, I stayed in my old, small office. The general manager's domain at the end of the hall was now a "conference room," and its once-private john was open to anyone who wanted to use it. But not a lot of conferencing went on in there. One morning I went in to use the lavatory and found soprano Aprile Millo asleep on one of the sofas. Rudolf Bing's elegant domain had become a dormitory. I called Joe Clark, and that night, without asking anyone's permission, Joe and I moved my furniture down the hall into what was no longer a conference room. A few weeks later, I brought up the question of my title at a meeting of the board. On May 13, 1993, the board voted to name me general manager.

Jimmy Levine was the first to congratulate me. I told him that he would retain the title of artistic director, but that I now had final authority over all matters at the Met. I also reassured him that nothing, as far as he was concerned, had changed: what Jimmy really wanted was virtual carte blanche to pick repertoire that he loved, decide what and when to conduct, and choose the people he wanted to work with. All that, I said, was still his. Jimmy said in his usual soft way, "Thanks, Joe. I could never do the job that you do."

After that, our relationship just got stronger, even when, in 2001, I persuaded him to agree to drop the title of artistic director in favor of music director. He kept the artistic director title until 2004. Given Jimmy's aversion to discord, I was careful never to disagree with him. On the rare occasion when I felt differently about the casting of a singer or a choice of repertory or a question of scheduling, I listened and then thoughtfully suggested an alternative for *him* to consider. Usually, after giving the matter a moment's thought, Jimmy would nod and say, "Okay, Joe."

And if he didn't take me up on a suggestion, I didn't argue with him. One attribute that has made Jimmy so valuable is his endless reserve of enthusiasm—it radiates to the orchestra, the stage, and the audience. The worst thing I could do was to dampen it. Some writer once raised the question of how two such different animals could get along, and compared us to a street cat, me, and a Persian cat, Jimmy. Street cats know how to charm as well as snarl. With Jimmy, I never snarled.

Jimmy continued to play a critical role in all the repertoire and casting decisions. He worked night and day to make the Met Orchestra better and better. He delivered one breathtaking performance after another—sometimes as many as four in six days, including *Parsifal*, which he conducted as if he were in a trance. But he deferred to me when I wanted a director to change something onstage that I didn't like. He turned to me when deals with artists had to be made, or when any unpleasantness cropped up. And without someone like me in charge, he couldn't have rebuilt the orchestra the way he wanted it because I was the person whom unhappy musicians came to when Jimmy decided it was time for them to retire.

Between 1990 and 2005, we replaced about fifty of the players. In many cases, the meetings went smoothly. When Jimmy suggested that it was time for Jascha Silverstein, the principal cellist of thirty years, who was having leg problems and heart problems, to step down, it was up to me to break the news. Jascha and I went way back—we'd been drinking buddies at Paddy Joyce's bar in Cleveland when the Met was on tour. Jascha took the news bravely, and then said, "Joe, I've had an incredible flight here. All I ask is that you give me a soft landing." I did.

Other meetings were difficult. One longtime second violinist was moved from the first row to the back row. (Bob Sirinek, the orchestra's manager, ostensibly engineered the move to protect Jimmy.) The violinist, a man in his seventies, came to me and complained. "I'm playing better now than I have in fifty years," he said. When I backed Bob and Jimmy, the violinist sued the Met for age discrimination. (The suit was eventually settled.) What made the situation even trickier was the fact that his daughter happened to be one of the company's most valuable dramatic sopranos. When she opened in a new production of *Madame Butterfly*, I made sure that her parents were invited to the performance and given two of the best seats in the house.

# 12

## BATTLE HYMN

Kathleen Battle's first appearance in the small role of the Shepherd in *Tannhäuser*, in the fall of 1977, was one of the quietest debuts in the history of the Met. Here was this very pretty, petite (five foot three) African American young woman who, on the few occasions I happened to notice her backstage, seemed not much older than a giggling teenager. (She was actually twenty-nine.) Her three-minute performance got a passing mention in the *Times*. As Met debuts go, it was a nonevent.

At the time, all I heard about her was that she was a "discovery" of James Levine. Jimmy, who had recently been appointed music director, had conducted her in a performance of Mahler's Eighth Symphony at the May Festival in Cincinnati, not far from the little blue-collar town of Portsmouth, on the Ohio River, where Battle grew up. According to her Met biography, she was the youngest in a family of seven children, the daughter of a steelworker from Alabama. Before her opera career she worked as a schoolteacher of inner-city black kids.

Years later, I sent shock waves through the opera world by firing

this sweet young thing with the voice of an angel. It was my first public act as general manager, and the shock came not only from the fact
that Kathy Battle was by then a superstar. More shocking, I think, was
the press release I sent out announcing my decision to sever the Met's
relationship with an artist who for more than ten years had been one
of the most glamorous and critically admired singers on our roster.

In both the for-profit and the nonprofit worlds, it is usual to pretend
that the person being fired is leaving "for personal reasons" or to
"explore other opportunities." In February of 1994, when I terminated
Kathy Battle's contract with the Met, I felt that the time for being
polite was over. The reason I gave for my decision was the real one—
and there was a long history behind it: "Kathleen Battle's unprofessional actions during rehearsals for the revival of *The Daughter of the
Regiment* were profoundly detrimental to the artistic collaboration
among all cast members, which is such an essential component of the
rehearsal process. I could not allow the quality of the performance to

*Kathleen Battle in* L'Elisir d'Amore

be jeopardized. I have taken this step to insure that everyone involved in the production will be able to rehearse and perform in an atmosphere that makes it possible for them to perform at their best."

The press went to town with headlines such as the "Axing of Battle." One of the more thorough accounts of what led up to the incident was a story in *Vanity Fair* in which someone at the Met remembered the singer's behavior as being "downright raucous" when she first arrived: "She acted about eighteen and ran around in blue jeans." The article also went on to say that various men backstage "couldn't take their eyes off her." In retrospect, I wasn't surprised. But the only Kathy Battle I remembered was the one who became a troubled, continually troublesome woman whose behavior defined *diva* in the worst sense—a performer with a pattern of behavior that makes the working life of everyone around her miserable. By dismissing Kathy Battle, I wasn't just getting rid of an artist who had become a pain in the neck, I was also announcing to the people who worked for me, and to the opera world in general, that the financial, artistic, and *emotional* health of the Met mattered more than any one person in the institution.

In the complicated equation that brings people into an opera house—the musical thrills, the romantic stories, the theatrical spectacle, and, for some people, the social cachet—the most potent factor, especially at a house such as the Met, is the charisma of the singers. Without slighting the appeal of mezzo-sopranos, tenors, baritones, and basses, who have all supplied their share of big box-office personalities, the singers at the top of the pecking order are the ones with the highest voices—the sopranos.

In most operas, the sopranos have more beautiful music to sing than anyone else, and they wear the most beautiful dresses. They're the ones with the glamour, the sex appeal, and—because they're usually damsels in some kind of distress—the biggest emotional draw. You may go to an opera to hear a great tenor, but you don't root for Alfredo, Rodolfo, Otello, or Siegfried. You root for Violetta, Mimi, Desdemona, and Brünnhilde. Those are roles for the divas.

*Diva* hasn't always had negative connotations. Back in my early years at the Met, in the days before the term was applied to campy pop stars and hairdressers, the word was reserved for the top prima donnas—the sopranos who were larger than life offstage as well as on.

Zinka Milanov, Maria Callas, Renata Tebaldi, Leontyne Price, Mirella Freni, Kiri Te Kanawa, Montserrat Caballé, Joan Sutherland—these were divas in the good sense of the word, women who carried themselves in a way that reflected their regal status in the opera world.

They, too, could be pains in the neck. Callas, whom I never met or saw, drove Rudolf Bing nuts by refusing to accept contractual terms. He fired her—though she'd been a Met artist only briefly. But if you look back at their famous battle, most of what infuriated Callas seems justified for an artist of her stature. She was particularly upset that the Met never offered her anything but old, tired productions. For this failure, you can only blame Rudolf Bing.

Another demanding, though less tempestuous, diva was Jessye Norman, who had quite a list of special requirements during her years at the Met. She once insisted on having a dressing room without a carpet in it because she was worried that any lint would go straight to her throat. We put Jessye upstairs in a converted storeroom, and she occupied it like a queen.

The greatest artists can be nervous wrecks—especially if they're

*Teresa Stratas in* The Ghosts of Versailles

sopranos or tenors. I've often wondered whether their constant strug-
gle to sound beautiful in the thin air of their upper register puts some
kind of terrible pressure on their brains. You never hear about mezzos
or baritones or basses "losing" their voices, but sopranos and tenors
live in fear of that—especially of losing the so-called money notes at
the top, which is what the fans are waiting for. Those fears can make
sopranos and tenors as skittish as thoroughbred racehorses—and they
can be tough on the people around them.

In my years at the Met, one of the two most alluring stage animals
among sopranos was the little Greek Canadian fireball Teresa Stratas.
(The other is the Finnish soprano Karita Mattila.) Stratas was so self-
critical that she sometimes couldn't face a curtain call. I remember an
*Ariadne auf Naxos,* after which she felt she had done so badly as the
Composer in the prologue that she was terrified to step out in front of
the curtain. It's my habit to race backstage just before the end of a performance to be there with the cast. When Teresa wailed, "I was lousy,
Joe," I said, "Teresa, get out there! You were terrific. They're going to
love you." And, of course, they did.

But in my experience, when the good divas object to something,
they're usually right. Stratas, who is terribly smart, was always right.
During a rehearsal of *Dialogues of the Carmelites,* she sent for me. She
said, "Joe, the set absorbs too much sound. Can't we get rid of all this
black velour?"

I looked at the black velour maskings, which were essential to one
of John Dexter's most striking productions. "I'll find a way to fix it," I
said.

I had the carpenter shop make plywood wings, thirty feet high.
They were painted black and placed in front of the velour to reflect
the sound. The next day, I was there when Teresa sang her first notes.
Her tiny face lit up with that smile that could be seen at the back of
the Family Circle.

On another occasion, Stratas told me that her throat dried up as
she walked from her dressing room to the stage. For years, the Met
has had a spritzer system onstage that reduces flying dust and helps
keep the singers' vocal cords lubricated. After Teresa complained, I
had the system extended to the dressing rooms. It was a distance of
about seventy feet, but you don't argue with Teresa. The next time she
came in, she said, "I'm glad you finally got it right."

If you took a poll asking the Met audience to name the most memorable performance of recent years, the winner would undoubtedly be Karita Mattila as the deranged title character of *Salome*. For daring intensity, I've never seen anything like it. Karita is one tough Finn, and Finns don't whine. "I don't want to cause any problem," she'll say, tossing that gorgeous mane of blond hair. Karita gives everything she's got. While she was rehearsing *Salome*, she worked with a personal trainer every day (she's always in perfect shape), and she banished her husband to Florida because she didn't want to lose focus.

But even Karita has her moments. She'd been doing her opening scene with John the Baptist in the rehearsal room on C level, standing on a slightly raised platform. When everyone moved upstairs to the main stage, she was suddenly confronted with a staircase that went about thirty feet down below the stage. She freaked. "I'll fall in and kill myself," she protested. "Okay," I said. "Go home and take it easy. We'll do something." We put a railing around the pit, and the next day she came over and hugged me. "You saved my life!" she said.

A few days later, Karita freaked again—this time during a dress rehearsal at which a photo call had been arranged for *The New York Times*. At the climactic moment when Karita shed her last article of clothing during the Dance of the Seven Veils, a *Times* photographer snapped a picture. How she noticed it, given the frenzy of the scene, I don't know. But she did. She grabbed her robe and walked off.

I called Jim Naples, the house manager, and said, "Lock the doors. Don't let anybody out of the building!"

I stopped the photographer, a young woman, as she was heading out of the auditorium. Since

*Karita Mattila as Salomé, 2004*

her camera was digital, I couldn't snatch it away and rip the film out. I said, "You're not leaving this building until you give me that camera."

The photographer jumped back. "What are you talking about?" She said.

"The camera. I want it."

She said, "But this is a photo call for the *Times*!"

"Let's talk this over quietly," I said.

I persuaded the photographer to show me every shot she'd taken. When we got to the shot of Karita in the nude, I said, "Erase it."

"I will," she said.

"How do I know you'll do it?" I said.

"I promise," she said.

"Okay," I said. "But if I see any nude photo of Karita Mattila in the *Times*, you'll pay a terrible price."

I guess the photographer knew her opera. She kept her promise.

I told Karita that everything had been taken care of, and she came back to the rehearsal.

The press returned for the final dress rehearsal, with orders to take no photographs during the two or three seconds when Karita was totally naked.

Karita's reviews were beyond any raves I've ever seen for an opera performance. In the American press, the nudity was no big deal. In Finland, however, it was a different story. Karita was distressed. "All they're talking about is the fact that I take my clothes off!" she said. "My family is very upset!"

I expected more trouble when we taped *Salome* for television, but I hadn't taken the full measure of Karita. We taped her dance, nudity and all. Backstage, I said to her, "Gorgeous performance! Now, don't worry about the nude scene. We can deal with that in the editing."

Karita tossed her blond mane and said, "You'd better show the full nudity! I didn't strip down for nothing!"

I said, "But what about your relatives in Finland?"

"To hell with the relatives in Finland!" she said.

Kathleen Battle had everything the great divas had—beauty, musical talent, a distinctive voice, a sense of style—but there was one fatal flaw: all she worried about was Kathleen Battle. Kathy, more than any artist I've ever been involved with, was oblivious to the feelings of the people she worked with, to the inconvenience and the wounds she caused when she insisted on doing things *her* way. Some of her colleagues defended her behavior as that of a perfectionist—they said she was an artist who was as hard on herself as she was on others. Baloney. That's not perfectionism, that's a lack of professionalism.

Kathy is not the only outstanding singer who has behaved like a law unto herself. The Romanian soprano Angela Gheorghiu is one of the most beautiful, exciting, and sought-after singers in the world. She brings audiences to their feet. Like Kathy, she carries herself beautifully—like the great divas of old. But she's also a diva in the bad sense—ridiculously demanding and unreliable about showing up for a rehearsal or even for a performance. (As I write this, she's just skipped an opening night of *La Rondine* at the Paris Opera, without bothering to tell anyone in advance.) Maybe it's because she grew up in Romania under that tyrant Ceauşescu, but every time you say something to Angela, she thinks you're lying. It gets exhausting. Is her talent and star appeal worth the aggravation? Time—and the tolerance of the opera house intendants who hire her—will tell.

I'm no psychiatrist, but anyone who's interested in the fear-of-success syndrome should look at what happened to Kathleen Battle after she joined the Met. Under Jimmy Levine's tutelage, she went from triumph to triumph. With her tiny champagne voice—it had what singers call a "ping," which enabled it to be heard at the back of the house—and her sparkling stage manner, she specialized in the saucy soubrette roles: Zerbinetta in *Ariadne auf Naxos*, Nanetta in *Falstaff*, Zerlina in *Don Giovanni*, Rosina in *The Barber of Seville*, Despina in *Così Fan Tutte*, and so on. Critics rated her among the all-time best as Sophie in *Der Rosenkavalier* and as Susanna in *The Marriage of Figaro*. Her conductor, most of the time, was Jimmy, who was so enamored of her that he sometimes blew kisses her way from the podium.

In the mid-eighties, Kathy became that rare Met star—a personality in her own right. She had her own designer, Rouben Ter-Arutunian, who dressed her like a Greek siren. She was profiled in *Vanity Fair.* Her recitals, for which she was sometimes accompanied by Jimmy Levine, were sold out, especially after she did a concert version of Handel's *Semele* at Carnegie Hall in 1985 that brought out the scalpers and earned her a standing ovation in the days when a standing ovation meant something. (Marilyn Horne, who knows a thing or two about Handel singing, led the applause.) Kathy became a top-selling recording artist for Deutsche Grammophon—second in popularity on the label's roster, I'm told, only to Karajan himself. In Japan, she was number one—a deity. And as her career went up, her behavior got weirder and weirder.

It started with her coming in late to rehearsals. Most singers at the Met, including the stars, arrive an hour ahead of time to vocalize and prepare themselves. But Kathy habitually showed up after the rehearsal had started, sometimes with an excuse, sometimes with a look that said she couldn't care less about keeping a hundred people waiting. Many rehearsals had to start with the singer who was covering her—and when Kathy walked in, she'd dismiss the stand-in without so much as a nod.

In 1982, while she was rehearsing *Barber*, I began hearing complaints about her rudeness to people in the makeup and costume departments. It wasn't that she was imperious, as divas could traditionally be. She was nasty—constantly at everyone and complaining about everything, from the eye shadow to the wigs, changing her mind about what was or wasn't right on her, and speaking in a way that made the people who only wanted her to look her best, as one of them told me, feel "smaller than a crumb." The makeup and wardrobe people are pros; they're used to singers who get insecure in front of a mirror. They muttered, but they didn't complain to management.

During the 1987–1988 season, Kathy arrived to rehearse *Figaro* and had a fit about her dressing room. Although the role of Susanna is the longest in the opera, it's a tradition at the Met and at other houses to give the "first" dressing room to the soprano who's singing the Countess—in this case, Carol Vaness. Kathy had a virtually identical dressing room next door. While Vaness was onstage rehearsing, Kathy went into the Countess's dressing room, threw Carol's clothes out into the hall, and moved herself in. Carol was understandably outraged, but she decided to rise above it—for the time being.

I had just become the head of operations. When I heard about the incident, I went to Joan Ingpen, the artistic administrator, and said that something had to be done. Joan promised to "look into it." Joan worked hand in glove with Jimmy Levine on casting and repertoire, and if she discussed Kathy's behavior with her mentor, I never heard about it. Here was the worst instance to date of what had become known as the "Kathy Problem." The Met's top management did nothing about it.

Two seasons later, Kathy trained her sights on a figure whom no real professional ever messes with during a rehearsal—the conductor. During preparations for *Julius Caesar,* she stopped in her tracks, went up to the English maestro Trevor Pinnock, and demanded that he follow *her* tempo—a slower pace that would allow her to caress her notes as long as she liked. Milking a part was not uncommon at the old Met. But we were now in a more rigorous era—especially when it came to Baroque opera, which was a specialty of Pinnock's. At the Met, a singer's differences with a conductor are generally discussed in private. But Kathy had it out in front of everyone. Pinnock, a newcomer to the house, did his best to adjust.

During the company's tour of Japan in 1988, Carol Vaness finally had enough. After the last performance of *Figaro* in Tokyo, Jimmy and I were walking back to the dressing room area when Kathy came running up to give Jimmy her usual post-performance cuddle. Carol marched up to Kathy and said, "You're a horrible colleague, and I'll never work with you again!" I smiled—the passive, aloof Countess had put clever little Susanna in her place. Jimmy looked miserable behind his glasses. Kathy shrugged and walked off. I grabbed Carol and led her to her dressing room. We didn't need words, we were thinking the same thing: when would the Met finally have the guts to do something about the Kathy Problem?

During the 1988–1989 season, Kathy's arrival times for rehearsals got later and later. She never spent an extra moment at the Met—her appearances were always fleeting, limited to the minimum time required of her. She was known for not accepting phone calls. If you wanted to talk to Kathy, you talked to one of her representatives. I called the agent at Columbia Artists Management, Michaela Kurz, who dealt directly with Kathy and told her that her client was a "disruptive force" backstage. Michaela listened and said that she would do what she could do.

After that, I made it a point to go to the artists' dressing area before Kathy's rehearsals and performances to see if she was there on time and behaving. For a while, she was perfect. Then, before a performance of *The Barber of Seville,* she didn't turn up at the usual time. The dressers were frantic. I waited. Fifteen minutes before curtain time, she raced in. She slowed down when she saw me, but I didn't want to hear any excuses. "Get ready," I growled. After that, any reasonable person would have realized that I was on her case. But Kathy wasn't any reasonable person. Nor, of course, did she bother to apologize.

Kathy was always a kitten when she was working with Jimmy. During my first year as general director, he conducted her wonderful Pamina in the David Hockney *Magic Flute,* and during that season, she gave no cause for complaint. At the beginning of the next season, however, she went head to head with Luciano Pavarotti—without Jimmy's protection. The two superstars were cast together for the first time in a new production of *L'Elisir d'Amore,* an opera that Pavarotti had done dozens of times.

Rehearsals started without Luciano, who had called to say, "I don't come for two weeks for what little I have to do." Kathy had to rehearse with Luciano's cover—which didn't do a lot for her belief in herself as the best thing since Nellie Melba. She showed up, but she wasn't happy. Finally, the Great One arrived, sort of.

On the morning of the first orchestra rehearsal, there was no sign of either Luciano or Kathy. By the starting time of eleven, they still hadn't shown up. I told the conductor, Marcello Panni, who was one of Luciano's handpicked maestros from the region of balsamic vinegar, "Get the covers." Never, in my experience at the Met, had an orchestra rehearsal started without the stars.

Ten minutes later, Luciano strolled onstage. He looked at the cover; the cover looked at Pavarotti. Luciano started to sing; the cover stopped singing. I yelled to the cover, "Keep going." Luciano glared at me and stopped singing.

I let the awkwardness continue for a few minutes, then I went onstage. "Luciano," I said, "this rehearsal is very important to the Met, and I fully expect that it's important to you." He looked sheepish, and the cover took his seat in the auditorium. One star had turned up.

Battle still wasn't there by the time of Adina's entrance in the second scene. "Keep going," I said. Just as the cover for Adina was starting to sing, Kathy came flying through the door. I raised a hand to tell her to stay where she was. The cover kept singing.

During the break, I assembled the cast. Without looking at Kathy or Luciano, I said, "I fully expect everyone to be here on time—all the time."

The next morning, Kathy and Luciano arrived an hour early. When

I arrived backstage at 10:55, Luciano came over, wearing his mega-watt grin, and said, "Where have you been, sire? I was waiting for you in the canteen so we could have coffee together."

"I had my coffee at home," I growled.

Then came the rehearsal—and I wished they'd both stayed home. Luciano wanted one tempo—fast; Kathy wanted another tempo—slow. As she dragged her feet, Luciano stood off to one side holding a wine bottle like a guitar and beating the air with his fist to get his buddy Panni to speed things up.

Kathy was smart enough not to go to the mat with the Great One in public, so after the rehearsal, she came to me. "I can't get through this," she said. "It's too fast."

I suggested that she and Luciano work things out together. Pavarotti—a superb colleague—would have been happy to sit down with her, but she wasn't about to sit down with him. Kathy never even went into the canteen; she was afraid that she might find herself sitting over coffee with a colleague.

The performances of L'Elisir went well enough, though Luciano did a lot of conducting with that wine bottle during the second performance. Still, I began to wonder whether Kathy's behavior hadn't been brought on by the fear that, at forty-four, she was beginning to lose her magic. Her singing had become mannered, which is usually a sign of vocal insecurity. It wasn't just her constant dragging of the tempo, it was the breathiness, the crooning, the lack of musical discipline. One critic wrote that she wasn't Kathleen Battle anymore—she was a singer imitating Kathleen Battle.

I'm sure that Jimmy would have done something about this, but Signor Panni had seen enough. One word from him, and there would have been another Vesuvius. After the third performance, Kathy complained again. "I can't continue," she told me. "Everything is too fast."

I wasn't sympathetic—she only wanted to draw more attention to herself—but I asked Luciano if he could talk to Maestro Panni and maybe slow things down, just a little.

Luciano laughed—everything was a joke to Luciano. "I don't understand Kathy Battle," he said. "She's beautiful; she has a lovely voice. Everyone wants to hear her sing. There must be something missing in her life. She needs a good man to . . ." He made an unmistakable Italian gesture and added, "And I'm just the man to do it!" That's Luciano: a worse psychologist than I am.

During the following season, in February of 1993, Kathy was cast for six performances in a signature role—Sophie in *Der Rosenkavalier*. The conductor was Christian Thielemann, who was making his Met debut. Like most Germans, Thielemann was super-prepared and he knew exactly what he wanted. *Rosenkavalier* is, in many ways, a conductor's opera, and Jimmy had always done a terrific job with it. But I was pleased to have this brilliant young German in the Met's pit and curious to see what he would do with the piece. Three years earlier, Carlos Kleiber had electrified the orchestra and everyone else in the house with his fresh insights into this often played score.

There was trouble right away. Thielemann had his ideas; Kathy had hers. Kathy wasn't about to yield, or even talk about it. Thielemann wasn't used to singers who wanted to be the conductor, too. After the first rehearsal, Kathy came to me and gave me the same old story. I called in Thielemann and told them to find a workable solution. The meeting seemed to go well, and I kept my fingers crossed.

During the next rehearsal, Kathy stopped singing in the middle of the first scene in Act 2. She went up to the footlights and told Thielemann how she wanted him to conduct the passage. "The orchestra is supposed to *accompany* the singer, not the other way around," she snapped. Thielemann looked at her as though she were a bothersome fly, and started up again—his way. Kathy fled to her dressing room.

A minute later, my assistant picked up the phone and heard Kathy say, "I need Mr. Volpe right now! And I want him in my dressing room!"

I was in a meeting. When my assistant poked her head in the door, I said, "Tell her I'll talk to her later." My assistant relayed the message. Kathy said, "If he's not in my dressing room in five minutes, I'm going home."

An hour later, Ronald Wilford, the head of Columbia Artists, called. "We have to work this out," he said.

"There's nothing to work out," I said. "She's not the conductor, Thielemann is. And I'm on his side."

A few hours later, Ron called again. "She won't do it, Joe. She wants out."

"Fine," I said.

Columbia Artists issued a statement: "Ms. Battle has withdrawn, and there will be no further comment."

This is it, I thought. Time to tell her that her relationship with the Met is over. But ahead was the spring tour in Japan, and the Japanese wouldn't take kindly to the news that their favorite Met soprano wouldn't be singing opposite Pavarotti in *L'Elisir d'Amore.* I didn't want to jeopardize the tour, and since I knew that Kathy was also going to be filming a commercial for a Japanese whiskey, I figured she'd have enough on her mind to keep her happy. In any case, since she never stayed at a hotel where other members of the Met were staying, there was little chance of running into her offstage. I decided to wait and see.

Her next assignment was the title role in *The Daughter of the Regiment,* which was scheduled in the spring season on February 14, 1994. Three months earlier, she was to sing Marie, the spoiled darling of the grenadiers, opposite the same tenor, Frank Lopardo, at the San Francisco Opera. I was optimistic that she would arrive at the Met having worked out all the kinks.

In December, Martin Bernheimer's review of the San Francisco production in *Opera* magazine alerted me to trouble:

> Apparently lacking forceful stage direction, the prima donna contented herself with a series of poses in lieu of a characterization. She spent most of the evening flashing her devastating dimples, rolling her pretty eyes and—at the slightest hint of a cadence—adopting an o-so-saucy-salute. She was cute, cute, cute. Also mannered, mannered, mannered. She did sing the introspective portions of the role exquisitely, but she missed maximum brilliance and focus, not to mention rhythmic punch, in the bravura outbursts. And her habit of sliding up to climactic top notes became a bit irksome when her pitch repeatedly failed, just by a hair, to reach the desired goal.

There was another warning signal from the coast: I heard that, after the run, members of the San Francisco Opera chorus had T-shirts printed with the slogan I SURVIVED THE BATTLE.

At the beginning of every rehearsal period, I go down to the rehearsal room on level C and greet the cast in person. Then I leave them pretty much alone, until they move up to the main stage. Not

*Rosalind Elias in* Daughter
of the Regiment

long after the rehearsals for *Daughter* started, I began hearing that Kathy was up to no good: she was making disparaging comments about the conductor, Eduardo Miller; she was disappearing during the lunch break and not returning in the afternoon.

Kathy's costar, the tenor Frank Lopardo, is one of the most professional, most agreeable guys in the business. I went down to C level and, during a rehearsal break, went over to Frank.

"How's it going?" I asked.

Good Met colleagues don't like to rat on other colleagues, but even Frank, who had survived the Battle in San Francisco, couldn't hold back. "She's become impossible," he said. "During our duets, she says, 'Stop looking at my mouth!' If I'm supposed to embrace her, she says, 'Don't touch me!' If someone happens to look in her direction, she screams at the conductor, 'They're looking at me!' "

I thought she must be going off the deep end. I called Ron Wilford. When I told him that Kathy had disappeared during the lunch break and not returned, he said, "The reason she leaves at lunchtime is because she can't face going into the cafeteria and eating with her colleagues.' "

"Ron," I said, "this woman needs help."

"You're probably right," he said, "but I'm not going to get into that. Can't you adjust the schedule so she can rehearse without having to take a break?"

I did. From then on, rehearsals began after lunch and ran the whole afternoon.

Kathy returned and worked all afternoon. I thought I'd solved the problem, but that evening I got a knock on my office door. My visitor was the mezzo-soprano Rosalind Elias, one of the company's most beloved artists. Roz, who was singing the role of the marquise who takes Marie into her castle and gives her singing lessons, had been a member of the company for thirty-three seasons. She had performed with some of the most difficult singers in opera, and she had never uttered an official peep against anyone. But she'd finally had enough.

"Joe," she said, "I hate to bother you, but I'm having a real problem with Kathy. During the music lesson, she does nothing but complain about me with one crude remark after another. For heaven's sake, the marquise isn't supposed to play the piano well. It's a comedy, right? But Kathy wants it her way. Now she's decided she doesn't want me to play the piano, she wants someone in the pit to play. It's become impossible."

I listened.

Roz continued: "Seriously, Joe, it's become so bad that I'm not sleeping. I'm on Valium. I've never taken Valium in my life."

"Stop the Valium," I said. "Give me a few days to work things out."

"Okay, Joe," Roz said gamely.

Maybe it was the look of weariness on this great lady's face as I led her to the door, but at that moment I made up my mind: Kathy Battle's days at the Met were over.

The next day, a Friday, Kathy didn't appear after lunch. At one thirty, one of her assistants called and said that she was "stuck in the tunnel." What tunnel? Her apartment was three blocks from the Met.

That night, I told my wife, Jean, that I had come to a decision about Kathy Battle. Jean went white. "But Joe," she said, "Kathy's one of the Met's biggest stars. How can you just fire her?"

"After what she's put us through, I have no other choice," I said.

Jean said, "But what will the patrons think? The subscribers? *Jimmy?*"

"Darling," I said, "I have no other choice."

On Saturday morning, I called Jonathan Friend, the artistic administrator, and told him that I was dismissing Kathleen Battle from *The Daughter of the Regiment* and replacing her with her cover, Harolyn Blackwell. "Let Ron Wilford know," I said, "but no discussion."

My next call was to Jimmy Levine, who was in Key West on a winter break. I told him the latest developments, and said, "That's it, Jimmy. She's finished."

All he said was, "Oh, my goodness."

I said, "Jim, this is the way it has to be."

Silence, then: "Joe, I have to fly to Cincinnati tomorrow to see my father. He's very sick. Can this wait until Monday?"

I said, "Jim, I've made up my mind."

"Wait till Monday, okay?" he said. "I'll be in your office at nine in the morning."

For Jimmy, that was an unheard-of hour. "Good luck with your dad, Jim," I said.

I had barely hung up when the phone rang. It was Wilford. "What's all this about Kathy Battle?" he said.

"You're surprised, Ron? After all the conversations we've had about her? What do you mean, 'What's all this?'"

"Joe, you can't fire her."

"Yes, I can," I said. "I can't let this go on any longer."

"Can we talk about this on Monday?" he said.

"Sure," I said. "But I know what I'm going to tell you on Monday."

"Don't do anything until we talk," he said. "Okay?"

I grunted.

Both Ron Wilford and Jimmy Levine were waiting outside my office when I arrived at nine o'clock on Monday morning. I met with Ron first.

"Joe," he said, "if you go through with this, think of your obituary. All it will say is that you're the guy who fired Kathy Battle."

"In that case," I said, "more people will come to my funeral."

Wilford, the most powerful agent in the business, isn't famous for his sense of humor. He doesn't like to be slapped down. He went on to argue that it was not in the interest of either Kathy or the Met to discharge her. I told him that my decision was precisely in the best interests of the Met.

He pressed on: "You'll be like Rudolf Bing—known only as the guy who fired Maria Callas."

"Ronald," I said, "Kathy Battle is no Callas."

He started to speak, but I put up my hand. "It's done," I said. "The only thing to discuss now is how we handle it in public. I'll send you the press release before it goes out."

Jimmy's greeting was the one he always gives when he pokes his head in my door: "Is this a good time now?"

"Come on in, Jim."

"Well, Chief," he said (he'd never called me that before), "it's your call, but if I were in your position, I'd let it go. Allow her to do the performances, and we won't hire her again."

I said, "Jimmy, I appreciate your position, but my mind is made up. This is what's best for the company."

We've never spoken about Kathy Battle again.

And that was it. I asked David Reuben, the Met's head of publicity, to get to work on a press release with the orders to "tell the truth— none of the usual excuses such as 'Ms. Battle is indisposed.'"

I put out the word that I wanted everyone involved in *Daughter* to gather onstage at eleven—the cast, the chorus, the conductor, the stagehands, the stage directors. When everyone was there, I said, "Kathleen Battle will no longer be singing in *The Daughter of the Regiment*. I'm happy to announce that the role of Marie will be sung by Harolyn Blackwell." I paused to let the implications sink in. Then, just in case they hadn't, I added, "No artist is more important than the art form. No artist can be excused for the abuse of colleagues. It's my responsibility to protect the integrity of this great company."

The company broke into applause. There were cries of "Bravo!" Frank Lopardo came over and shook my hand. Roz Elias kissed me.

After the news was made public, I was especially pleased by the congratulatory faxes I received from opera managers and arts executives throughout Europe and America. As Ernest Fleischmann, the executive director of the Los Angeles Philharmonic, wrote, "Somebody has to stay 'Stop.' It's good for everyone."

Since then, I've played over many times in my mind the decision to dismiss Kathy Battle and wondered whether it was partly prompted by my desire to establish my authority at the Met. Perhaps it was. Unquestionably, that single act made it a lot easier for me to handle difficult divas of both genders. From then on, everyone who came to work at the Met knew that there was a limit to the company's tolerance of unprofessional behavior. And everyone knew where the buck stopped.

In the media storm, I wasn't surprised by a story in the *Times* that described the press release as an "extraordinary statement [of dismissal] from an institution that usually maintains an air of patrician diplomacy." The *Times* was out of date. The Battle incident signaled a new era at the Met. The charade of the company as a bastion of "patrician" behavior was over. As long as I was running things, the first order of business would be to maintain the Met as a hardworking opera house on the highest possible artistic level.

When the dust had settled, I called Kathy with the intention of telling her that she needed help. I left a message, but I've never heard back.

Like every father, I've had to see some of my kids through periods of trouble. I've sometimes felt that I should have been able to find a way to help this beautiful, talented woman avoid the catastrophe. I've also wondered whether Kathy's behavior might have been her way of asking to be fired, a way that this former schoolteacher from small-town Ohio could escape the crazy pressure of being one of the world's most glamorous divas. She had never really graduated from all those perky ingenue roles—all those "ina's" and "etta's"—that had made her a star. And she was forty-six. Perhaps she just wanted out. Perhaps she and I had been collaborators, after all.

Ron Wilford and the American Guild of Musical Artists filed a complaint charging that the Met had fired Kathy Battle without just cause. The case went to arbitration during the summer of 1995. Dozens of witnesses testified that Kathy Battle's behavior had been "disruptive and abusive," and they detailed her "maltreatment of colleagues" during rehearsals. One stage director testified that at one rehearsal she had demanded that the rest of the cast leave the room for forty minutes while she rehearsed alone with the pianist.

At one point, the arbitrator, a woman named Carol Wittenberg, asked Kathy's costar, Frank Lopardo, to describe how Kathy had rebuffed his attempts to embrace her. Deciding that actions spoke louder than words, Frank pulled the arbitrator out of her chair and embraced *her.*

Wittenberg ruled that the Met's dismissal of Kathleen Battle was entirely justified.

# 13

## THE NEW PRIMA DONNAS

My bible is the memoir of the company's longest-serving general manager, Giulio Gatti-Casazza, who held the position from 1908 to 1935. When Otto Kahn hired "Gatti" from La Scala, where he'd been the intendant for ten years, he didn't speak a word of English. Like me, he'd learned on the job. By all accounts, Gatti was a brilliant administrator, both artistically and financially. His posthumously published account of his years at the Met, *Memories of the Opera*, which I dug out of the company's archives one day, is full of wisdom about opera in general and the Met in particular.

When all is said and done, every general manager is judged on the quality of the productions brought to the Met during his tenure. The Met's 2005–2006 season listed twenty-nine different productions. They included a world premiere (Tobias Picker's *An American Tragedy*); the premiere of an older opera new to the Met (Tchaikovsky's *Mazeppa*); two new productions of old favorites (Gounod's *Roméo et Juliette* and Donizetti's *Don Pasquale*); and twenty-five revivals of productions in the current repertory. These range from Verdi's Egyptian

A caricature of
Giulio Gatti-Casazza,
the Met's first general
manager, 1912

blockbuster *Aida*, a perennial sellout, to Alban Berg's masterpiece *Wozzeck*, which opera connoisseurs love and the general public shuns. When I glance through the list of titles and the names of all the different directors and designers involved, one thing is obvious: the Met, which has been accused of being unadventurous in its approach to staging, embraces a greater variety of production styles than any other opera house in the world, from the picturesque romanticism of Zeffirelli's *Carmen* to the circus-like exoticism of Julie Taymor's *The Magic Flute* to the stylized minimalism of Robert Wilson's *Lohengrin*. One reason for this department-store approach is purely practical. Unlike the situation that prevails at European houses, government handouts do not guarantee the company's financial health. To stay in business, the Met has to appeal to a broad array of tastes, musical and aesthetic. This is America, not Germany. Keeping all these disparate operatic balls in the air at one time is a considerable juggling act. For me, Gatti best described the dilemma in a passage in his memoir that I underlined in pencil:

There are two elements which chiefly concern the impresario in opera production. The one is the artistic, and the other is the practical and financial. I am well aware that pure criticism despises the commercial phase of the opera and concerns itself wholly—and quite rightly—with the artistic. But the director must consciously keep both these ends in view. And he who knows his business must have the courage to sustain his opinions in the face of this criticism. Criticism represents the idealistic point of view. The director must be an idealist only so far as it is practicable for him to do so . . .

It is always the same story—that of Don Quixote and Sancho Panza—the idealist and the realist. I must be both . . . the matter-of-fact Squire and the questing Knight of Rueful Countenance.

I feel qualified to play both roles. But my countenance has never been mistaken for rueful, and there's no question about which character is the better fit. Like Gatti, I have more in common with the practical squire than with the deluded knight. Indeed, according to one of the most idealistic of opera composers, Giuseppe Verdi, when it comes to running an opera house, a Sancho Panza is far better equipped than his windmill-tilting master. As Gatti writes:

> Well do I remember the day—it was in 1898—when Verdi gave me this bit of advice:
> "Read most at-ten-tive-ly (emphasizing each syllable) the reports of the box-office. These, whether you like it or not, are the only documents which measure success or failure, and they admit of no argument, and represent not mere opinions, but facts. If the public comes, the object is attained. If not—
> "The theater is intended to be full, and not empty. That's something you must always remember."

This passage I underlined with a Magic Marker.

For years at the Met, there was a foolproof way to keep the theater full: perform tried-and-true favorites over and over again. There are certain operas—*Aida, Carmen, The Barber of Seville, La Bohème, Tosca, Madame Butterfly, La Traviata, Rigoletto,* Wagner's *Ring* Cycle, *Faust, The Magic Flute, Der Rosenkavalier,* and the double bill of *Cavalleria Rusticana* and *Pagliacci*—that are guaranteed to attract a virtually full house regardless of who's singing. But not even the Met could keep that up very long. For one thing, we'd quickly lose our core audience of sophisticated operagoers, who are always hungry for new experiences. For another, we'd bore ourselves silly.

From the beginning, I felt that broadening the company's repertory was essential to our reaching the largest possible audience and keeping the company alive artistically. Unlike many American and European opera houses, the Met doesn't merely present opera. It *creates* opera. It's a house of artists, and everyone who contributes to a Met production—the wigmakers, the costume makers, the scenery builders and painters, the stagehands, the dancers, the chorus, the musicians, the directors and designers, the singers, the conductors, and even, as far as I know, Zeffirelli's dogs, donkeys, and horses—considers him- or herself an artist. Artists are creative people. They're restless. They need challenges.

With this in mind, I authorized more productions of operas that
had never been given at the Met than any general manager since
Gatti. In the course of twenty-seven years, Gatti produced thirty-one
Met premieres—twelve of them world premieres. The Met premieres
included operas that have since become standards (Smetana's *The
Bartered Bride*, Puccini's *The Girl of the Golden West* and *Il Trittico*, Offen-
bach's *The Tales of Hoffman*, and Verdi's *La Forza del Destino*), as well as
quite a few that have long since disappeared from memory. I doubt
whether anyone is going to rummage through the Met's attic for *La
Fille de Madame Angot*, *The Pipe of Desire*, *Madonna Imperia*, *The Canterbury
Pilgrims*, or *Mona*. But it must be pointed out that in Gatti's time new
operas were being turned out like sitcoms.

Gatti's successor, the Canadian baritone Edward Johnson, who was
in charge of the Met from 1935 to 1950, brought fifteen operas into
the repertoire, notably Gluck's *Alceste*, Mozart's *The Abduction from the
Seraglio*, Britten's *Peter Grimes*, and Mussorgsky's *Khovanschina*. Johnson's
three world premieres, which have not gone down in history, were
*The Man Without a Country*, *The Island God*, and *The Warrior*. Not even Bob
Tuggle in the Met's archives could tell you who wrote them.

Rudolf Bing's primary goal was not to expand the repertoire but to
improve the Met's tattered production values. During his twenty-two
years at the helm, he authorized eighty-nine new productions—only
twelve of them Met premieres. (Four were world premieres.) Eight of
the works he introduced had legs: Stravinsky's *The Rake's Progress*,
Strauss's *Arabella*, *Ariadne auf Naxos*, and *Die Frau ohne Schatten*; Offen-
bach's *La Périchole*; Verdi's *Macbeth* and *Nabucco*; and Berg's *Wozzeck*.

During my sixteen years of running the company, I enlarged the
repertoire at roughly the same rate as Gatti-Casazza, producing
twenty-six Met premieres (and four world premieres). At the same
time, I've restaged revivals at the same rate as Rudolf Bing—seventy-
three new productions in all. From a geopolitical standpoint, my
broadening of the repertory reflects the end of the cold war: four of
the premieres were Russian operas (*Lady Macbeth of Mtsensk*, *The Gambler*,
*War and Peace*, and *Mazeppa*). Three were Czech (*Rusalka*, *Kát'a
Kabanová*, and *The Makropoulos Case*). Like all my predecessors, I was
swayed by a certain degree of patriotism when it came to commis-
sioning new operas. All four world premieres—John Corigliano's *The
Ghosts of Versailles*, Philip Glass's *The Voyage*, John Harbison's *The Great
Gatsby*, and Picker's *An American Tragedy*—were by American com-

posers. (*Ghosts* and *The Voyage* were commissioned during the tenures of Anthony Bliss and Bruce Crawford.)

One phenomenon that none of my predecessors had to contend with was the rise of the prima donna director. As *regie* (director's) opera exploded in Europe during the nineties, the Met began to experience fallout in the form of some pretty bizarre behavior by directors who felt that their vision of a particular opera superceded that opera's dramatic requirements and the practical needs of the company.

This presented a new challenge. During the 1970s and '80s, five European directors of different nationalities—the Englishman John Dexter, the Italian Franco Zeffirelli, the Austrian Otto Schenk, the German August Everding, and the Frenchman Jean-Pierre Ponnelle—were entrusted with most of the new productions and premieres. Dexter, who had the biggest impact on the company—he staged fifteen new productions in nine seasons—was, of course, a special case.

I can't imagine a group of stronger, more diverse personalities. Zeffirelli has had the longest career of any director at the Met. His first assignment for the company was *Falstaff*, in 1964. His most recent production was *La Traviata*, in 1999. In manner, Zeffirelli was as grandly theatrical yet as controlled as his stage spectacles. His flare-ups were never tantrums, they were calculated for effect. Zeffirelli was all about the show, not about himself. As a master of every aspect of stage production, he was a much-admired figure backstage. When he yelled at me and I yelled back, we had a perfect understanding of each other.

Otto Schenk, who was a celebrated comic actor in Vienna before he became an opera director, has staged sixteen new productions at the Met since 1968. Each one has shown his (and his usual designer Günther Schneider-Siemssen's) magical sense of Romantic realism—even if the setting is the outskirts of Valhalla. All of them have demonstrated his knack for presenting opera so that it enters the audience's bloodstream intravenously. Schenk's productions, which teem with people in all their wonderful foibles, range from the bubbly, sardonic *Die Fledermaus* to magical realizations of most of the Met's Wagner repertory (*Tannhäuser*, *Meistersinger*, the *Ring*, and *Parsifal*).

Otto is all heart, and he's very funny. When he came to New York to discuss a new production, he'd enter my office on all fours, look up at me with a crooked smile, and make me get down on the carpet with him to sign the contract. As a personal favor, he came out of retire-

*Otto Schenk in his own production of* Die Fledermaus, *1986*

ment to stage my last production, Donizetti's *Don Pasquale.* After we signed the contract, he said, "When I arrive for the rehearsals, I'm bringing an urn so that when I die you'll have it for my ashes."

I said, "Bring a big one so I can join you."

August Everding directed five productions at the Met between 1971 and 1989. His first was the lost-in-the-clouds *Tristan und Isolde* for Jess Thomas and Birgit Nilsson. His last was a *Flying Dutchman,* which still retains its spectacular atmosphere of cosmic peril. Everding, who died in 1999, was the dean of European opera directors. He was a cultivated man with a deep classical education. He was also a superb politician. He ran most of the German opera houses at one time or another, and when Tony Bliss retired, the Met offered Everding the general manager's job. He sensibly turned it down because Jimmy Levine's agent, Ronald Wilford, had, in effect, blackmailed the Met into naming Jimmy artistic director. Wilford's threat that Jimmy would walk unless given the title was an empty one, but it worked.

During rehearsals, Everding would get so focused on the task at hand that he wouldn't realize he was chewing his tie. He organized and presided over the Association of International Directors of Opera, or AIDO, as it was called (a nice echo of both *Aida* and *addio*). I was a member of the group's executive committee, along with the heads of the principal opera houses and festivals. We met three times a year in various European cities to discuss artistic and economic issues of common interest, including ways to control artists' fees. I was always struck by the deference with which we were greeted in the grand hotels. In America they wouldn't have had the foggiest idea who we were. In Europe, they bowed to us like statesmen. We all bowed to Everding.

The late Jean-Pierre Ponnelle, Jimmy Levine's favorite director, staged five new productions between 1978 and 1987, including Mozart's *Idomeneo* and *La Clemenza di Tito*, and Massenet's *Manon*. Unlike Schenk, the colorful storyteller, or Everding, who addressed each work on its own terms, Ponnelle had a distinctive approach that was as exquisitely elegant as Zeffirelli's was hot and extravagant. Each of his wonderfully detailed productions had the stamp of "Ponnelle"— very structured, very clean, very ordered—an approach especially suited to Mozart. As a man, Ponnelle at first seemed closed—a typical overeducated Frenchman. He had no patience for fools and would quickly decide who was a "theater person" and who was a phony. Dexter, Zeffirelli, Schenk, Everding, and Ponnelle—these stage artists set the standards by which we still measure ourselves.

As stimulating as their different approaches have been for the Met, their similarities were even more important. Each of these directors— "the Pros," Joe Clark calls them—had a complete understanding of the opera they were working on. In some cases, they had a deeper one than the composer himself. Rather than superimposing a concept on the piece, they worked with the piece. During the process, they could display irritation, impatience, or temper—or, as in Franco's case, could walk out and yell at me from the safety of their apartment. But deep down, they were collaborators. They knew that the Met had put at their disposal not only the world's best singers but also the most skilled costume makers, scenery builders, lighting technicians, choreographers, and choristers. The Pros reveled in working with us, not against us.

The Met mounts new productions with the idea that they will last at least twenty years. They come in various sizes and budgets, but they're all expensive. (Today, they range in cost from $1 million to $3 million.) The Met's donors are paying for them, and they expect a return on their investment. When a new production opens at the Met, it's only one of four or five operas playing that week. Getting it mounted stretches the capacities of the house to the limit—artistically, logistically, and psychologically. Everyone feels the excitement and the strain. Until we see the thing up onstage, we're all holding our breath.

Operas aren't one-shot deals. Opera lovers want to see the great musical and dramatic works over and over again. There are several reasons why the best Met productions last. They serve the opera and the singers, rather than competing with them. They give the audience an exciting theatrical experience. And they hold up in their own right, no matter how many times the cast changes. Met regulars fall in love with certain productions—they want to see them around for their grandchildren. The best testament to the stage genius of Dexter, Zeffirelli, Schenk, Everding, and Ponnelle is that, of the fifty-two productions they created for the Met, thirty-nine are still in the repertory—including Zeffirelli's forty-two-year-old *Falstaff,* which had its latest run in the fall of 2005.

W hen I became general director, it was clear that the Met had to establish relationships with a younger, even more diverse assortment of directors. Like everything else in American culture, tastes in opera were fragmenting. The younger generation had not been steeped in the tradition of "grand" opera. Art—along with language, food, fashion, and sex—had become political. Sincerity was out; irony was in. It wasn't enough for opera to thrill; it had to provoke, explain, comment. Enter the new prima donnas.

The first new production on my watch, a staging of Verdi's *The Masked Ball,* brought me into the clutches of the Italian director Piero Faggioni. The Met had last staged the opera in 1979, using the British director Elijah Moshinsky for the first time. *The Masked Ball* has one of Verdi's most beautiful scores and most awkward librettos. Verdi originally set the story—a true tale of a Swedish king whose hanky-panky with the wife of his secretary got him assassinated—in Stockholm. When Neapolitan authorities found the story too close for comfort, Verdi transferred the setting to colonial Boston. Somehow the names of the characters never got sorted out—King Gustavus, who becomes the governor of the Massachusetts Colony, is referred to as Riccardo; two Swedish conspirators are called Tom and Sam. Moshinsky's production opted for Boston over Stockholm. The first insurmountable problem was the casting of Luciano Pavarotti as the governor. Pavarotti sounded wonderful, but it was hard to imagine him as a Puritan in a New England saltbox (or, as Moshinsky later referred to Peter Wexler's set, an "orange crate").

In 1984, the Met, upon the recommendation of Plácido Domingo, hired Piero Faggioni to direct the company's first production of Zandonai's *Francesca da Rimini* since 1916, an opera that Jimmy Levine and David Stivender, the Met's chorus master, thought was a neglected masterpiece. A post-Puccini verismo vehicle, it wasn't a masterpiece, and neither was Faggioni's grandiose staging, with elephantine sets by Ezio Frigerio. But Faggioni, an ex-actor with the manner and looks of an aging matinee idol, demonstrated an impressive command of stagecraft on the Met's scale.

Sybil Harrington's dislike of the imperious Faggioni quashed his chance to direct *Tosca*, but I approached him in 1990 for a new *Girl of the Golden West*, which he had just staged with success at Covent Garden. Faggioni told me that he would be happy to create an entirely new *Girl*, as long as he could do everything himself—the direction, the set designs, the costumes, the lighting. "The Met doesn't work that way," I said. "The house is too complicated for one person to assume all those responsibilities. We work as a team." Whatever the Italian word for "team" is, it wasn't in Faggioni's vocabulary. The Met decided to look for someone else. When I couldn't find anyone, I went back to Faggioni.

Joe Clark and I flew to Rome to discuss ideas for returning *The Mask-ed Ball* (as Faggioni pronounced it) to eighteenth-century Sweden. Imme-

*Italian director, Piero Faggioni*

diately, we sensed trouble. It turned out that Faggioni had a long memory. In 1979, he'd met with John Dexter about a new production of Puccini's *Manon Lescaut*. The discussion went rapidly downhill when Dexter
informed him that the designer on the project was to be the distinguished American Ming Cho Lee. "How can I work with a Chinaman?"
Faggioni complained. Dexter showed him the door.

Faggioni never got over it. The immense injury to his Italian
pride—along with the immense insult added by the Met's failure to
engage him promptly after the immense success of *Francesca da Rimini*—was all he wanted to talk about. After several days devoted to
raking over the history of Faggioni and the faithless Met, we finally
got down to business. As before, Faggioni insisted on doing everything himself. As before, I said no. The Met would find a designer.
Reluctantly, Faggioni agreed.

Unfortunately, the sketches by the Met's designer were a dud, and
by the time they came in we were down to the wire. I had no option
but to let Faggioni take over the whole show. The result was near
anarchy, caused by the necessity of consulting with the jack-of-all-
trades on every aspect of the production—discussions that invariably
began with another Faggioni rehashing of ancient history.

Things got really crazy when I was called during a rehearsal by an
assistant director who said that it was "urgent" that I have a word with
Mr. Faggioni. Apparently, during the ball scene, he had ordered two
African American women in the chorus to vacate their customary
positions downstage and get as far out of sight as possible. "Blacks to
the back!" he barked. "There are no blacks in Sweden!"

The Met choristers had heard it all, but this was a new one. Duti-
fully, the two women had moved to the back of the bus. The assistant
director, however, thought (correctly) that Signor Faggioni needed to
be brought up to date on race in America.

"There were maybe blacks in Boston, but there are no blacks in
Sweden," Faggioni reiterated.

"Piero," I said quietly, "this is America."

He looked as though I'd said "Macedonia" and continued to argue
the point. In the end, the two African American women returned to
their original positions in full view of the audience. Faggioni, however, doesn't give up easily. He insisted that the black American bass
Terry Cook, who was singing the conspirator Sam, put on white

makeup. At the same time, it was fine if the black American soprano Harolyn Blackwell, who was singing the page Oscar, retained her natural complexion. "The conspirator can't be black," Faggioni declared. "Oscar can be black, because he's a servant." I gave up.

Perhaps I was too indulgent. I had just assumed the responsibilities of general director, and this was my first show. Jimmy and I were still working out our choreography. We both agreed that Faggioni's desire to have a commedia dell'arte troupe pantomime the story during the opening prelude was ridiculous. But Faggioni, the master of Italian irony, wore us down, and the mimes stayed for opening night. After hearing the hoots in the audience, I did away with them, as well as with several other exercises in Faggioni overkill.

The production featured Pavarotti in fine form and looking more plausible as a fun-loving king than he had as a Puritan governor. Aprile Millo, an exciting young soprano with a huge top register, sang Amelia, the king's secret lover. Millo was immediately touted as that rarity—a real Verdi dramatic soprano, which the Met hadn't had since Leontyne Price. (When Renata Scotto, a wonderful artist, took on the heavier Verdi roles, she developed a wobble you could drive a train through.) The evening, as with many other productions of Verdi at the Met, was a hit with the audience but not with the critics. Still, I couldn't disagree with the *Times* reviewer who wrote, "The Piero Faggioni staging, having begun with a feeble cliché [the commedia dell'arte bit] stumbled on to one absurdity after another." When Faggioni and I sat down to reopen the possibility of his staging *The Girl of the Golden West,* I said, "This time you'll only direct."

"I had an *immense* success, and this is how you treat me?" he said, the picture of wounded Roman pride. "And you come to me at the last minute! Nobody else could have done it!"

"Sorry, Piero," I said, and we parted ways.

Or so I thought, until the following season, when I brought in another hotshot Italian director, Giancarlo del Monaco, for the new—and, as it turned out, splendid—*Girl of the Golden West.* Faggioni sent a letter threatening to sue the Met, claiming that we had "stolen" the staging of the saloon scene from his Covent Garden production. Nothing came of the suit, but it was undoubtedly good for another hour or two in the Faggioni book of grievances.

. . .

During the 1990–1991 season, another prima donna, the English director Jonathan Miller, came to the Met. Miller was a transatlantic celebrity. He'd studied neurophysiology at Cambridge and given up a medical career to become one of the clever comics in *Beyond the Fringe*. He'd directed Shakespeare plays and operas—notably, for the English National Opera, a landmark production of *Rigoletto* transplanted to New York's Little Italy. Every article said the same thing: Jonathan Miller knows everything or at least a little about everything.

Miller's debut was auspicious—a beautiful staging of *Kát'a Kabanová*, the Met's first production of the opera by the Czech composer Leoš Janáček. The spare set, designed by Robert Israel, looked like a stunning Russian folk painting of life along the Volga. The cast, led by the wonderful Czech soprano Gabriela Benacková as the rebellious title character and the formidable Leonie Rysanek as her stern mother-in-law, was topnotch. So was the conducting by the Janáček specialist Sir Charles Mackerras. The event was a critical success—and a breath of fresh air for the Met.

The critics also loved Miller's next two productions—Debussy's

*Jonathan Miller at work*

*Pelléas et Mélisande*, which opened in March of 1995, and Stravinsky's *The Rake's Progress*, which opened in November of 1997. Both were done with remarkable thoughtfulness. Still, I was beginning to wonder if this brilliant character was the director everyone was saying he was. After awhile, I found John Conklin's set for *Pelléas*—a manor house in serious need of renovation—stifling. ("Proustian" was how Miller and Conklin described the concept, which made the critics delirious.) It wasn't long before Miller's heavy-handed approach to the characters as a dysfunctional family lost in their private dreams sent me (and others in the audience) into my own dreams.

With *Rake*, Miller tried to make the cartoon-like characters into human beings, but I didn't feel that he really had his heart in it. When I closed my eyes, I could hear the love that Jimmy Levine in the pit felt for *Rake* and *Pelléas*, two difficult scores. When I opened my eyes, I saw a director showing us how clever he was.

During the rehearsals for *Pelléas*, I got a taste of Dr. Miller's encyclopedic expertise. The subject was the company's plan to introduce supertitles at the beginning of the next season. For several years, we'd been debating the pros and cons of installing instant English translations of librettos on some kind of screen. The argument for titles was a populist one: they would make opera more accessible to more people. The argument against them, led by Jimmy Levine and Jonathan Friend, was elitist: titles would dilute the sensuous, challenging experience of taking in opera on its own musical and dramatic terms. Several board members decided that titles were another instance of "dumbing down." Since those board members had been coming to the opera for years and knew the librettos backward and forward, why shouldn't everyone else go to the same trouble?

My only problem with titles was a practical one. The Met's proscenium arch is so high—and its height changes, depending on the opera—that I could see no way of installing titles above the stage without giving the people in the orchestra seats stiff necks. One day, when I was in the auditorium trying to figure out where else the supertitles might go, it occurred to me that we'd been looking at the wrong place. Why not put the titles on the backs of the seats?

I called Joe Clark. He had recently been on a plane where he'd observed such a system during the movie hour. He thought back-of-the-seat titles were a great idea. A special drive raised $3 million to fund the project. Joe put his technical staff to work. Countless hours were spent developing filters that would restrict the view of each screen to the person facing it. Countless hours were spent devising an electrical system that would enable each patron to activate or deactivate the screen. After nine months and a lot of trial and error, Joe Clark's shop came up with a system that worked. The Met's super-discreet titles were introduced at the performance of *Otello*, which opened the 1995–1996 season.

Met Titles, as the system is called, was an instant success. Since then, they've become a luxury that every Met patron takes for granted. They've made an incalculable difference in enhancing the experience of operagoing at the Met and in the company's ability to attract—and retain—audiences. Jimmy Levine, who once said that he would allow titles into the Met "over my dead body," loves them. Only Jonathan Friend, as a matter of principle, still refuses to turn them on.

Jonathan Miller, the world's expert on everything, said that super-titles would never work. "Neurologically speaking," he said to me, "it's impossible to take in the information on the screen with the eye and transfer it to the brain while keeping your focus on what's happening onstage." Well, Darwin was right—even operagoers are part of evolution. When Plácido Domingo made his entrance in Act 1 of *Otello* shouting, "Esultate! L'orgoglio musulmano sepolto è in mar!" ("Rejoice! The Muslim pride is buried in the deep!"), four thousand opening-night patrons instantly understood that the storm was over, and they got goose bumps. The titles have brought a new level of electricity to the Met.

In 1998, Jonathan Miller returned with an excellent new production of *The Marriage of Figaro*, adapted from one he had done in Europe. Like his *Pelléas*, this one (designed by Peter Davison) featured a lot of peeling paint to let the audience know that the house of Almaviva was on the way out, like the rest of the rotten European aristocracy. We assembled a dream cast: Bryn Terfel, the larger-than-life Welsh baritone, as Figaro; Renée Fleming, the world's most beautiful Countess; Dwayne Croft, the handsome American baritone, as the Count; the elegant American mezzo Suzanne Mentzer as Cherubino; and, as Susanna, Cecilia Bartoli, the Roman candle.

Bartoli was box-office gold. Her previous appearances at the Met—

as Despina in *Così Fan Tutte* in 1996 and as Cinderella in Rossini's *Cener-entola* the following season—had sold out the house. Her vocal tech-nique and authority in the Italian bel canto style began where those of other singers ended. At thirty-two, she was the world's bestselling female classical artist on disc and the most in-demand singer of her generation. But she seldom appeared in operas, preferring to give recitals in which she could trill all night for astronomical fees. She belonged to that rare species of opera singer whom Jonathan Miller, with all his Cambridge education in the human anatomy, feared and loathed—a superstar.

Cecilia is not a diva in the bad sense of the term. She is funny, warm, and down to earth. She throws herself into a part, and she's always respectful of her colleagues. As a musician, few singers in the world can touch her. But she did have insecurities about singing in a house the size of the Met. During *Così* and *Cenerentola*, I had to reassure her constantly that although her voice wasn't large, her ability to draw listeners in was so extraordinary that nobody at the back of the house could possibly miss a nuance in her astonishing arsenal of nuances.

As the millions of people who buy her recordings know, Bartoli loves vocal rarities. When she discovered that Mozart had written an alternative pair of arias for Susanna as star turns for his new prima donna Adriana Ferrarese del Bene, in a revival of *Figaro*, she had to sing them. Before she signed her contract for *Figaro*, both Jimmy and I agreed that she could replace "Venite" in the second act and "Deh, vieni" in the fourth act with the del Bene arias. The revived *Figaro* of 1789 was a bigger success than the 1786 Vienna premiere, but the alternative arias were dropped after Mozart's librettist, Lorenzo da Ponte, got dumped by his mistress, who was none other than Adriana Ferrarese del Bene.

I hadn't completely loved the idea—dramatically, the original arias made more sense—and I insisted that Cecilia sing the familiar arias on opening night. But both Jimmy and I thought that the departure from tradition would create additional excitement around the run of *Figaro*s. We decided that Cecilia could sing the showstoppers in three of the eight performances, including a *Live from the Met* telecast. We apprised Miller of the novelty long before he showed up for rehearsals. He frowned with displeasure, but I emphasized that it was a done deal.

When Cecilia arrived a week before opening night, she asked

Miller to rehearse the alternative arias. Miller nodded vaguely and then did nothing about them. Instead, he complained. Not to me or to Jimmy, but to everyone else within earshot. Miller loves the sound of his own voice more than most opera singers love theirs, and everyone who came into the Met's cafeteria was treated to an aria about what a terrible thing Bartoli had inflicted on him, what moral cowards Jimmy and I were, and so on. Miller is a virtuoso talker, and it must have been a good show. (I recall that he once described the Royal Opera as "a kind of wife kennel, a place where businessmen dump their wives in order to keep them quiet." This is a man who loves opera?) But coming from someone in his position, the behavior was unprofessional. It was hard to believe that a man of his stature was falling to pieces over two arias.

Miller's complaints soon reached the newspapers. (Since he'd stopped writing *Beyond the Fringe* sketches, he'd saved his best lines for the press.) Anthony Tommasini, who was then a junior critic at *The New York Times* (he is now chief music critic), took me and Jimmy to task for deferring to the diva.

A few years later, I was amused to read in *The Guardian* Miller's version of what happened when the two of us finally met in my office. As he recalled the meeting, I reminded him that he had agreed to the replacement arias. Then his memory got more interesting. "I agreed in much the same way that France agreed in 1939," he told the reporter. "You could see a cloud of unknowing pass across [Volpe's] eyes, and he just said, 'Don't f*** with me.' "

Miller is an ex–comedy writer. If I'd wanted to play Tony Soprano, I could have come up with a better line than that. All I said to him was that an agreement was an agreement and that Cecilia Bartoli would sing three performances with the new arias.

Left largely to her own devices, Bartoli did just that. The critics grumbled. The audience went nuts. The world survived. Some months later, *Opera News* interviewed Miller about the incident, and I was asked for a comment. I sent a carefully worded statement: "Jonathan Miller is a wonderful stage director with a vivid imagination. Everyone at the Met loves and admires his work."

When I didn't offer him any more new productions or invite him back to direct the *Figaro* revival, Miller began telling everybody that the Met had "fired" him. Baloney. He was stroking his ego. I was running an opera house. He fired himself.

. . . .

Early on in my tenure, two directors—Giancarlo Del Monaco and Elijah Moshinsky—became Met dependables. As time went on, they became undependables. From the very beginning, the red meat on the Met's menu has been the Italian repertory—chiefly, the operas of Verdi and Puccini. When staged and sung with color and passion, they can't miss. This is the stuff that sends the audience into the night with their blood racing. And yet, for many reasons, this repertory is the hardest to stage freshly. The operas of Verdi and Puccini tell their tales loud and clear. Romantic in style, they're as realistic as a good cop series such as *Law and Order.* The characters aren't gods or monsters, they're people caught up in the moral and political issues of their time. Any attempt to relocate these operas, update them, stylize them, or add a layer of contemporary irony risks making them look silly.

Giancarlo Del Monaco, a newcomer to the Met, was raised on this repertory. His father was the great Italian tenor Mario Del Monaco. As a kid, Giancarlo was dragged from one opera house to another, running around backstage while his dad belted out "Celeste Aida" and "Vesti la Giubba." In the process, Giancarlo acquired a deep knowledge of the Italian repertory and a difficult personality. He worked mainly in Germany, where he made a name for himself doing controversial productions—a *Butterfly* set in Vietnam, a Saddam *Nabucco,* which opened a year before the Gulf War. After his initial success at the Met with a beautifully traditional *Girl of the Golden West,* he told *Opera News,* "I have a Eurotrash face for Europe and a classy face for the Americans." I was relieved that he wasn't thinking of bringing his Eurotrash face through U.S. Customs.

Del Monaco's *Girl of the Golden West* had a strong cast led by Plácido Domingo and Barbara Daniels, vivid conducting by Leonard Slatkin, and a ghost town in the third act instead of the redwood forest that Puccini asks for. This Del Monaco production was followed, two seasons later, by the Met premiere of *Stiffelio,* which honored Plácido Domingo's twenty-fifth year with the company. The production made a good case for a neglected Verdi masterpiece despite the uneven singing and unalluring figure of Sharon Sweet as Lina, the title character's adulterous wife, and a forty-foot-long table that made the two principals squint when they wanted to see each other.

With a new *Madame Butterfly,* in 1994, the Eurotrash face of Del

Monaco began to show. His take on Lieutenant Pinkerton wasn't just that the U.S. Naval officer turned out to be a liar, he also had to symbolize the Ugly American—a smoker, a drinker, and a brute. I hated the shallow anti-Americanisms. (An American flag was hoisted when Pinkerton sarcastically quoted "The Star Spangled Banner.") But I was more concerned with the self-indulgent conducting of Daniele Gatti, an Italian maestro new to the house, who was taking certain sections so slow that the singers were finding them difficult to sing. I had Ken Noda, Jimmy's assistant and extra pair of eyes and ears on everything, attend a rehearsal to make sure that my judgment wasn't off the wall. Ken agreed with me. This sort of problem would normally have fallen to Jimmy to deal with, but he was away. I called Gatti's agent and said, "I don't want to make a big deal of this, but . . ."

Gatti turned out to have the same Italian pride as Faggioni. He got huffy and demanded that I specify exactly where I thought things were too slow. I replied that I could only indicate the problem, not fix it. As I pointed out, *he* was the conductor. During the run, Gatti grudgingly managed to move things along. When the run was over, he grandly announced that he would never return to the Met.

When Jimmy got back, I reviewed the situation. "But, Joe," he said, "I was only a phone call away."

I said, "I know, but sometimes those phone calls aren't answered or returned."

From then on, Jimmy always returned my calls.

The most passionate singing on *Butterfly's* opening night came not from Catherine Malfitano's Cio-Cio San or Richard Leech's Pinkerton, but from one of the Met's most beloved divas of years past. At the end of the Act 1 love duet, when Pinkerton ripped off his shirt, pulled Cio-Cio San's kimono down, and buried his head in her breasts, Licia Albanese, who had sung more Cio-Cio Sans in the 1940s and '50s than anyone else, let go with the most ringing boo I've ever heard at the Met. Licia later wrote me a letter saying how "tasteless" she'd found the scene. I did get Pinkerton to cut back on his smoking and drinking, but I retained the raw passion during the love duet. As the last notes lingered in the air, I was with Pinkerton all the way.

Two months later, Del Monaco unveiled a new *Simon Boccanegra*. It was a dud, despite one of Verdi's most powerful scores and a cast led by Domingo, Kiri Te Kanawa, the baritone Vladimir Chernov, and the bass Robert Lloyd. The Eurotrash impulse to make fun of traditional conventions reared its head in a confrontation between ax-wielding plebeians in black and sword-toting patricians in red. The singers tried hard to bring humanity to their roles, but the direction was more interested in turning them into caricatures. There was nothing so bad that it had to be yanked out—just a flatness, which can settle in when a director's whims are fundamentally at odds with the material.

Del Monaco's last production at the Met was *La Forza del Destino*, which opened in March of 1996. The opera features some of Verdi's most exciting music and one of his lumpiest librettos. The vengeance story travels all over the map, and it's tough to pull together. This *Forza* never got off the ground. When Del Monaco showed up for rehearsals, he wasn't the same bright-eyed, focused fellow I'd met five years earlier. I later learned that he'd left his position as intendant of the Bonn Opera. His marriage had ended, and the woman he now introduced as his wife was really his girlfriend. I began hearing tales that he was fighting with everyone.

One night, the doorman in my building, where Del Monaco had taken a temporary apartment, roused me out of bed at three in the morning. I threw on some clothes and went downstairs. There was Giancarlo cursing the doorman in Italian. Apparently, he'd come in stinking up the lobby with a big cigar; when he was told that he couldn't smoke in the elevator, he threatened the doorman's life. The police were on their way. Fortunately, I knew the cops in the Twentieth Precinct and I was able to assure them that Mr. Del Monaco was an important visiting artist and that he was under terrible pressure to produce a wonderful new show ("You know how Italians are . . ."). Everybody calmed down, and Giancarlo went up to his apartment, minus the cigar.

His behavior was particularly unpleasant to the large-figured Leonora in *Forza*, Sharon Sweet. In rehearsals, Del Monaco either ignored her or ordered her around like a servant. She fled to her dressing room in tears, and I was called.

"I don't work with mountains," he said loftily, when I asked him why he was treating her so badly. "That's why I don't work with Pavarotti."

I said, "And that's why some people don't work."

*Forza,* even with Domingo and Chernov in the cast and Jimmy in the pit, was a spiritless black hole. Del Monaco hasn't returned.

For nine seasons, from the spring of 1994 to the fall of 2001, Elijah Moshinsky was the closest thing the Met had to a house director. After the fiasco of the Boston *Masked Ball,* he came back in 1986 with a worthy but forgettable Handel's *Samson,* borrowed from Covent Garden. But it was not until March of 1993, when he and the designer Michael Yeargan teamed up for a gorgeous production of Strauss's *Ariadne auf Naxos,* that he demonstrated what a good fit he was for the Met. The production elegantly captured the work's tricky blend of satire and loftiness, grandeur and farce. It more than fulfilled my hope of mounting productions that were right for the piece in a way that was fresh, stylish, and beautiful.

Moshinsky's return to the Met came at the urging of Jessye Norman, the Ariadne of the production, who had loved working with him in *Tannhäuser* at Covent Garden. At the opening night, I told him that I thought the *Ariadne* was one of the best new productions the Met had had in years, and I added, "I've completely forgotten your *Ballo* [*The Masked Ball*]." Moshinsky grinned and said, "So have I."

From that point forward, we were on a roll: a handsome, durable *Otello,* which marked the Met debut of a secret weapon from St. Petersburg, the whirlwind conductor Valéry Gergiev; a film-noir staging of Tchaikovsky's creepy masterpiece *The Queen of Spades;* a strong, expressionistic production of our third Janáček opera, *The Makropoulos Case;* an appropriately garish *Samson and Dalilah;* and an old-fashioned crowd pleaser, and Verdi's first popular success, *Nabucco.*

Between *Nabucco,* which opened in 2001, and a lackluster production of Verdi's *Luisa Miller,* something happened to this gifted director. Like others before him—notably his countryman John Dexter—Moshinsky was prone to paranoia. During *Ariadne,* he had battled with one of the assistant directors, Lesley Koenig. When Koenig, a protégée of Jimmy's, was entrusted with a new production of *Così Fan Tutte* and Michael Yeargan agreed to design it, Elijah suspected a plot. I heard that his personal life was in disarray, which can't have helped.

For all the success of most of Moshinsky's productions, he became increasingly difficult to work with. Perhaps he had done too many

Verdi operas, with their love of plots within plots, but he was always trying to stir up a conflict that would divert everyone's attention from the real problems at hand. During *Otello*, he tried to play the two Desdemonas, Carol Vaness and Renée Fleming, against each other—building up or putting down one at the expense of the other. Both Carol and Renée were too smart to fall for it.

When I objected to his setting *Luisa Miller* in a placid English village far from its German Romantic roots, arguing that Victorian gentility was out of keeping with Verdi's music, Moshinsky refused

*Elijah Moshinsky directed operas for nine seasons at the Met.*

to discuss the matter; by then, he couldn't be told that any of his ideas might need rethinking. I knew that I was dealing with a troubled man—his wife had divorced him—and I dropped the issue.

I had always promised Moshinsky that a Met staple ripe for a new production, Gounod's *Faust*, was his to direct. We agreed that Michael Yeargan was the best choice as designer. The production was scheduled for the spring of 2005. Over many months, Michael turned out perhaps fifteen different designs; each was unacceptable to Moshinsky. When Michael suggested that Moshinsky sit down with Joe Clark to work out a solution to something objectionable, Moshinsky put up his hands in horror: "Absolutely not!" he said, fearing that yet another conspiracy was afoot. When he began skipping meetings with Michael, I stepped in and canceled his contract.

My relationship with the director who had done more distinguished new work during my tenure than any other had come to an end. Once again, it was the eleventh hour: we had committed the Met to a new *Faust* and had signed up a topflight cast, including three of the biggest male names in opera—Roberto Alagna, René Pape, and Dmitri Hvorostovsky. There was no backing out. Yeargan reminded me that some years earlier he had worked with the Romanian director Andrei Serban. Serban had directed a lively, if wildly overpopulated production of Berlioz's *Benvenuto Cellini* for the Met in December of 2003. He lived in New York, where he taught a theater course at Columbia. He was available. He was sane. Or so I thought.

## 14

## THE PLAYGROUND

Unlike Italian opera houses, where opera is a blood sport, the Met isn't generally a place where people feel it's their birthright to boo when they don't like what they're hearing. Americans get awestruck over high art, even when it comes in low forms, as opera sometimes does. We feel sorry for a singer who, after all that training, is having a bad night. But Met patrons can get highly offended when a director's pursuit of artistic liberties violates their pursuit of happiness.

In 1982, Peter Hall's new production of *Macbeth* featured a swarm of flying goblins and latex Oracles. It turned the Met audience into jeering Italians who would happily have tossed Sir Peter into the witches' cauldron. "They thought we were mocking Verdi," the lord of the English theater later said in disbelief.

I don't think so. Met patrons come from many different cultures, but essentially they're Yankees with common sense. They know when someone's opened the doors to the nuthouse. In March of 1979, the Met, at Jimmy Levine's urging, borrowed Jean-Pierre Ponnelle's *Flying Dutchman* from the San Francisco Opera. Conceived as the Steersman's dream, the production was a nightmare of interpretive license (the sleeping Steersman was doubled by a writhing mute). The audience turned into a lynch mob. Some loved it; some hated it.

Three new productions during my watch provoked a similar response. The first, in November of 1992, was a staging of *Lucia di Lammermoor* by Francesca Zambello, a newcomer to the Met with a résumé of strong-minded productions in American regional opera. She had been enthusiastically endorsed by Jimmy, who nodded sympathetically when she described her vision of *Lucia* (as she later wrote in the program) as a "tale of psychological terror, of emotional blackmail, and of sexual politics set in the half-seen realm of the unconscious." The trouble with relocating nineteenth-century opera in the half-seen realm of the unconscious is that the audience is apt to get left in the dark.

There was virtually no trace of the Scottish landscape in the sketches that Zambello and the designer, John Conklin, showed me. All I saw were fragments of a ruined castle—ruins for Act 1, ruins for Act 2, ruins for Act 3. In postmodern opera, fragments had become mandatory. This was especially true of Conklin, a clever man who did the sort of designs that made me wonder, "Why is that upside-down chair hanging from the ceiling?"

"Where are we?" I asked Francesca.

"In Lucia's mind," she said.

"But she doesn't go mad until Act 3," I said. "This design makes it look like she's lost it from the beginning. Why not begin with a castle in good shape and have it disintegrate as she does?"

Zambello, a very forceful woman, wasted no time telling me that the audience would have little trouble understanding that this was a new look at an old warhorse.

I wasn't convinced, but I didn't dig in my heels. I was still only general director; Zambello had Jimmy's enthusiasm, and I didn't want to be a stick-in-the-mud. In any case, I was hardly nostalgic for the Met's old *Lucia*, for which I'd built all those "stone" columns in the old house. Zambello and Conklin seemed to take my point, and they assured me that they would cut back on the ruins and maybe even throw in a real room or two.

For the intendant of any opera house, supervising a radically new staging of a familiar work is like being an anxious parent. If you second-guess the child from the beginning, the child won't get a life of its own. If you don't apply a steadying hand, he or she might go off course to a point of no return. With a new production, you have to give the director the leeway to see what works and what doesn't. At the Met, the possibilities are endless. Unlike most European houses, the Met doesn't just offer a shell for the director to fill; it provides a playground where anything you want to happen can be made to happen. If you want the moon to jump over a cow, the Met will give you the cow and the moon and make it jump.

For a first-time director, this can present too much temptation. In the case of a newcomer like Zambello, the Met's resources reinforced her vision of *Lucia* to the point of wackiness. Despite modifications, the ruins became so ruinous that they looked, as the *Times* critic wrote, like a "ruin of a ruin." The production's underlying feminist agenda grew so insistent that Arturo, Lucia's arranged fiancé, rose from under the stage on a pedestal, dressed like a Russian czar. Despite a virtuoso performance by June Anderson as the madder-than-mad heroine, the audience bellowed at Zambello.

Zambello's *Lucia* was performed twenty-five more times before it was mercifully buried. In 1998, I replaced it with an ultraconventional

*Francesca Zambello directed* The Trojans,
Cyrano de Bergerac, *and*
An American Tragedy.

production by the French director Nicolas Joël. As the critics rightly pointed out, we swung too far in the other direction, ending up with an empty-headed *Lucia* tailored to the dazzling vocal work of Ruth Ann Swenson without going anywhere near her mental work. Ruth Ann sang beautifully, but the production was a bore.

Few directors would want to return to the scene of such a fiasco, but after gaining maturity in Europe, Zambello returned to the Met in February of 2003. This time, she was able to take the measure of the house, and she delivered a stunning production of Berlioz's *The Trojans*. She had Jimmy in the pit, leading a powerful performance of one of his favorite composers. She had the choreography of Doug Varone, whose ritualistic dances had an emotional charge equal to that of the music. And she had three magnificent principals—Ben Heppner as Aeneas; Deborah Voigt as Cassandra; and as Dido, Lorraine Hunt Lieberson, an exquisite artist who hushed the house with every vocal and physical gesture and who should have long since been a Met star. Who would have imagined that Berlioz's unwieldy epic, a notorious problem child, would become the hottest ticket in town?

Zambello's next two projects for the Met—a witty production of Franco Alfano's rarely heard *Cyrano de Bergerac* and an intelligent staging of Picker's *An American Tragedy*—further vindicated Jimmy's original enthusiasm for her as a resourceful director who could bend the Met's forces to a fresh point of view and make it work.

With certain European avant-garde directors, the nuances of transatlantic communication can mysteriously (or purposely) get lost in translation (*"Scusi*, Joe, but I thought you said . . ."). When I asked the cult American director Robert Wilson to stage a new *Lohengrin* for the spring of 1998, there was no mystery about who or what we were working with. Bob Wilson is Bob Wilson, and that's what we got. Courteous, meticulous, and a thorough professional, Wilson, with his cadre of quiet disciples, created a magnificent light show as self-effacing as his name. The shimmering hues illuminated the opera's obsession with purity, enhanced its dramatic shifts, and allowed Wagner's familiar strains (conducted with reverence by Jimmy) to be heard as though they were written that morning.

What I didn't sufficiently anticipate was how hard it would be for the two principal singers, Deborah Voigt and Ben Heppner, to move in

*Robert Wilson, who directed the minimalist* Lohengrin

the ritualized Wilsonian manner. I also failed to register a recent development in the history of booing. For months, anti-Wilson forces had been peppering the Internet with appeals for the Met audience to give his *Lohengrin* the same treatment it had dished out to Zambello's *Lucia*. Perhaps Elijah Moshinsky was right: opera is a world of conspiracy.

I'm happy to say that this magical *Lohengrin*, which I regard as a triumph, survived the catcalls Wilson got on opening night. In subsequent performances, Voigt, Heppner, and Deborah Polaski, as a hyperactive Ortrud, settled more comfortably into Wilson's scheme. When we revived the production the following fall, with Karita Mattila as Elsa, everything clicked. Wilson had micromanaged the first performances to such an extent that the production, as one critic said, looked like "frozen Kabuki." For the revival, Wilson mostly sat around opening mail. Karita worked for weeks with Wilson's "movement coordinator," Giuseppe Frigeni, so that she could make the clockwork choreography look completely natural. Her body language was as eloquent as her voice. It's taking nothing away from Debbie Voigt's gloriously sung Elsa to say that sometimes at the Met, a casting change can make all the difference.

Some of the company's new productions are chosen primarily to flatter a star. I wouldn't have presented *Cyrano de Bergerac* or, a few years earlier, Wolf-Ferrari's *Sly*, about the drunken English poet Christopher Sly, if Plácido Domingo hadn't been so eager to do them. For Kiri Te Kanawa, we mounted Strauss's last opera, *Capriccio*, which gives the audience two hours of pedantic Viennese chatter before cutting loose at the end with fifteen minutes of gorgeous soprano singing. Sam Ramey, the Met's leading hometown bass, got to cavort devilishly in Arrigo Boïto's *Mefistofele*. Renée Fleming was the glittering reason for new productions of Bellini's *Il Pirata* and Handel's *Rodelinda*.

My biggest fiasco, a new production of *Il Trovatore*, was prompted by the Met's desire to promote the career of the American tenor Neil Shicoff. Although *Trovatore* is one of Verdi's most popular works, it's tough to stage for modern audiences because the plot, which concerns two enemies who don't know they're really brothers, has inspired more parodies than any other opera. If you want to get a laugh about grand opera, sing the Anvil Chorus and pound the table. The Met hadn't done a successful *Trovatore* in years. Still, the opera has some of Verdi's best tunes. We were coming up to the centenary of the composer's death in 1900. I wanted to lick the *Trovatore* curse, once and for all.

Although *Trovatore*'s famous arias are evenly distributed among the four leading roles, the opera requires above all a Manrico on the order of such all-out dramatic tenors as Caruso and Giovanni Martinelli. In the post-Domingo generation, the closest thing was Shicoff. Neil had been one of the Met's most promising young tenors in the mid-1970s. He then decided that the grass was greener in Europe. In 1996, he returned to the Met after a long absence and sang a heartfelt Lenski in Robert Carsen's undernourished production of Tchaikovsky's *Eugene Onegin*.

No one would ever accuse Neil of subtlety, but alone among American tenors he sings with a plaintive intensity that marks him as a true descendant of the last great American Manrico, Richard Tucker. (Both singers had fathers who were celebrated cantors.) The assistant manager for artistic affairs, Sarah Billinghurst, and I wanted to build a real following for Neil at the Met. When his manager, Matthew Epstein, suggested *Trovatore* as the perfect vehicle, I was intrigued but not completely convinced. Did Neil really have the heroic sound and the fearless top notes necessary to pull off an aria like "Di quella pira," which has the most famous high C in opera? In the Age of Irony, what director would be willing to risk his neck with *Trovatore*? As Jimmy Levine put it, "It's a death sentence, Joe."

On our very short list of directors who might have been willing to go to the gallows, the likeliest name was that of Graham Vick. In the fall of 1994, Vick, who was the young, smart head of the Glyndebourne Festival, had given the Met one of its most controversial productions—the company premiere of Shostakovich's *Lady Macbeth of Mtsensk*. Vick took his cue from *Pravda*'s devastating pan of the work in 1936 as "crude, primitive, vulgar"—a review that appeared after Stalin walked out of a performance. The Met's staging, which featured a wanton Maria Ewing in the title role, was stylishly crude, primitive, and vulgar—though it required a good deal of editing down from the extravagant production that Vick first envisioned.

"Think John Dexter," I told him, and little by little he did. Afterward, he paid me a compliment unheard of from most directors: "Thanks for pushing me, Joe," he said. "It's much better now." The audience was loudly divided between those who were infuriated by the harshness of the production and those who thought it appropriate for a work that could now be seen as a savage anti-Soviet satire. I thought that both the controversy and the production were terrific.

A few years later, Vick returned with an impressive production of another notoriously difficult twentieth-century opera, Schoenberg's *Moses und Aron*. Vick's bold staging wolfed down this ungodly stew of head-splitting music, theological argument, and orgiastic carrying-on. (The Golden Calf scene, choreographed by Ron Howell, had more glitz than skin.) Jimmy's affection for the score, and the committed singing of John Tomlinson and Philip Langridge in the title roles, helped make the six-performance run, if not a box-office smash then a hit among the operagoers who like to suffer for their art and talk about it all night afterward. Who said the Met always played it safe?

Jimmy and I agreed: Graham Vick was the man for *Il Trovatore*.

Vick's first designs (the work of Maria Bjornsen, who had created the look for *The Phantom of the Opera* in the London West End) were too grand for comfort and too spacious acoustically for Neil. (Neil had already battled against the acoustical shortcomings of Carsen's wide-open *Onegin*.)

"Let's strip everything down," I said, remembering the failure of the Met's last *Trovatore*—Fabrizio Melano's leaden staging of 1987. Here, I thought, was one Verdi opera that could benefit from a simpler, more abstract design. Paul Brown, who had worked so well with Vick on *Lady Macbeth* and *Moses und Aron*, replaced Bjornsen.

Brown's designs came in during the spring of 2000—late for a production that was opening in early December. But the basic concept was strong, simple, and acoustically good for Neil—essentially, a square-off between two movable, sometimes intersecting walls, one

*A scene from Graham Vick's* Trovatore

charcoal gray, the other white, to underscore the fraternal conflict. Then Vick got into the Met playground.

Graham talks an exceptionally good game, and he had almost everyone, including Neil, believing that the more stage technology he employed, the livelier things would be. Floating stairs appeared out of nowhere. A religious cross became a ramp. If Vick could have found a cow for his flaming moon to jump over, he would have used it.

Verdi was more concerned with the psychological clash of human conflict than he was with a Spanish Civil War that pitted the two brothers against each other. Vick, however, wanted to make sure the audience realized that he was no militarist, so he dressed Count di Luna's troops like Keystone Kops and decorated the stage with hanging corpses. When I finally saw the whole thing onstage, I got a stomachache. Out came my scissors—I should have used an ax.

It was too late. Despite all the ludicrous bits I managed to get Graham to excise, the production was what it was—a cold, abstract vessel whose pyrotechnics only heightened the absurdity of the story. I prayed that the Met's patrons wouldn't laugh thanks to Neil's passionate high notes; the powerhouse presence of Dolora Zajick as Azucena, the gypsy mother; the suave baritone of Roberto Frontali as the Count; and the soft glow of the Russian soprano Marina Mescheriakova as Leonora.

My prayers were no use. In Act 2, when Manrico made his entrance on the falling cross in Leonora's chapel (the image was supposed to heighten her feeling that he's coming from heaven), the audience howled. When he sang "Di quella pira" balanced precariously on a swinging staircase, they were too worried about his safety to howl. In the final scene, when Manrico and Azucena were in prison awaiting their execution, the house broke out in laughter at the sight of Neil and Dolora trying to keep their footing on a rippled floor that Joe Clark and I dubbed "the potato chip." When Graham Vick took his curtain call (Paul Brown had wisely headed for the hills), the audience screamed for his head.

After the opening, I called Vick and told him that I was making some changes. He said fine. Out went the flaming moon, the hanging bodies, the swinging staircase, the falling cross, and the potato chip. Vick became incensed, took his name off the production, and vowed never to work at the Met again. I couldn't blame him. What was left was an empty shell. The curse of *Trovatore* lived on.

. . .

Carmen, oddly enough, has been another hard-luck opera for the Met. In my time, the Met has produced four *Carmens*. The first was Jean-Louis Barrault's 1967 staging, which set everything in a bull-ring as big as the Coliseum. Next came Goeran Gentele's 1972 production (finished, after his death, by Bodo Igesz), which seemed underdirected and which used unconvincing projections to suggest the mountain pass. In 1986, Peter Hall's ugly arts-and-crafts production became such a hodgepodge after the Carmen, Agnes Baltsa, demanded certain changes that Sir Peter took his name off it.

The Met's current *Carmen* will be ten years old in the 2006–2007 season. It has held up better than I thought it would. In 1995, I decided that my old friend Piero Faggioni might be a good match for a new *Carmen*. Running an opera house, among other things, gives you a short memory. Faggioni, in his Roman splendor, liked the idea, and he was even agreeable to the idea of collaborating with the designer of our choice, Dante Ferretti, who had worked on many Martin Scorcese films. Ferretti's first sketches were more cinematic than theatrical, and when Faggioni saw them, he reverted to his old self: "I'll do everything myself," he said.

"Sorry, Piero," I said, reverting to my old self, "we're sticking with Ferretti."

I asked Ferretti to suggest another director, and he came up with Liliana Cavani, whose film *The Night Porter*, with Dirk Bogarde and Charlotte Rampling, had been a kinky international sensation. Interesting, I thought.

Cavani and Ferretti arrived on my doorstep with a new vision of *Carmen*. Cavani was a pale woman whose manner suggested that she wanted to grind me under her heels. Her *Carmen* was all over the place. In Act 2, we went from a highly realistic railroad station to an abstract landscape in the mountains. "This doesn't make sense," I said.

"Take it or leave it," she said and walked out, clicking her heels.

It was too late in the day to go after an untested director, so I called Franco Zeffirelli. "You're in luck!" he said. "I happen to have a very good *Carmen* in Verona right now. It's similar to the one I did in Vienna twenty years ago."

European Zeffirelli tends to be cheaper than Met Zeffirelli, but Zeffirelli is Zeffirelli. "How big is the cigarette factory?" I said.

"No cigarette factory," he said. "This is a simple Zeffirelli *Carmen*. Perfect for the new Met."

"It's not exactly a *new* Met, but I like the sound of it."

"You can use the Verona rocks as they are," he said, "but I'll have to adapt some things for the Met."

"Economically, Franco," I said. "Economically."

"*Ecco*," he said. "Who's the Carmen?"

"Waltraud Meier."

"No! No!" he said. "She can't sing Carmen. She can only sing German! Get the American black."

"Denyce comes in later," I said. "Jimmy wants Waltraud. It's an interesting choice."

"I don't think so," he said.

"I'll arrange for the two of you to meet," I said. "You'll be wonderful together."

Zeffirelli's preference for the beautiful African American mezzo-soprano, Denyce Graves, over the magnetic German soprano with mezzo capabilities made some sense. In recent years, Graves had been the Carmen of choice. She had made the gypsy temptress hers— much as the Met's beloved Risë Stevens had virtually owned the role back in the 1940s and '50s. Meier, one of the world's most formidable Wagner singers, had never sung *Carmen*. But she was a redhead with a

*Waltraud Meier as Carmen*

blazing stage presence, and if she could pull it off, the Met would make international opera news. Zeffirelli had a point, but he had objected in much the same way to the casting of another superb German-singing actress, Hildegard Behrens, in his 1985 production of *Tosca*—and then been won over by her tremendous intensity. Meier was a similar stage animal, and I was sure that the two of them would get along.

When Waltraud, Franco, and I met for lunch before rehearsals began, I realized that their chemistry was worse than nonexistent. Waltraud got right down to business. "*Who* is Carmen?" she demanded of Zeffirelli.

Zeffirelli looked into the distance and said airily, "Carmen is an animal, controlled by no one."

"I know all that," she said. "What about *this* Carmen?"

Franco isn't used to such questions. He twirled a forkful of pasta and said, "We shall see."

"See *what*?" Waltraud persisted.

"A *beautiful* Carmen" was all Franco would say.

This was going nowhere.

Which is where it went. For the next few weeks, Zeffirelli busied himself surrounding the rocks from Verona with as many dragoons, cigarette girls, gypsies, smugglers, bullfighters, and bullfight fans as he could cram onstage. I drew the line when he wanted to import real gypsies from Rome. His promise of a "simple *Carmen*" was valid for the production's relatively spare scenic elements, but not for the costumes. The writer Justin Davidson spent weeks backstage, watching the production take shape. In an article in *Newsday*, he described the Zeffirelli approach to "economy": "The most abject gypsy will be dressed in a tailored costume, an intensively aged patchwork of different-colored fabrics that has been dyed, bleached, scrubbed, crumpled and re-dyed to create a glamorous stage version of misery." That's Franco.

Zeffirelli's *Carmen* required a menagerie that even by his standards was extensive—seven horses, three dogs, and two donkeys. I was amused until two of the horses buckled during a rehearsal and collapsed onstage. "We can't have that!" I said. "Get rid of them." Franco didn't want animals collapsing onstage either. One of them was a big white steed on which Plácido Domingo, as Don José, made his entrance in Act 3. "Franco," I said, "what is this, the Lone Ranger? He's only a corporal!"

"But, Joe," Franco said, "it's so *beautiful!*"

Franco had eyes for the horse but not for Waltraud. Even the most resourceful singers need direction—and Waltraud Meier is one of the most resourceful singers in the world—but she got no help from Zeffirelli, who increasingly preferred to direct the scenery and the extras rather than the principals. After a rehearsal during which he paid her not the slightest attention, he called out an Italian pleasantry as she went to her dressing room. Waltraud was heard to mutter, " '*Ciao, bella,*' my ass!"

After a few days of this treatment, she came to me. "Joe," she said, "this is not going to work. Maybe I should go home."

"Keep your focus," I said. "We'll get this done."

Before long, Zeffirelli stopped coming to rehearsals when Waltraud was in the scene, sending one of his assistants instead. "Franco," I said, "she needs help. You must work with her."

He waved dismissively. "She doesn't listen," he said. "And as I told you, she's no Carmen. She's a hausfrau."

We brought in a European director, Angela Zabrsa, to help Waltraud. From that point on, Franco ignored her completely. Diligently, she went to work putting together her own Carmen.

The result on opening night was two *Carmens*—one eye-filling, the other perplexing. Waltraud had worked out every detail of a complex woman of lethal sensuality, but it was an assemblage not a character. She looked as though she'd sashayed in from another production and was surprised to find herself in this one. In subsequent performances, she gamely came up with ways to integrate herself better into the surroundings, but it was a mismatch from the beginning—a mistake on the part of Jimmy and me that caused this distinguished artist unnecessary pain. When Denyce Graves took over the role for four of that season's performances (she later did thirty more in revivals), Zeffirelli finally got the Carmen he'd been directing all along—a force of nature that fit in perfectly with his gaudy street fair.

One of the Met's most rewarding collaborations has been with the Russian conductor and artistic director of the Maryinsky Theater in St. Petersburg, Valéry Gergiev, for whom I created the new position of principal guest conductor in the fall of 1997. My relationship with Gergiev—who, with his Kirov Opera and Orchestra, circles the globe more tirelessly than the Flying Dutchman—began in 1992 when he brought his Russian troupe to the Met for a series of summer performances. At his Met conducting debut with *Otello,* in the spring of 1994, I sensed that here was an interesting foil to James Levine. Under Jimmy's baton, the Met's performances have a steady, radiant glow. Valéry conducts from feeling, not precision. In his quivering hands the music is volcanic, unpredictable. Valéry's performances can be erratic, and he can drive you crazy with his habit of racing in at the last minute. Some members of the orchestra and the chorus squirm when he stops and asks them to think not just about the music but about what's going on in the opera. ("Remember, you're Cossacks!") But certain top singers (including Karita Mattila and Renée Fleming) love him for the excitement he can generate like nobody else, not only in the Russian repertoire he introduced to the company, but in Mozart, Strauss, and Wagner.

Occasionally, the Met is happily startled by the success of an opera that seemed destined to become a "warehouse production"—that is, a production headed for a good long stay in storage. One such surprise was Tim Albery's lovely, childlike production in November of 1996 of Britten's *A Midsummer Night's Dream,* which punctured the axiom that the last century's greatest English composer is box-office poison—notwithstanding the Met's superb stagings of *Peter Grimes, Billy Budd,* and *Death in Venice.*

Another surprise hit was Temur Chkheidze's 2001 production of *The Gambler,* an adaptation of the Dostoevsky story that sounds more like a sung play than a full-fledged opera. I wondered if the audience was more hooked on the story's parade of sadists, masochists, narcissists, cynics, and hysterics than on the music. In any case, they were hooked. *The Gambler* marked the Met debut of the brilliant Russian designer George Tsypin, who went on to create the look for two subsequent hits, *War and Peace* and Julie Taymor's production of *The Magic Flute.*

The 2002 production of *War and Peace* was one of the most ambitious undertakings in the Met's history. The Met threw the works at it—a $3 million budget; the famous Russian film director Andrei Konchalovsky; fifty-two singers (for sixty-eight roles), most of them Russian. The principals included the stunning young soprano Anna Netrebko as Natasha, and Dmitri Hvorostovsky, the handsome young baritone, as Andrei. There were 120 choristers, 41 dancers, 227 super-numeraries, a horse, a dog, and a goat. I even got into the act on opening night after one of Napoleon's defeated soldiers seemed to lose his footing on Tsypin's rotating platform and disappeared into the orchestra pit. Gergiev, who was conducting, stopped the show, the retreat halted, and the audience stood up and craned to peer into the pit. The performance picked up after ten minutes. At the curtain call, I marched the wayward soldier out in front of the audience and told everybody that "our retreating French grenadier had lost his way in the storm" but was unhurt.

The grenadier was a twenty-one-year-old, thirty-dollar-a-day extra named Simon Deonarian. It turned out that he hadn't lost his way at all. In a bid for fifteen minutes of fame, he'd jumped into the pit, just clearing a safety net and landing on the bow of the associate principal violinist, Sylvia Danburg, and snapping it in two. *The New York Times* and the other media outlets responded with their usual enthusiasm for mishaps at the Met, and the kid got his fifteen minutes. I dismissed him from the other nine performances. But perhaps he did the Met a favor: *War and Peace* sold out the rest of the run.

For Gergiev, who led a brilliant musical performance, the event was a triumph. Konchalovsky, who had done a terrific job holding everything together (including the Met chorus, which had to be schooled in the Russian foot-stomping tradition of "One! Two! Three! Squat!"), was dismayed by the media's lack of interest in him. Konchalovsky was a big name in Russian cinema, and he'd had a Hollywood triumph some years back with *The Train*. He couldn't understand why Prokofiev, Gergiev, Netrebko, Hvorostovsky, and the jumper were getting all the attention. I tried to tell him that this was opera, not the movies.

Four first-time German directors took to the Met and its ways like longtime members of the family and produced illuminating productions of familiar operas. In 1999, Dieter Dorn created a magical *Tristan und Isolde*. In 2000, Jürgen Flimm, who is now the head of the Salzburg Festival, staged a *Fidelio* that was vibrantly theatrical without trying to out-manifesto Beethoven. Flimm returned to the Met with a contemporary, steamy *Salome*, which set the biblical horror story in a garish four-star hotel in the Persian Gulf. The cheering by champions of deftly handled stage irony drowned out the scattered booing of the traditionalists, who preferred a *Salome* out of DeMille.

In the spring of 2004, the international film actress and director Marthe Keller banished memories of Zeffirelli's grandiose *Don Giovanni* with a clean, stripped-down take on Mozart's complicated moral comedy that evenly distributed the foolishness and sweetness among the don's victims on both sides of the gender line. The production also demonstrated that not since Ezio Pinza had the Met had such a charismatic bass as in the towering young German René Pape, a stage natural with a huge voice who could be as powerful projecting King Marke's wounded dignity in *Tristan* as he was inhabiting the sly boots of Leporello.

Herbert Wernicke undoubtedly would have gone on to a distinguished career at the Met if he hadn't suddenly dropped dead of a heart attack on a street in Basel in April of 2002. A year earlier, he had unveiled a wonderful *Die Frau ohne Schatten*, which replaced the opera's usual fairy-tale setting with a hall of mirrors for the Emperor and the Empress and a dingy factory room for the Dyer and his wife. Rarely since Karajan's *Rheingold* and *Die Walküre* in the seventies had the Met entrusted someone with all aspects of a production. Under Wernicke's guidance, the singers' stage movements were as seamless as the scenic elements—all designed by Wernicke himself.

With Wernicke, the process of creating a production was both flexible and practical. Like August Everding, he had no one-size-fits-all approach to opera. His ideas were vague at the beginning, but they took shape through discovery and experimentation. When he mentioned to Joe Clark that he envisioned the Dyer's hut as a kind of squatter's hovel in a tunnel, Joe rummaged around and found a horde of old pipes that gave the set its industrial look. Wernicke was a dream to work with, and we were thinking of asking him to direct a new *Ring* when we heard about his untimely death. In an obituary, a German colleague wrote the best description I've ever read of what makes a superior opera director: "[Wernicke's] analytical style, combined with his exceptionally visual imagination, keen sense of magic and exacting observations of the sheer complexity of reality outside the theatre repeatedly enabled him to uncover in opera the secret interrelationship between past and present."

. . .

Julie Taymor of *The Lion King* fame is another director on that order. Her production of *The Magic Flute*, with stage designs by George Tsypin, has become the Met's biggest hit since Zeffirelli's *La Bohème*. It took Taymor, a control freak with a million ideas, some time to settle down. When Joe Clark said something about a proposed stage effect, such as "This won't work—it's too big and we can't get it onstage in time," Julie's first reaction was "I did this before and it works." She had done *The Magic Flute* before—in 1994, she and Tyspin staged a version of the opera that was kindergarten compared with the show we were putting on at the Met. But it didn't take long for Julie to get into the Met's collaborative spirit. Working with Joe and his staff, she created a fantastic spectacle that enhances and tweaks Mozart's Masonic fairy tale at the same time.

Logistically, Taymor's *Flute* was beyond anything the Met had ever done before. The centerpiece of Tsypin's design, a crystal palace of moving walls and stairs, had to appear onstage quietly out of nowhere before going into kaleidoscopic gyrations. Twelve Indonesian birds and seven bear puppets, carried by twenty running puppeteers, had to come and go during arias and duets. Three spirits—kids in diapers, fright wigs, and Methuselah beards—had to fly over the stage on a gliding perform suspended from the wings of a giant dove. Flames had to emerge from the furnace-like heads of puppets that doubled for the guards to Sarastro's Temple of Wisdom. A Las Vegas chorus of bird-headed showgirls on stilts had to peck and prance around Papageno as he fantasized about finding himself a girlfriend. I thought of calling up the police department and asking if we could borrow some traffic cops.

Night after night, Julie and her team were in the house well into the early hours of the morning, trying to make it all work. Somehow, opening night, in the fall of 2004, went off without a glitch. The ovation, from grandparents and eight-year-olds, was as enthusiastic as any I've heard at the Met.

## 15

## SIAMESE TWINS

My timing was fortunate. During the boom years of the 1990s, the Met increased its endowment from $110 million to $235 million. My friend Rudy Giuliani, a longtime Met fan, put the city on a roll. Smart policing made the streets and the subways safe. New York was awash in tourists, many of whom happened to love opera. The Met's relations with the unions were stable and friendly. For a dozen seasons, the company broke even. By the end of the nineties, we were even operating slightly in the black. Financially, the Met was in better shape than at any time in its history.

An important reason for the company's good health in these years was the presence of two tenors who would be on every opera lover's list as among the legendary singers of all time. Luciano Pavarotti and Plácido Domingo were already world famous when they joined forces in 1990 with José Carreras, who had miraculously survived leukemia. Their international concert act—the Three Tenors—became a franchise and went on to fill soccer stadiums around the world, bringing in unprecedented numbers of new and old opera fans and selling millions of recordings. It was an irresistible combination of great singing,

*Luciano Pavarotti in* Daughter of the Regiment, *1972*

great packaging, and great camaraderie—which is not something that happens every day among tenors. Although both Pavarotti and Domingo eventually made a lot more money out of the Three Tenors than they earned at the Met, they remained loyal to the house that had made them stars in the first place.

They were the Siamese twins of opera, though they never appeared in an opera together, and it would be hard to imagine them joined at the hip. They both made their Met debuts in the fall of 1968, in circumstances that foreshadowed their later careers. On October 8, Domingo filled in for an indisposed Franco Corelli as Maurizio in *Adriana Lecouvreur.* His leading lady was Renata Tebaldi. On November 16, Pavarotti canceled his scheduled debut as Rodolfo in *La Bohème,* pleading some kind of illness. On November 23, a week later, he made his debut in *Bohème* opposite the Mimi of another exciting young singer from his hometown of Modena, Italy—the soprano Mirella Freni.

*Plácido Domingo as Otello, 1987*

Both men got strong reviews in the *Times*. Donal Henahan went all out for Domingo, whom he described as the Met's "hottest young artist in the tenor category . . . a strapping fellow with a plangent and sizable voice, as well as considerable stage magnetism." Henahan noted a Herculean quality in Domingo—an ability to galvanize the evening through sheer intensity—that he would later demonstrate countless times at the Met: "Again and again," Henahan wrote, "[he] lifted the performance out of the depths of fatuity into which it relentlessly lapsed."

Peter G. Davis was more mixed but also astute about Pavarotti. "The tenor," he wrote, "triumphed principally through the natural beauty of his voice—a bright, open instrument with a nice metallic ping on top that warms into an even, furnished luster in mid-range. Any tenor who can toss off high C's with such abandon, successfully negotiate delicate diminuendo effects, and attack Puccinian phrases so fervently is going to win over any *La Bohème* audience, and Mr. Pavarotti had them eating out his hand. As far as acting tenors go, Mr. Pavarotti is not the worst, but his generally stiff and unconvincing stage presence did leave something to be desired."

Fair enough—though it wasn't long before that big, beaming stage presence left nothing to be desired.

But nobody could have anticipated how much these two singers would come to mean to the Met. Over the years, Pavarotti and Domingo have appeared in a combined total of 925 performances of 49 different operas in the house. (Plácido, who is still the Met's leading dramatic tenor, has sung 570 performances of 43 operas; Luciano, who sang his farewell *Toscas* in the spring of 2004, has been featured in 355 performances of 20 operas.) When Domingo opened the 1999–2000 season it was his eighteenth Met opening night, surpassing Caruso's record of seventeen. He has sung in three opening nights since then.

The marketing value of both men has been phenomenal. New productions and Met premieres attract the most attention from the press and the public. In the course of his Met career, Domingo has appeared in twenty-two new productions, including the Met premieres of Verdi's *Stiffelio*, Léhar's *The Merry Widow*, Wolf-Ferrari's *Sly*, and Franco Alfano's *Cyrano de Bergerac*. Pavarotti has sung in thirteen new productions, including the Met premieres of Mozart's *Idomeneo* and Verdi's *I Lombardi*. Both singers have been prominently featured in Met audio recordings, radio broadcasts, telecasts, and home videos. Because they are among the handful of international stars around whom operagoers plan their visits to the Met, we've made sure that virtually all our subscription series include one or more appearances by Pavarotti or Domingo. Over the years, they've been the big draw at many of the Met's fund-raising galas, at hugely elevated ticket prices. One of the most successful was the silver anniversary evening of September 27, 1993, which celebrated their twenty-five years with the company. I've always thought that a key to their appeal is the fact that they're opposites—as complementary as the two greatest New York Yankee sluggers. Pavarotti is Babe Ruth; Domingo is Lou Gehrig.

Pavarotti is boisterous, larger than life, as immediately recognizable offstage as he is on. No matter what role he's singing, he's not

Rodolfo, Mario Cavaradossi, or the Duke of Mantua—he's Pavarotti. Opera fans have a personal identification with him that no other singer can claim. A few years ago, as I was coming through U.S. Customs at JFK Airport after a trip to Italy, I was asked by the man in the passport booth, "Is it true, Mr. Volpe, that Pavarotti cracked in *Don Carlo* at La Scala?" Like one of the Babe's mighty swings that sent the ball out of the park, a high C from Pavarotti always had the audience on its feet.

Domingo, on the other hand, is a striver intensely dedicated to his craft, quiet and formal in manner, totally dependable in professional habits. He works hard at everything—mastering the style peculiar to each new role, from Mozart to Wagner; challenging himself as a conductor; running two regional opera houses at opposite ends of the country—those of Los Angeles and Washington. In 1995, Cal Ripken, Jr., finally broke Lou Gehrig's endurance record of playing in 2,130 consecutive games. But I'll bet that nobody ever breaks Domingo's record of having sung, as of the latest count, 122 different leading roles throughout a career that began when he was sixteen. Now in his sixth decade, he's the Iron Man of opera and still going strong. He's probably the most admired opera singer of the past forty years, and though his ringing sound is unmistakable, you can't recognize *him* inside his roles. Domingo gets off a plane in Wichita and nobody turns a head. Pavarotti—undoubtedly the most beloved opera singer of the past forty years—gets off the plane, and everybody yells, "Luciano!"

Pavarotti and Domingo are both intensely proud. Neither man would stoop to put the other one down. As far as I've seen, they've always been on good personal terms—being so different helps. If there's any envy on Plácido's part over Luciano's greater popularity with the public, he's got too much Spanish reserve to show it. Someone once described Luciano as a "rock star for adults." That's one of the few things that Plácido has never aspired to.

Both men are real pros. Never, in my experience, has either one indulged in the sort of competitive, insecure behavior that has distinguished more than a few of their lesser colleagues in the tenor category. I'm thinking of Roberto Alagna, who arrived on the scene hyped as potentially the "next Pavarotti" or "next Domingo." Roberto—a very fine singer, especially in the French repertoire—once got so upset that Domingo was autographing recordings at the Met on a day when he, Roberto, was to perform in the evening, that he had to be talked out of canceling the performance. Of course, the two titans both love a standing ovation as much as the next singer, but if one of the ladies or even a baritone gets a bigger hand, they'll never say a word about it. (In this regard, my favorite story happened before my time during the 1944–1945 season after the mezzo-soprano Jenny Tourel's first performance as Adalgisa in *Norma*. The Met's leading dramatic soprano at the time, Zinka Milanov, was singing her sixteenth Norma, and at the end, Tourel got the bigger ovation. When Tourel walked past the star's dressing room, Madam Milanov stuck her head out and said in a voice that could have curdled milk, "*Happy?*")

Domingo and Pavarotti realize that a lot rides on their performances, and they've never failed to give everything they've got. Like every top opera star, they have an uncanny sense of the audience—in entirely different ways. When Plácido's not feeling his best, he won't hesitate to ask me to announce that he's suffering from a cold or whatever ailment but will go on nonetheless. Somehow the announcement relaxes him and makes him less concerned about making a mistake and surer that the audience will forgive him if he does.

Luciano, on the other hand, would have to be really sick to ask me to make such an announcement. He'd say, "I have a cold, but if you tell them that, they'll listen for the mistake." He knows that all he has to do is go out there with that million-dollar smile and the audience will be his—cold or no cold.

Both Pavarotti and Domingo have de facto veto power over the artists they sing with. (All the top singers at the Met have some say in casting decisions that affect them.) Luciano has generally preferred a relatively slim leading lady—Carol Vaness and Maria Guleghina are two of his favorites. He vetoed the casting of the Bulgarian soprano Ghena Dimitrova as Tosca, saying, "What's the point of having two elephants onstage?"

Offstage, Pavarotti behaves like a king; Domingo, like a prime minister. Luciano travels with an entourage of assistants. (One of them, Tino, is a wonderful cook.) He insists that he be picked up at the airport in a Mercedes, and he'll ride only in the front seat. He has to have the presidential suite, which he calls "my apartment." Except for his long-scarf fetish—the scarves come in more colors than Baskin-Robbins flavors—he's not vain about his appearance. Most of what's in his forty or fifty bags of Louis Vuitton luggage is food-related: pots, pans, pasta, prosciutto, and lots of parmigiano reggiano, which he thinks has the power to solve every human problem, including a bad complexion. In social gatherings, Luciano doesn't work the room: he shows up only because it's part of his job, and then he sits down—near the food. You go to him.

Plácido travels with his vigilant wife, Marta, a score in his lap, and a cell phone at his ear. At social functions, especially ones where there are important board members to be stroked, he strokes—with Spanish dignity. Offstage, Plácido is all business; onstage, he's all art. Uncomfortable in a concert setting (as far as I know, he has given only one New York recital in his entire career), he comes to life in costume and makeup. The stage is his world.

For Luciano, who's happiest just being himself singing Puccini arias and Tosti songs, and clutching his signature big white handkerchief, the world is his stage. He's Pavarotti all the time—performing, joking, testing, and seeing how much he can get away with.

As soon as rehearsals started for the new production of *I Lombardi* in November of 1993, I began hearing from Luciano's manager, Herbert Breslin, that his client didn't want to sing on December 21, as scheduled, because he wanted to fly home to Modena before Christ-

*Domingo as Cyrano, 2005*

mas. I repeatedly told Breslin that the request was out of the question. *I Lombardi* was opening on December 1 and was scheduled to be televised after the holidays. The final taping was scheduled for December 21.

In the middle of the run, I got a call from Luciano. "Joe," he said, "can you tell me why I have to be here on the twenty-first? Let's do the final taping on December seventeenth."

I said, "Where are you?"

He said, "In my apartment."

I said, "Don't move. I'm coming over, and I'm going to tell you why you're going to be here on the twenty-first."

A pause. Then: "I need ten more tickets for the next performance."

I said, "Tickets? Why are we talking about tickets? I thought we were talking about your going home."

He said, "Oh, that. Forget about it."

Luciano is street smart. You don't have to say no to Luciano.

Both Plácido and Luciano have always relied heavily on prompters. Luciano knows all the arias, but he tends to forget the words in between. Plácido, with his ever-expanding repertoire, has forgotten more roles than most singers have ever learned. Both men are so magnetic onstage that the average operagoer thinks that what they're hearing is effortless. Don't believe it: Pavarotti and Domingo are masters of illusion. A friend of mine once remarked that he'd never seen Domingo so riveting as he was during a performance of *Idomeneo* a few seasons back. After the performance, one of the other singers told him that Plácido was not riveting but rather *riveted*—on the Met prompter, Susan Webb, in the prompter's box. Only the greatest opera performers have the stage savvy to pull that off.

Both men are nervous before a performance; both like me to be there for them. I'll go backstage to wish them good luck, and they'll tell me exactly how they're feeling—that's what I'm there for. Then Plácido will adopt an air of fatalism: "God willing, everything will be all right," he'll mutter to himself. After the final curtain at the end of his last performance every season, he bends down and kisses the Met stage—his way of saying, "I'll be back."

Before a particularly difficult evening (such as *The Daughter of the Regiment*), Luciano will put on his tragic clown's expression and say, "I go to die. . . . In two hours I may not be alive." Then he'll pull out one of the licorice pills he always has on hand, wet it, and stick it on his costume in case his throat goes dry. If he passes a good-looking dancer on his way to the stage, he'll murmur, "Pretty flower."

Domingo, the consummate man of the theater, is always in perfect order before a performance—with makeup, wig, and costume exactly as they should be. Pavarotti, on the other hand, is a wild card. He likes to do his own makeup, and he can come out looking pretty weird. Before a telecast of *L'Elisir d'Amore* he emerged with the right eyebrow higher than the left one. The director complained to me (you don't complain to Pavarotti). "This will look terrible on television," he said. "Please tell him to make the eyebrows the same level." I knew it was hopeless, but I went up to Luciano and said, "The director doesn't like the way you do your eyebrows."

"What?" he said.

"Make them the same height," I said.

"Okay," he said and went back to his dressing room. When he came out, he'd reversed them: now the left eyebrow was higher. I looked at the director and shrugged.

After a performance, Luciano would rarely comment on how things had gone. He would become Pavarotti, king of the opera world, collect his entourage, and head out to greet the hundreds of fans waiting for his autograph. Often, he'd be wearing the costume of the character he'd just sung. (A wardrobe man would be sent to his apartment the next morning to pick up the costume.)

Plácido, on the other hand, never unwinds. He replays every moment of the evening, thinking about how to adjust a phrase or a tempo, an inflection or a color, so that the next time, his performance will be not only richer but also more comfortable. When he took on the title role of Verdi's seldom-sung *Stiffelio*, in the 1993–1994 season, I was amazed at how during the run he was able to find so many little things to deepen the characterization. Pavarotti gives audiences the sense that, vocally, he's pushing the limits of rational human control. Domingo thrills listeners with the sense that he is in superhuman control.

Both men are supportive of their colleagues. Every soprano who has ever sung opposite Domingo will tell you how secure his presence makes her feel, how his alertness to everything that's happening onstage brings out the best in her. Pavarotti is extraordinarily sensitive to his costars. After Aprile Millo missed a high note in the second act of *I Lombardi*, she said that she was going home. Luciano, who was standing nearby, said, "Go home now? You'll never come back into the theater if you do. Come into my dressing room." Aprile followed him in, and for the rest of the intermission, he went through every note of her part in Act 3 until she felt confident about finishing the opera.

Over the years, I've had a more personal relationship with Luciano, partly because we're both Italian and partly because we got to know each other back when he was new at the Met and I was master carpenter. In those days, he was slimmer (though hardly svelte). Even so, he was always concerned about the amount of traveling he'd have to do onstage. He wanted to see the plans of a new production before it got built, not only because he regards himself as an expert on everything, including architecture, but also because he wanted the set tailored to his special capacities. Most of what he wanted involved reducing the number of steps that he might have to climb. He liked staying on one level—the closer to the audience, the better.

Luciano is always thinking about food and weight, two subjects on which he's also the world's expert. During the second act of *L'Elisir* in the spring of 1998, he suddenly looked as though he were going to pass out onstage. His diction got slurry, and he leaned on the proscenium arch. He made it through the act, and I raced backstage. "Water, water," he was gasping. "Bring water." He downed a couple of glasses and staggered into his dressing room. Everyone followed. He slumped into a chair and waved the others out.

"What happened?" I said.

He said, "I thought I could lose some weight if I tried some new diuretics. Then I drank some salt water."

"For God's sake," I said to the great medical expert. "No wonder you got so dizzy. You were completely dehydrated."

Luciano is an expert not only on how to lose his own weight but also everyone else's weight, particularly mine. At the beginning of every season, he'd look at me and say, "You're in bad shape, Joe. I'd say ten kilos have to go." The next season, he'd say, "Twenty kilos." Then, "Thirty kilos." He may have been right.

Every fall I would go over to Luciano's apartment on Central Park South to discuss his rehearsal and performance schedule. One year he came into the living room swathed in towels and bigger than ever. We were going through the schedule when the doorbell rang. In came a fellow whom Luciano introduced as "my yoga teacher"—an apparently very famous one, who catered to the stars. Everything that Luciano does, you have to do, too. "Pay attention, Joe," he said as the yoga teacher began with some breathing exercises. "Bend your knees." I made a stab at joining in. Luciano's knees were bent, but they weren't supporting him. He was perched comfortably on the edge of his desk, which was covered with the usual pharmacy of throat medicines and pills. Making sure that I was keeping up with him, Luciano inhaled, exhaled, inhaled, exhaled. I couldn't see his chest move, but he wanted to make sure mine was moving. "Deeper, Joe," he said. "That's right."

We never got to the lotus position. After ten minutes of "in, out, in, out," Luciano said, "Okay. That's enough yoga." He waved the famous yoga teacher away.

Then he said, "Fox [one of his nicknames for me], I hope you're not hungry. We're having a no-pasta lunch so you can lose some of those kilos."

Tino arrived with fruit salad in a big bowl. Luciano piled up my plate with strawberries, pineapple, melon, and grapes. "You have to eat all of it or you don't get the next course," he said. What I ate would have satisfied me for the rest of the day, but Tino returned with a platter of roasted chicken, string beans, and mashed potatoes. "See," Luciano said, "no pasta!" We finished off the platter. Then came an enormous green salad. "The lettuce is good for the digestion," Luciano said. "The vinegar is *balsamico*, from Modena—good for the arteries." We finished off the salad. Then came dessert: four scoops of ice cream in Luciano's bowl, four in mine. That, too, was topped with *balsamico*—a Pavarotti sundae.

"The key to losing weight," Luciano said, "is not to eat all the ice cream. Always leave some of it in the bowl." He dispatched three of the four scoops. "See, Giuseppe Volpe [as he sometimes calls me], you follow this diet, you'll lose those kilos."

With Luciano, the world runs according to Luciano. Once, when Jean and I were visiting him in Modena, he invited us to lunch at a racetrack in which he had a financial interest. We got there first and were sitting on the terrace, sipping wine, when he arrived in his red BMW. He roared up the driveway, knocked over a bush, and proceeded around to the back of the building so he could park as close as possible to the kitchen. After lunch, he offered to drive us to our "apartment."

"You mean our hotel," I said.

He said, "I'll drive you to your apartment."

"No, you won't," I said. "Not after I saw what you did to that bush."

"I always hit that bush," he said.

I didn't realize the depth of our relationship until Luciano found himself going through a bitter divorce with Adua, his wife of forty-one years. During a rehearsal of *L'Elisir* in 1998, he called me into his dressing room and shut the door. "Are you busy?" he said.

"What do you mean 'are you busy'? I'm here," I said.

"I have twenty minutes before I have to go back onstage," he said. "You know, Joe, this divorce is very difficult."

"I know," I said. "I've been through a couple of them."

"I have another problem," he said. "I have no man friends to talk to about it."

I listened as Luciano told me about how bad he felt about the divorce—especially because of the hostility his daughters now had toward him. I told him that he could count on my support. After he made his way to the stage, I thought, "Here's a guy who's loved by more people than anyone but the pope, and he's all alone." I felt honored that he'd turned to me.

In the mid-nineties Pavarotti's performances began to drop off. During the 1996–1997 season, he canceled his appearance in a new production of Verdi's *La Forza del Destino* because he hadn't been able to learn the part of Don Alvaro. He lost twenty-four kilos, then gained them back. In 1997–1998, he did six *Turandots*. His voice was in good shape, but he could hardly move. The following two seasons he did eight *Toscas*. In 2001, he sang five *Aidas*. The part of Radames, which is one of the most punishing tenor roles in the Verdi canon, taxed him beyond anything he'd done before. He all but crooned "Celeste Aida," but it still brought down the house. In the meantime, he paid $12 million in back taxes to the Italian government; went through operations for bad knees and a bum hip; survived his divorce from Adua, who asked for a settlement of $112 million (she didn't get it); and became romantically involved with his former personal assistant, Nicoletta Mantovani, who was thirty-five years younger than he. They are now married and have a toddler named Alice.

I knew that Pavarotti probably had only one or two seasons left in him when we agreed on his last contract with the Met—two *Toscas* in the spring of 2002, in his signature role of the painter Mario Cavaradossi. The second *Tosca* would be performed as a closing-night gala, a fund-raiser whose top ticket price ($1,875) would include dinner. The appearances would mark the conclusion of Pavarotti's thirty-fourth season with the Met. He was turning sixty-seven, but no one officially described them as his "farewell performances"—that would have wounded his pride. Nonetheless, by the time of the first *Tosca*, on Wednesday, May 8, all the major newspapers were asking, Was this Luciano Pavarotti's *arrivederci* to the opera stage?

As things turned out, it wasn't. On Wednesday morning, I called Luciano at his apartment to see how he was doing—a call I'd made on the day of every performance of his for years. Luciano said, "I just got up—it's too early to tell, Siré [another nickname]."

At noon, I called back: "Luciano, how are you feeling?"

"It's too early to tell," he said. "I just got up. But maybe I got a little cold coming back."

"Okay. I'll call you later."

At three, I called again.

Luciano said, "I still don't know how I feel."

"Well," I said, "see how you do with Gildo."

Gildo DiNunzio, a vocal coach at the Met, had been helping Pavarotti warm up since his Met debut in 1968. He was on his way over.

At five thirty, I got a call from Herbert Breslin: Luciano wasn't feeling well—I'd better alert his cover, the Dominican tenor Francisco Casanova.

I called Luciano.

"I can't do it, Joe," he said. "Better I take this performance off and I'll be ready for Saturday night."

Luciano was not capricious about canceling, especially at a time like this. "Okay," I said. "Are you seeing a doctor?"

It was a ridiculous question. Of course Luciano was seeing a doctor. A throat specialist whom he often consulted had already been there. So, I'm sure, had his internist. Luciano liked to have at least two doctors in attendance while he called his doctor in Italy. Regardless of what any of them said, he would then decide on the medication for his condition and reach for the pharmacy on his desk.

"They've given me a cortisone shot and sinus pills," he said. "Give me a half hour to see if they save my voice."

I called Casanova.

I had never heard such booing when I stepped out in front of the curtain a few minutes after eight and announced to four thousand opera lovers that their idol was suffering from a cold and would be unable to sing. I put a hand up and continued: "Mr. Pavarotti asked me to say to you how so, so sorry he is and to apologize. He knew you would be understanding."

The booing got worse.

I went on: "I know you're disappointed. You can boo some more if it makes you feel better." The booing turned to laughter, and the show went on.

Perhaps it was a slow news season. In any event, Pavarotti's "no-show" became an international story. The *New York Post* ran a front-page picture of him in a Borsalino and a ten-foot-long scarf. The headline read "Fat Man Won't Sing." A headline in the *Daily News* read "The Plot Sickens at the Met."

Francisco Casanova had done a more than respectable job filling in, but I knew I had to come up with someone special if Pavarotti canceled again. I recalled a videotape I'd seen of a performance of *Il Trovatore* at La Scala. It featured a promising young tenor named Salvatore Licitra. He was thirty-three, the age at which Pavarotti had made his Met debut, and he was creating a stir in Luciano's repertoire in the Italian opera houses. As far as I could tell from the tape, Licitra had a gorgeous young voice and a convincing stage presence. The Met had signed him for nine *Toscas* during the 2004–2005 season. I asked Jonathan Friend to find out if Licitra was free on Saturday night.

Jimmy Levine, who was conducting the performances, was

*Pavarotti's replacement,*
*Salvatore Licitra*

opposed to the idea of our using Licitra. "Casanova's a known quantity," he said. "Why take a chance?"

"I want the excitement of flying a kid over from Italy to replace Pavarotti," I said. "This is a gala. We have to give them something special."

On Friday morning, Licitra, who in the previous twelve hours had flown from Milan to London and then to New York on the Concorde, arrived in my office with his New York agent, Jack Mastroianni. He hadn't had time to obtain a proper work visa, so I'd told Jack to tell him to tell the people at passport control, "I'm visiting Mr. Volpe at the Metropolitan Opera."

Licitra was a stocky, sweet-faced young man with curly black hair. He didn't look the least bit terrified. He said, "Mr. Volpe, this is a great opportunity. But if Luciano can sing, then I will sit with you in the box and watch the performance. If he can't, then I'll sing."

I liked him at once.

"Thank you for coming," I said. "Now it's time for you to get measured in the costume shop."

The Met keeps half a dozen costumes in different sizes for every major character in the company's inventory of productions. I went down to the costume shop with Licitra, and we found a Cavaradossi outfit that, with a few adjustments, would fit him perfectly. "Now, go home and rest," I said.

"Rest?" he said. "I'm fine."

In the afternoon, I called Luciano. "How are you feeling?" I said.

"Not so good," he said. "I have a lot of . . . what is the English? . . . catarrh."

I listened as he spelled out the symptoms of catarrh in detail. "Well, take care of yourself," I said. "I'll talk to you tomorrow." I didn't mention Licitra.

On Saturday, I didn't call Luciano until three in the afternoon.

"I'm doing a little better," he said. "I'm going to warm up."

At four thirty, I called back. "How are you feeling?"

"A little better," he said. "Not great, but I think I'll be okay."

At five thirty, he said the same thing. I called Jack Mastroianni and told him I wanted Licitra in the house.

At 6:15, I went over to the Met. Hundreds of people had already taken up a position in the plaza. The demand for tickets was so great that we'd set up an outdoor screen to show the performance free of charge to Pavarotti fans in the plaza. I called Luciano. "When are you coming over?" I said.

"I don't know, Joe," he said. "Gildo's here. You better talk to him."

Gildo, whose judgment is unimpeachable, said that Luciano wasn't up to it. "Too much phlegm, Joe," he said. "He can't do it."

"Put Luciano on the phone," I said.

"If you're not going to sing, Luciano," I said, "you must at least come to the house, stand in front of the curtain, and apologize for canceling the performance. These people have paid a lot of money just to hear you."

A long pause, then: "I can't do it, Joe. I'm too sick."

I knew him too well to argue. For Luciano, the love he got from his fans was better than oxygen. To have stood there and felt their disappointment would have been more than he could bear.

When I arrived at the Met, Breslin was outside Luciano's dressing room. "Herbert, he's not singing," I said. "Salvatore Licitra will be Cavaradossi."

Breslin looked as though I'd driven a stake through his heart. "Joe," he said, "can we have a drink in your office?"

When I handed him a drink, he called Luciano and begged him to come to the house and face the audience. Again Luciano refused: he was too sick.

I went backstage to see Licitra, who was vocalizing in a dressing room. "Okay," he said. "I'm here. Don't worry."

Well before the curtain time of eight, the Met's auditorium was filled to capacity with people in evening dress. The TV cameras were in place for the simulcast. At last count, the crowd out on the plaza numbered more than three thousand.

I was thinking about how I was going to tell everybody the bad news when Paul Plishka, who was singing the Sacristan in Act 1, came over. "I sure wouldn't want to be in your shoes," he said. "This reminds me of the time I was doing *Anna Bolena* at La Scala. When Caballé canceled, they went berserk."

"Tell me about it," I said.

Paul told me the story—and gave me my speech. Out I went.

Thank God for friends. When the black-tie crowd saw my unhappy face, one of the Met's diehard patrons, Kit Gill, started clapping. No one claps louder than Kit, and soon the whole place started clapping—even Rudy Giuliani, who had a front seat in my box. I managed a smile and took a deep breath. Luciano's yoga teacher would have been proud.

"Thank you and welcome to The Metropolitan Opera," I said. "No doubt many of you are very knowledgeable operagoers, and you'll remember that February fourteenth at La Scala in 1992 was known as the St. Valentine's Day Massacre."

The clapping stopped. I continued: "It seems that for a performance of *Anna Bolena*, Montserrat Caballé was supposed to sing when an announcement came out over the audio system saying that she had canceled. The audience went crazy and began shouting for the intendant to come out. 'Badini! Badini!' They shouted for forty-five minutes, but Mr. Carlo Badini, the head of La Scala, wouldn't come out. Giulietta Simionato [the celebrated mezzo-soprano] went out—she had no success. Renata Tebaldi went out—she had no success. Well, everybody got sent home. And of course that was a terrible thing for an opera audience."

I paused, then I said, "Tonight I'm afraid I have some bad news for you. And I'm happy to say that I have some good news for you. At five fifteen, when I called Maestro Pavarotti to see if he was going to sing, he said he was. He called me at ten after seven and said, 'My dear friend, I'm sorry, I cannot sing.' I said, 'Luciano, come to the theater and make your apologies. This is a hell of a way to end this beautiful career of yours. At least come.' He said, 'I cannot do that.'"

Pause. Then: "Fortunately, we have a replacement for Luciano. We called him in Milan. He took a Concorde to London, arrived at nine thirty at Kennedy, was here at eleven forty-five in my office. Rehearsed for an hour or so. Had a costume fitting. He said, 'Mr. Volpe, I knew I was going to make my Met debut in this role in the 2004–2005 season, but if Luciano Pavarotti can sing, I will sit with you in your box and enjoy the performance. And if he cannot sing, I will be there for you and the Metropolitan Opera and Maestro Levine.' Salvatore, I think you'll find, is a lovely, wonderful young tenor, and I'm very thankful that he will sing for you. Thank you very much for your understanding."

When I got to my box, Rudy whispered, "Good job, Joe. Well, I told you how to handle it: 'Tell 'em, 'If you don't behave, you won't get a performance.'"

They behaved.

*Pavarotti as the painter Cavaradossi in* Tosca

The press notices were glowing about Licitra and scathing about Pavarotti, even after Breslin released a statement in which Luciano tried to explain his reasons for canceling: "A proper vocal condition is the basic rule for any singing performance. Without it, no matter how much willingness, talent, discipline or passion there is, it is simply impossible to offer the public the performance for which they have paid."

True enough. Still, the press wasn't having any of it. I'd never seen an editorial in *The New York Times* about a tenor's cancellation before, but now the Gray Lady got up on her high horse and treated this one almost as a breach of national security: "The vast majority of that audience at the Met on Saturday night would have been grateful merely for the concession of an appearance, a gesture of acknowledgment and respect. A few words, a few bows, a recognition of the extraordinary role the Met and its audiences have played in his career—that would have been more than generous and more than enough."

I'll say this about the opera press: they love rubbing salt in wounds.

I also felt bad that, in my nervousness, I'd announced that the incident would seal Pavarotti's career. Luciano called and said, "Joe, this isn't the end. You have to let the public know—particularly the European press. I've got lots of engagements over there. I'm going to come back to the Met. We'll do *Tosca* next year."

"Luciano," I said, "you're right. I said that under pressure, and I apologize. I'll write a public letter to the European press and tell them that the Met still wants you."

I sent the letter. This was no way for a king to go out. If Pavarotti wanted to sing *Tosca* as his farewell to the Met, then the Met owed him that.

Since no *Toscas* were scheduled during the following season, Pavarotti eventually said farewell to the Met with three *Toscas* in the spring of 2004. For the most part, he sounded like a ghost of himself. But in Cavaradossi's two great arias, "Recondita armonia" and "E lucevan le stelle," there were goose-bump moments when everybody knew they were listening to the most haunting voice of our time.

# 16

## THE TRAPEZE ARTISTS

In June of 2004, Jonathan Friend got a call from an agent in Stockholm about an unknown Swedish dramatic soprano named Erika Sunnegårdh. The fact that Jonathan hadn't heard of her was unusual. Jonathan's mind (and computer) is a storage bin for most of the information the Met uses when it casts singers for each season. Agents are constantly badgering him and Sarah Billinghurst to check out the golden throats of budding Domingos and Flemings. Even more unusual was the Stockholm agent's answer to Jonathan's first question: "Where has she sung?"

"Nowhere," the agent replied.

"Nowhere?" Jonathan said, wondering why he'd answered this call in the first place. "Are you suggesting that we audition a singer who's never been on a professional stage anywhere? The Met is generally interested only in singers who have sung *everywhere*. How old is Erika Sunnegårdh?"

"Thirty-seven," the agent said.

Hmmm, Jonathan thought: thirty-seven and she's never been on an opera stage. She must weigh three hundred pounds. "Where does she live?" he asked.

"New York," the agent said.

This was getting stranger. Aspiring opera singers in New York live in a hothouse. Among the tight little network of voice teachers and their students, agents and presenters, anyone with serious potential gets talked about. Sooner or later, the talk reaches the Met.

"What has she been doing for a living?" Jonathan asked.

"Making sandwiches," the agent said. "She works for a caterer."

Four hundred pounds, Jonathan thought.

"I've just heard a tape of her," the agent said. "Trust me."

Skeptically, Jonathan agreed to arrange an audition in the Met's auditorium. "Two arias," he told the agent. "Ten minutes."

Jonathan later reported to me about Erika Sunnegårdh's audition. "In the first place," he said, "she's *very* attractive. And she wasn't the least bit nervous—this is a woman with her feet on the ground. She sang 'In questa reggia' [from *Turandot*] and 'Anch'io dischiuso un giorno,'

*Rosa Ponselle in* Forza del Destino

[the Babylonian slave Abigail's killer aria from *Nabucco*]. Both were exceptional. The voice is a little light in the middle and lower registers, but she's got a huge top. For Verdi and Puccini, she has what it takes. She came back to sing for Jimmy, and he flipped."

"Why are we only hearing about her now?" I asked.

"She left Sweden when she was nineteen—family problems," Jonathan said. "She told me that it took her fifteen years to sort out her life. She's been taking voice lessons. Until now, she said, she hasn't felt ready for a career."

"I wish more of them were that smart," I said.

A few months later, Jonathan flew to Sweden, where he heard Erika Sunnegårdh make her professional debut in the title role of *Turandot* at a provincial opera house. Jonathan later reported, "She was everything I hoped she'd be." The Met immediately engaged her to cover Karita Mattila in six performances of *Fidelio,* in the spring of 2006. As of this writing, she's scheduled to make her Met debut as Leonore on April 13, unless she has to step in for Mattila before then. Not since Rosa Ponselle's debut in 1918, opposite Caruso in *La Forza del Destino,* has the Met given an unknown singer such an opportunity. If Erika Sunnegårdh makes anything like the splash Ponselle did, it will be front-page news.

Until Ponselle came to the Met to tackle one of Verdi's most challenging heroines, the only professional singing she'd done was in movie houses and cafés around New Haven and in a vaudeville act with her sister, Carmela. (They were known as the Ponzillo Sisters.) At twenty-one, she was one of the youngest singers ever to make her Met debut in a leading role, just as in 1950 a twenty-year-old named Roberta Peters, who had also never been on an opera stage before, sang Zerlina in *Don Giovanni.*

Ponselle became one of the legendary divas of the last century. Peters became the Met's "sweetheart soprano" for thirty-four seasons and appeared sixty-five times on *The Ed Sullivan Show*—more than any other performer, classical or popular. Today, it's almost inconceivable that a singer would be granted a major Met debut at such a young age. The idea that Hollywood or network television would also give that kind of prominence to a classical singer is also unthinkable. Maybe Erika Sunnegårdh will be the next

*Roberta Peters, a star at twenty*

Jenny Lind, the Swedish Nightingale, who conquered America in the nineteenth century. But I wouldn't bet on it. Let's face it: opera stars don't enjoy the popular esteem they used to. For the Met, which has been a house of stars from the beginning, the decline of opera celebrity has presented a real challenge.

The media have not helped. For some years now, the national news outlets, even *The New York Times*, have made it a practice to follow culture, not lead it. This means that the entertainment monoliths, which churn out mainly kiddie litter, dictate where the media direct most of their attention. Can you imagine one of the news magazines, which have all but abandoned regular serious coverage of the arts, putting Maria Callas on the cover with the understated billing "Callas, Opera Singer"—as *Time* magazine did in 1958? Come to think of it, when was the last time you saw an opera star on the cover of any mass-circulation magazine?

The shrinking of the classical recording business has also played a part. Caruso, John McCormack, Lawrence Tibbett, Lily Pons, Elisabeth Schwarzkopf, Callas, Tebaldi, Sutherland, Price, Horne, von Stade, Battle, Pavarotti, Domingo—these and countless other singers saw their careers propelled by the steady release of new recordings that reached millions of people. Today, only a handful of the very top singers have long-term recording contracts, and few of their new releases are promoted beyond the narrow niche of classical music listeners. Who was the Harvard Business School graduate who decided that all Americans were created demographically?

Then there's the jet plane. Before jet travel made it possible for singers to appear in twenty different opera houses in any given season, the stars came to the Met and stayed around for months. Unlike today's stars, the old ones didn't come for only one or two roles in a season; they sang a variety of roles. In the 1953–1954 season, Zinka Milanov appeared thirty-one times in five different operas. In the 1955–1956 season, Richard Tucker made thirty-three appearances in eight different operas. In 1971–1972, Franco Corelli performed thirty times in seven different operas, nine of them on tour.

Of course, being an opera singer wasn't quite the same thing in those days. It was easier to take on multiple roles in a season because no one expected singers such as Milanov or Tucker to do much more than stand up and sing. Before the Bing regime, some leading Met artists, such as Lauritz Melchior and Jussi Bjoerling, rehearsed only when they felt like it. (Bing publicly castigated Bjoerling as a singer in decline after replacing him with a young tenor for a Met broadcast.) At today's Met, everybody from the prima donna to the spear-carrier comes to rehearsals. And the rehearsals are more demanding than ever. Productions are increasingly elaborate, and there's a much greater effort to integrate the singers into the staging. Even the biggest stars have to work hard to satisfy the vision of the new prima donna directors.

In the pre-jet days, the stars may not have been as physically—or as emotionally—active onstage, but opera lovers were able to get to know them. The top singers—Tebaldi, Tucker, Price, Corelli, Rysanek, Sutherland, Nilsson—regarded the Met as home. The Met audiences regarded the singers as family. The great singers were beloved figures. Of course, claques grew up around them. I remember a *Bohème* in which Tebaldi stood on one side of the stage and sang to her claque, while Corelli stood on the other side and sang to his claque. Neither of them bothered to look for Mimi's lost house key, and nobody wanted them to.

Today the stars drop in for one role, sing it a few times, and then dash to the next gig a thousand miles away. Even Renée Fleming, the Met's most popular prima donna, who lives just a few blocks from Lincoln Center, generally appears for only one or two operas a season, sells out the house, and then splits for parts unknown.

More than most corporations, the Met is vulnerable to fluctuations in the economy. The recent drop in the value of the dollar against foreign currencies has made the stars more reluctant than ever to commit themselves to the Met for extended periods. During the last five years, the dollar has lost 25 to 30 percent of its value against the euro, the British pound, and the Swiss franc. The top fee for a performance at the better European houses averages eighteen thousand euros—or, as of this writing, twenty-five thousand dollars. The Met's highest fee for singers has just gone up to sixteen thousand dollars. (Leading conductors receive the same.)

The cutback in classical CDs has also diminished the Met's clout with leading singers. During the 1990s, artists knew that singing at the Met, which has the world's largest opera audience, was a sure way to boost sales of their recordings. Today, only a few top artists have enough new solo recordings to worry about.

Still, the Met remains a house where singers love to sing. Artists used to smaller halls in Europe are sometimes intimidated by the size of the Met's auditorium, but I've never heard anyone complain about the excellence of the acoustics. And everybody agrees that the Met's musical staff is the best in the world.

Jimmy Levine, of course, is a tremendous asset. He can "read" voices better than anyone, and he has an uncanny knack of coaxing singers to a higher vocal level without making them feel pushed. With artists who are doing a role for the first time, Jimmy spends hours coaching them on when to sing softly and when to sing loudly; on tempos; on phrasing and the places to breathe. By the time they begin rehearsing with the orchestra, they're as comfortable as they can be. Jimmy even does the same for singers in operas he's not conducting.

No other opera house has so many musical coaches, or "assistant conductors," as they are called. Each of them is an expert in one or more vocal styles, from Italian to German, French, Russian, and Czech. Karita Mattila told *Opera* magazine a few years ago, "[the Met] is a fantastic place for singers—I love working there. The music staff is one you can't compare with any other opera house. Even in good houses like Covent Garden you can feel that they are trying to save money, and these cuts are very sad because they *do* affect the musical results. But at the Met it is all very safe. Everyone on the music staff can conduct. Everyone can prompt—it's a wonderful help that makes a big difference and the Met is a very secure place."

In his memoir, Gatti-Casazza was shrewd about the lifeblood of every opera house—the human voice: "The voice is a distinctly personal thing," he observed.

> There are some people who sing for the very reasons that others do not. Some singers have faults that, for others, constitute good qualities, and vice versa. There are some who cannot sing at all if they do not sing through the nose. Take Tamagno, for example. [The outstanding nineteenth-century Italian tenor Francesco Tamagno was the original Moor of Venice in Verdi's *Otello.*] He had a truly remarkable and powerful voice. But if anyone else tried to sing the way he did, he would lose his voice in fifteen days.
>
> The voice in its meritorious qualities, also, is a very special

thing, each one having its own peculiar characteristics. It is, of course, entirely unpredictable. By examining the throat one cannot say that here is a person who can sing or not. I have seen throats that were frightfully formed, having enormous tonsils, yet their owners could sing. I have seen singers who became thoroughly pink and even rose-colored in the face and the throat while singing and they could continue to sing, nevertheless, for many years without doing any harm to themselves.

What Gatti was saying is something that I've had to remind myself of every day: there are as many different kinds of opera singers as there are people.

The Met's roster of singers for the 2005–2006 season lists 81 sopranos, 47 mezzo-sopranos, 4 countertenors, 76 tenors, 54 baritones, 17 bass-baritones, and 34 basses. The total number—313—is roughly the same as it was when I became general director in 1990.

Within each vocal category is a handful of top singers around whose availability the Met builds the premieres of new productions and the revivals for each season. At the moment, they include, among the sopranos, Natalie Dessay, Renée Fleming, Barbara Frittoli, Angela Gheorghiu, Hei-Kyung Hong, Soile Isokoski, Karita Mattila, Waltraud Meier, Anna Netrebko, Deborah Polaski, Sondra Radvanovsky, Ruth Ann Swenson, Violeta Urmana, and Deborah Voigt; among the mezzo-sopranos, Stephanie Blythe, Olga Borodina, Susan Graham, Denyce Graves, Magdalena Kožená, Jennifer Larmore, and Dolora Zajick; among the countertenors, Bejun Mehta and Andreas Scholl; among the tenors, Marcelo Álvarez, Johan Botha, Plácido Domingo, Juan Diego Flórez, Marcello Giordani, Ben Heppner, Salvatore Licitra, Neil Shicoff, Ramón Vargas, and Rolando Villazón; among the baritones, Thomas Allen, Carlos Alvarez, Vladimir Chernov, Dwayne Croft, Thomas Hampson, Dmitri Hvorostovsky, Juan Pons, and Bo Skovhus; among the bass-baritones, John Relyea and Bryn Terfel; among the basses, James Morris, René Pape, and Samuel Ramey.

I'm often asked why the Met can't "get" a particular notable singer or why we're "the last ones" to hire someone who's made a big splash elsewhere. The truth is, there are as many answers to these questions as there are singers. For one thing, the Met isn't a house for everyone: there are a number of topflight singers whose voices and personalities

*Bryn Terfel as Falstaff,* 2002

just don't project as vividly in an auditorium with 3,800 seats as they do in smaller halls, particularly ones in Europe. (Projection isn't a matter of vocal heft; it comes from the carrying quality of the voice and the intensity behind it—witness two singers with "small" voices and incredible projection: Kathleen Battle in her prime and Cecilia Bartoli.) In general, there are two types of singers: those who sing with what might be called a broad brush, and those who sing with a fine brush. The Met tends to favor the former type—singers such as Karita Mattila, Plácido Domingo, and James Morris, who can really get it out there. Two superb fine-brush singers who have sung only a few times at the Met—and perhaps not been heard to their best advantage—are the British soprano Felicity Lott and the Swedish mezzo Anne Sophie von Otter.

Then there's the matter of house chemistry. Certain top singers are just more comfortable in other halls than they are at the Met. I sometimes think that Roberto Alagna, a huge favorite at Covent Garden and other European houses, has never quite gotten over his much-hyped 1996 Met debut in *La Bohème,* during which he cracked in the first-act duet and had trouble finishing the performance. It's always been a mystery to me why another leading international tenor, José Carreras, whose New York career began at City Opera and who became beloved in London and Vienna, never became a big draw at the Met. It will be interesting to see if the wonderful Lithuanian dramatic soprano Violeta Urmana becomes a star of the first magnitude. Since she moved up from mezzo roles a few years ago, she's been touted by critics as "the real thing" and "a throwback to the Golden Age." She had the guts to sing her very first Ariadne in *Ariadne auf Naxos* at the Met in the fall of 2005, which is a role most sopranos wouldn't dream of doing in New York without trying it out somewhere else beforehand. All the critics loved her, and so did I. But her singing is a rare combination of broad brush and fine brush—the best combination—

and you have to have been around the opera world awhile to realize just how good she is.

Certain singers who are naturals for the Met choose, for personal reasons, to become only occasional visitors. As a result, they fail to build a real New York following. In both voice and personality, the phenomenal bass-baritone Bryn Terfel was born to burn up the Met. Nobody has ever gotten a better lift-off than he did when his debut as Figaro in 1994 made front-page news in the *Times*. But Bryn is super-selective about what roles he will sing, and he seems increasingly reluctant to spend significant time away from his wife and kids in North Wales.

Dmitri Hvorostovsky, Bryn's only rival for star power among baritones of their generation, has followed the opposite course. At first, the Met audience was cool to him, perhaps because he seemed cool— a bit arrogant—toward them. Since then, in such roles as Prince Yeletsky in *The Queen of Spades*, Prince Andrei in *War and Peace*, Posa in *Don Carlo*, and Valentin in *Faust*, he has really enjoyed himself, matching the natural beauty of his voice with natural charm. Now the Met audience can't get enough of him.

For singers, the Met is the ultimate test—the house that gets the most international press coverage and the most attention from the world's opera fans and connoisseurs. Many young singers with rising reputations prefer to put off coming to the Met for their debut or a new role until they feel entirely secure. As of this writing, the dazzling Russian soprano Anna Netrebko still won't say yes to the Met's offer of Violetta in *La Traviata*. She sensibly feels that she first has to get quite a few Violettas under her belt elsewhere.

Dmitri Hvorostovsky,
*natural charm*

S ingers come to the Met in many ways—not all of them via a call from Sweden. The Met employs a full-time scout, Eva Wagner-Pasquier, who constantly scours the opera houses of Europe for promising new talent. (Eva happens to be a great-granddaughter of Richard Wagner.) Everyone on the artistic staff—led by Jimmy Levine and his deputies, Sarah Billinghurst and Jonathan Friend—is constantly on the lookout for young singers who just might make it.

Visiting conductors and stage directors also contribute suggestions, and so do the top singers themselves. Both Pavarotti and Domingo seem to have an endless supply of "protégés." Some are winners of the two tenors' own singing competitions. Most are female and, at least in appearance, fetching. Both Ponselle and Peters were "discovered" by renowned tenors: Ponselle by Caruso, Peters by Jan Peerce.

In 1980, Jimmy Levine realized that the company had to begin growing its own vocal talent. That year, the Met launched the Young Artist Development Program. The program has been financially sustained by George and Frayda Lindemann. They are an unusual couple: he's run businesses whose products range from contact lenses to natural gas pipelines; she's a managing director of the Met, a musicologist specializing in the French Baroque period.

The program, which has been supervised musically by Jimmy's assistant, John Fisher, is fertile breeding ground. Each season, about a dozen singers from around the world win auditions for intensive training by the Met's musical staff. Graduates who have gone on to stellar careers at the Met and other companies include Stephanie Blythe, Dwayne Croft, Alexandra Deshorties, Michelle De-Young, Christine Goerke, Anthony Dean Griffey, Paul Groves, Nathan Gunn, Aprile Millo, Heidi Grant Murphy, Stanford Olsen, Sondra Radvanovsky, Christopher Schaldenbrand, Tony Stevenson, Gregory Turay, Dawn Upshaw, and Jennifer Welch-Babidge.

Opera training, it turns out, can be more effective than rehab at Hazelden. Two alumni of the Lindemann program—the dramatic soprano Andrea Gruber and the baritone

*Charles Taylor in* Lucia

Charles Taylor—are recovered drug addicts. Most of the trainees have had a conservatory education, but not Taylor, who is now thirty-seven and singing major roles. Charles is from cowboy stock in Arizona, and he was a methamphetamine addict, a Grateful Deadhead (he's got the skull-and-roses tattoo), and a farmhand before he took singing seriously and changed his life. I like what he once said about his acceptance into the Young Artists Program: "I felt like a fraud. I never finished college. I can hardly read music and I have to learn everything by rote. Fortunately, I'm a good parrot. Opera's got heavy metal in it—there are riffs in Wagner, Verdi, and Puccini where I'll just get the horns up in rehearsal and start head-banging!"

Each singer at the Met may be unlike any other singer, but here's a safe generalization: the higher the voice, the more temperamental the person. In other words, when trouble comes it's likely to come from a soprano or a tenor, not from a mezzo, a baritone, or a bass. In the world of opera, life often imitates art. Operatic excitement feeds on anguish, and most anguished people are generally the hero or the heroine—the tenor or the soprano—who have a passion for each other that somebody is trying to thwart. It's not unusual for sopranos and tenors to be nervous wrecks offstage as much as on.

Vocally, sopranos and tenors are more fragile than mezzos, baritones, or basses. They're the high-wire act. When they push their voices to the upper limit, they're doing something the rest of us can't imagine doing. They're trapeze artists, alone up there on the thin wire of a vocal cord without a safety net. When a soprano or a tenor cracks, the audience feels as though it has witnessed a little death. Rudolf Bing once offered another explanation for the volatile temperaments of sopranos and tenors: "When God made high voices," he said, "he also made smaller brains." He was only half-joking.

Most emotional outbursts by singers are solo performances that are over quickly. But when they come in the form of a duet, they can reach gale force. In 1998, the French Italian tenor Roberto Alagna and his wife, the Romanian soprano Angela Gheorghiu, arrived in my office to discuss a new production of *La Traviata*, staged by Franco Zeffirelli. Joe Clark and I had gone to Rome a few weeks earlier and returned with Zeffirelli's sketches, magnificently executed as usual, for a straightforward, opulent *Traviata*. (Zeffirelli's sketches are so perfectly scaled architecturally and so beautifully detailed that they can be framed.) The "Love Couple," as opera wags had dubbed Alagna and Gheorghiu, were insisting on doing everything together at that point in their careers. (Nowadays, they tend to appear separately.) They had demanded a look at the production design before signing their contracts, and I'd agreed. With them was their manager, Herbert Breslin, perspiring and looking aggrieved, as usual.

During the Met's tour of Japan in the spring of 1997, I had been treated to a preview of the Love Couple's antics. In Nagoya, Gheorghiu was singing the part of Micaela in Zeffirelli's production of *Carmen*. When she appeared in the dress rehearsal, I noticed that she wasn't wearing the blond wig that Zeffirelli had called for as a way of showing that Don Jose's jilted fiancée was an innocent country girl from the north. With her black locks flowing, Gheorghiu looked more like another nickname the wags had pinned on her, the Draculette.

After the first act, I went backstage and said to one of the wardrobe mistresses, "Where's the wig?" The woman said, "Angela doesn't want to wear it." I said, "Tell her she has to," I said. Out came Angela in Act 2—no wig.

After the act, I went to her dressing room. "Angela," I said, "where's the wig?"

*Louis Lima and Angela Gheorghiu in* Carmen—*without the wig*

"I don't think the wig fits in this production," she said.

"But it's the same production you did in New York," I said. She stared at me as though she'd never heard of a place called New York. "So what's the problem?" I said.

"I'm not wearing the wig," she said. "If you insist on it, you can get someone else."

"Angela," I said, "the wig goes on, with or without you."

"I'm not wearing the wig."

We parted, and I said to Sarah Billinghurst, "Replace her with Ainhoa Arteta."

On the evening of the opening performance, I was greeted in the elevator by Gheorghiu and Alagna. They were in matching powder blue. That's carrying the Love Couple act a bit far, I thought.

"Where are you going, Angela?" I said.

"To my dressing room," she said.

"But you're not singing tonight," I said. "Ainhoa is the Micaela."

"I have a contract," she said.

"But you said you wouldn't wear the wig. You've been replaced."

The elevator door opened just in time.

A half hour before curtain time, Mr. Nakato, the president of the Japan Arts Corporation, which had organized the tour, approached me backstage. He looked as though he were thinking about hara-kiri.

"Miss Gheorghiu and Mr. Alagna are out front," he said. "They are stopping everyone and telling them that you won't permit her to sing. And they want seats for the opera."

"Give them seats for the opera," I said.

"But maybe she should sing?" Mr. Nakato suggested.

The Japanese hate confrontations. Mr. Nakato didn't want to go in front of the curtain and tell everyone that Gheorghiu, who has a huge following in Japan, would not be singing that evening.

"It's too late," I said. "I've replaced her with another singer, the beautiful young Spanish soprano Ainhoa Arteta. The audience will love her."

Sadly, Mr. Nakato went out onstage and delivered the news. I went out to the lobby and confronted the Love Couple. "What are you doing?" I said.

"I have a contract," Angela said.

Roberto looked as though hara-kiri had also occurred to him.

"If you decide to wear the wig, you can sing the next performance," I said. "In the meantime, enjoy the show."

Two nights later, Angela made her entrance wearing the blond wig—sort of. From my seat out front, I spotted a distinctly visible curl of black hair. At the end of the act, I went backstage and raised my voice. "Wear it right," I told Angela, "or I'll put someone else on." For the next four *Carmens*, the wig went on, right.

The Met choristers, as they often do, had the last word on the subject. They made up a joke that made the backstage rounds. It went: "Have you heard what Volpe-san tells Gheorghiu-san? 'Wig or Walk. Hair or Hike. Rug or Reave.' "

Now, two years later, the Love Couple were showing their matrimonial muscle again. After a glance at Zeffirelli's sketches for *La Traviata*, Alagna said, "I've got a much better production." He opened a briefcase and pulled out some sketches.

"What are those?" I said.

"My brother's sketches for *La Traviata*." His tone implied that every tenor of his stature had a brother who could sketch a better *Traviata* than Franco Zeffirelli.

"Thank you, Roberto," I said. "I'm sure they're very nice. But I can't use them. This," I said, pointing to the Zeffirelli sketches, "is the production we're doing. Now, let's get down to the contracts."

The meeting ended inconclusively. Breslin tucked the contracts, still unsigned, into his briefcase.

The next morning, I called Breslin. "Who does Roberto Alagna think he is?" I said. "I have a commitment to Zeffirelli. I want those contracts signed and on my desk Thursday morning. [This was Tuesday.] If they're not here, I'll withdraw them."

Nobody in the opera world ever believes that an intendant really means it when he threatens to pull a contract. Breslin and his clients didn't believe it this time. After all, these were great artists—how could the Met do without them? When Thursday morning came and went with no sign of the contracts, I called Breslin. "I'm faxing you a letter withdrawing the deal," I said.

"You can't do that," he said.

"Yes, I can," I said. I faxed the letter.

The next day, Breslin called and said, "I've got the signed contracts. I'm sending them right over."

"Forget it," I said. "The deadline has passed. They're out."

Breslin, who is a press agent as well as a manager, decided on preemptive action. He called the *Times* and told a reporter that Alagna and Gheorghiu were "reluctantly" withdrawing from the Met's new *Traviata* because the tenor, whose first wife had died a few years earlier, needed to spend more time with his children.

When the reporter called me for a comment, I gave him the real story and added, "Isn't it too bad that Herbert Breslin can't tell the truth."

The greatest singers, as opposed to the merely excellent ones, are risk-takers—they sing to save their souls, not their voices. In opera, risk-taking isn't just a matter of tackling challenging new roles, but of showing the audience who you really are. You can't fake it with opera junkies. They're waiting for that rush, and when they get it they know it.

I've felt it more times than I can think of, though certainly not every week at the Met. Two experiences come immediately to mind. In the fall of 1999, the German bass René Pape made a whole opera out of King Marke's fifteen-minute monologue in Act 2 of *Tristan und Isolde*. At the time, Pape was just thirty-five—an unusually young age for the Cornish king who's just discovered that his wife has been unfaithful to him with his most trusted knight. But with his agile, imposing stage presence, his incredibly flexible, penetrating voice, and his sheer imagination, René delivered the most deeply personal portrait of the dignified, wounded king that I've ever seen. Power and vulnerability in the same breath— that's what the finest opera singing gives you like nothing else. René

*René Pape as King Mark, 1999*

literally stopped the show, which is exactly what a great King Marke has to do.

Five seasons earlier, in 1994, another astounding German artist, the soprano Hildegard Behrens, was so riveting as the title character of Strauss's *Elektra* that when I checked my watch, as I always do when the curtain closes, I couldn't believe that ninety minutes had just passed. Anyone who had seen Behrens's amazing leap off the parapet of Castel Sant'Angelo in Zeffirelli's staging of *Tosca* knows how daring she could be onstage—she was one of the rare singers who love to *move*. Her Elektra was a magnificent madwoman in perpetual motion, vocally and physically. Somehow, at the end of the performance, you felt both drained and elated—another gift of the greatest singers.

Hildegard once said something that should be tacked to the dressing room wall of every aspiring opera singer: "Singers reach and touch the audience and get the message across in different ways. I love theater, and I love acting, and I love the music most of all, but I can't separate them. Opera is music theater, and acting and singing are one thing for me. Music for me comes out of the dramatic context. I never had the temptation to view the voice as a fetish. For me, it's just a vehicle. I cannot consider it as some kind of golden calf."

A handful of singers on the 2005–2006 roster have the ability to make that ultimate connection with the audience: besides René Pape, they include Domingo, Natalie Dessay, Bryn Terfel, Renée Fleming, Deborah Voigt, Ben Heppner, Dmitri Hvorostovsky, Karita Mattila, Anna Netrebko, Olga Borodina, Ro-

*Hildegard Behrens as Elektra, 1994*

lando Villazón, Juan Diego Flórez, and—if he stops taking on every part that's offered him—the young Sicilian who arrived on the Concorde to fill Pavarotti's shoes in his not-quite-farewell *Tosca*. My boy Salvatore Licitra has a natural openhearted appeal that makes audiences root for him the moment he walks onstage. You can't get that in a conservatory.

The risk-taker whose rise to the top most closely parallels my tenure at the helm of the Met is Renée Fleming. From the somewhat stage-shy young woman with an incredibly beautiful voice whom I first heard in her debut as the Countess in *Figaro* in 1991, to the complete opera performer who was so riveting in her recent *Manon*, I've watched the most brilliant American singing career of my time grow, opera by opera. Renée is one of the very few stars who define *state-of-the-art* in certain roles—Mozart's Countess, Desdemona in *Otello*, and the title roles in *Rusalka* and *Manon*. When she makes her entrance, the opera seems to hold its breath as everyone takes in her lovely heart-shaped face and melting eyes. Her vocal lines are so exquisite that listening to her is like watching a bird in flight.

Because Renée is at the top, she gets knocked for not having enough *this* or enough *that*—the "intensity of Callas," the "nobility of Tebaldi," and so on—as if any singer can have it all. One reason for the carping is that Renée is probably the most restless singer I know. She tries on different vocal styles as often as she changes her amazing wardrobe. One season, she's doing Previn's *A Streetcar Named Desire*; the next, it's Handel's *Rodelinda*. She sings in six or more languages—English, French, Italian, German, Russian, Czech . . . and Sarah Vaughan. Critics get huffy because they can't put her in a box.

*Renée Fleming and Marcelo Álvarez in* Manon, *2005*

I think Renée's chameleon ways say a lot about why she's the ideal prima donna for today. She wants it all. She's the girl next door; she's the diva who's dressed to kill; she's classical; she's pop; she's a serious musician; she's a celebrity; she's the mother of two daughters; she's a career woman. And she never gives up. A few days after I dropped Alagna and Gheorghiu from Zeffirelli's *La Traviata*, I got a call from Renée.

"Joe," she said, "would you consider me for Violetta?"

"Of course," I said without hesitation. "The part's yours."

Renée got down to work on a role that's one of the ultimate tests for a prima donna. Then, a few months before rehearsals were scheduled to begin, she called. "Joe," she said, "you'll probably never hire me again, but I can't do it. I've been through a terrible divorce, and I'm not able to focus right now. I won't bring anything special to it. Can I have another chance?"

"Of course you can," I said without hesitation. Four years later, Renée, a bigger star than ever, did her first *Traviata* at the Met. Some people thought she was a little too special in her determination to make this Violetta her own, but for her it was a personal triumph and another milestone.

Another thing I like about Renée is that she intends to be around a long time. Unlike Callas, her flame is not going to die out after ten years. She has more natural assets than just about any singer I can think of. The Met is lucky that she knows how to protect them.

What I, and audiences, love about Renée is that she's a work in progress. And so is the wonderful tenor from Argentina, Marcelo Álvarez, who was her Chevalier des Grieux in *Manon*. When Marcelo made his Met debut in 1989, in the opening cast of *Traviata*, he wasn't ready. But, like Renée, he's blossomed, and his steady growth has put him at the top among today's young tenors in the Italian and French repertoire. Curiously, very few of these tenors are Italian or French. Virtually all of today's most admired young leading men are Latin American—the Argentinian Álvarez, the Peruvian Juan-Diego Flórez, and the Mexicans Ramón Vargas and Rolando Villazón. Some people are already calling Villazón, who was an irresistible Duke of Mantua in this season's *Rigoletto*, "the next Domingo." The most realistic art form lives on unrealistic hopes.

. . .

Opera singing isn't just about the voice, it's about the whole body. It's an intensely physical activity. Crossing the Met stage during a performance can be more dangerous than crossing Fifth Avenue at rush hour. In 1974, when I was still master carpenter, a faulty step collapsed under Birgit Nilsson's Brünnhilde as she was ascending to a rocky knoll. Nilsson fell to the stage. I was mortified and ran over to help her up, apply first aid, the Heimlich maneuver, anything. But she got to her feet and said, "It's okay, it's okay." Still, she didn't finish the act. I felt so responsible for the mishap that I thought I might lose my job, especially when it turned out that she'd broken a collarbone. Nevertheless, there she was on opening night, her arm in a sling. I wanted to go up to her and say how sorry I was, but when the Valkyries' music started, the great Nilsson swept past me without a glance, thinking only of that wild ride.

Brünnhilde was struck again in 1990 during a performance of *Götter-dämmerung*. In the last scene, Hildegard Behrens ran upstage to throw herself on Siegfried's funeral pyre and set off the inferno that destroys Valhalla, sending it piece by piece into many elevator shafts. Behrens had just finished singing her last note when she was knocked down by a falling beam. She suffered a bruised forehead, two black eyes, and a damaged spinal cord. Three years later, she returned for those astonishing Elektras.

In the fall of 1996, I dropped in on a rehearsal of Zeffirelli's *Carmen*. Denyce Graves, who had taken over the title role from Waltraud Meier, was having trouble with the "Habanera." During the break, I went up to her and said, "Some-thing the matter, Denyce?"

"I'm sore here," she said, point-ing to a tender place on her neck, under her throat. "I really got slammed by my opponent in kick-boxing class."

*Denyce Graves as Dalilah, 2004*

*Kiri Te Kanawa as Arabella, 1994*

Denyce is a stunning woman who keeps herself in top physical shape. This is one Carmen you don't want to go up against. "Your *what* class?" I said.

"Kickboxing," she said. "It's great for the reflexes."

"Your reflexes are fine, Denyce," I said. "Stop the kickboxing."

Several seasons later, Kiri Te Kanawa arrived for six performances of one of her signature roles, the Countess in Strauss's *Capriccio*. Of all the prima donnas, Kiri is the most naturally aristocratic. Offstage, she's the gal next door. We've been buddies ever since she made her Met debut—unrehearsed—as Desdemona in a matinee of *Otello*, in 1974. I was standing in the wings, listening to her Act 1 duet with Jon Vickers, and I couldn't believe what I was hearing. When I got my first glimpse of her from the front, I couldn't believe what I was seeing. When Kiri came offstage, I took her by the arm and escorted her to her dressing room—a chore that wasn't in the job description of master carpenter.

Years later, during *Capriccio*, I was in Central Park on my bike when

I spotted Kiri on Rollerblades. "Kiri!" I called out as she whizzed by. "Are you out of you mind? What are you doing?"

She turned and said, "Rollerblading. What does it look like?"

"Take those things off, will you?" I said. "You want me to have a Countess on crutches?"

Kiri laughed and kept going, but the next time I ran into her in the park she was on her own two feet.

# 17

## NO LIGHT IN THE TUNNEL

Lincoln Center has the richest concentration of cultural activity in the country, but if anyone suggested building something like it today, they'd be considered certifiable. Since the 1960s, when the place was developed as a slum-clearance project, it has made a huge difference. You can quarrel with much of the high-rise construction that's gone up around Broadway and Sixty-fifth Street—I live near the top of one of those big, bland apartment buildings, and the view, architecturally speaking, isn't what it could have been—but you can't quarrel with what Lincoln Center has meant, both to the Upper West Side of Manhattan and to the whole city.

This may be America's most successful urban renewal project. Nearly five million people come to Lincoln Center every year. You can't measure the economic impact of that statistic. (A recent study put the annual contribution at $1.5 billion.) Moreover, when you see all those singers, musicians, dancers, actors, directors, and backstage people reporting for work every day, and then you watch the crowds strolling across the plaza as the sun is going down over the Hudson

*The Met, the biggest building on the sixteen-acre campus*

and the lights are coming up in the performance houses, you have to marvel at the cultural excitement that Lincoln Center injects into New York, day after day.

The three million ticket buyers who come every year to Lincoln Center do so for a variety of reasons: opera, symphony concerts, chamber music and solo recitals, theater, ballet, film, jazz, lectures, the Big Apple Circus, outdoor ballroom dancing, and other events too numerous to name. By far the largest number of these ticket buyers— one-third, in fact—come to the Met. The Met is the eight-hundred-pound gorilla in the room. It accounts for 50 percent of Lincoln Center's cash flow. It occupies the biggest and most inviting building on the sixteen-acre campus. I love the zany Marc Chagall paintings behind the Met's glass windows—all those Russian folktale figures swirling around a fiddler. The Chagalls are the only splashes of color in an otherwise almost colorless vista of glass, granite, and travertine. They're huge greeting cards inviting visitors into the special realm of opera. As you approach them, the world feels better. But I imagine that some of my Lincoln Center colleagues have a somewhat different view of them. Perhaps they wonder why Chagall didn't include a devil somewhere—a devil who looks like me.

Since 2000, when Lincoln Center officials announced a billion-dollar-plus campaign to renovate and enhance the campus facilities, I've been branded as the ogre—an obstructionist whose lack of concern for the project as a whole has blocked progress on this vital need.

Do I agree that much of Lincoln Center's physical plant—the central plaza and many of the facades and facilities—require refurbishment? Yes. I've renovated too many run-down houses myself not to understand the value of fixing up a place that needs fixing up.

Do I believe that Lincoln Center should undertake certain alterations to the existing campus that will make it even more attractive and accessible than it is now? Of course. In this country, the nonprofit performing arts leaders—Lincoln Center's constituents are all nonprofit institutions—must constantly think about ways of making themselves less elitist and more welcoming, or, as I hear them saying today, "user-friendly."

Do I think that the Met, given its premier position on the campus, should dictate to the other constituents the best way to go about the renovation? No. Lincoln Center is a collective of many different institutions, each with its own agenda and leaders. I believe in diversity. It's good for society in general and for Lincoln Center in particular. At the heart of New York's economic strength is the concept of "neighborhood." Lincoln Center's constituents benefit from being close to one another and they benefit from our shared mission of artistic excellence.

Have I acted the way I've acted during the redevelopment process because my primary obligation is to protect the interests of the Met? Absolutely. That's what I get paid for.

Do I regard the process as it has been conducted (as of this writing) to be sane, fair, open, and sensitive to the Met? No. Since the project was announced five years ago, there has been nothing concrete to show for all the meetings and studies and design plans. Millions of dollars have been squandered because of poor judgment and poor leadership. If the high-powered people from profit-making institutions who have been involved in this endeavor ran their businesses the way that the Lincoln Center Development Project has been run, they'd be out of business.

Lincoln Center was founded essentially as a real estate venture. As a result, its thirteen constituents—the Metropolitan Opera, the New York Philharmonic, the New York City Ballet, the New York

City Opera, the Lincoln Center Theater, the Juilliard School, the New York Library for the Performing Arts, the Lincoln Center Film Society, Jazz at Lincoln Center, the Lincoln Center Chamber Music Society, the School of American Ballet, City Center of Music and Drama (which operates the State Theater), and Lincoln Center, Inc.—have never enjoyed the feeling of community that you get, for example, at a university. Until the summer of 1996, when I heard about a harebrained scheme to install a standing clock on the plaza, I'd never thought much about Lincoln Center as an entity, or about the Met's place in it.

At the time, the top two executives of Lincoln Center for the Performing Arts, Inc., as the umbrella organization is officially known, were the chairman, Beverly Sills, and the president, Nathan Leventhal. For many years, Beverly Sills had been the beloved public face of Lincoln Center. She was "Bubbles"—the New York City Opera's prima donna in the 1960s and '70s whose rise to cover-story celebrity as America's "favorite" soprano coincided with the establishment of Lincoln Center as America's preeminent arts complex. Beverly is a woman with formidable charm and a formidable capacity for fundraising. She is also a diva who has the diva's desire to be loved by everyone, which is not always a quality helpful to decisive leadership.

Nat Leventhal was a political buddy of New York mayors—first of Ed Koch, then of David Dinkins. Although the primary responsibility of Lincoln Center's president is to take care of the physical campus, Leventhal was more interested in filling Avery Fisher and Alice Tully halls. For Leventhal, getting Jessye Norman or Yo-Yo Ma to open the Great Performers Series, or launching a something-for-everyone Lincoln Center Festival during the summer, was more fun than repairing cracked granite in the plaza or keeping the travertine panels from falling off.

In June of 1996, Beverly and Nat unveiled the mock-up of a new adornment to the plaza—an eighteen-foot-tall twisted bronze pylon with four clock faces, each emblazoned with the name of the clockmaker, Movado. In return for the rights to advertise its name on the city's most prestigious cultural site, Movado agreed to pay Lincoln Center $250,000 a year for five years toward the upkeep of the plaza, as well as $750,000 to produce the work.

Lincoln Center could certainly have used some financial assistance for maintaining the plaza, which in those days was costing the constituents $5 million a year. The clock tower was designed by Philip Johnson, a principal architect of the Center. But one look at the cockamamie thing, and I was incensed. Forget about aesthetic merit. To me, it looked like an overscale trinket, something you'd wear on a key ring. This would blight the single best element of the original Lincoln Center design—the big central plaza open to the sky and unimpeded by anything other than a glorious fountain. The insertion of a trendy grandfather clock ("time sculpture," it was called) would be a violation of the space's visual integrity and a piece of blatant commercialism in a setting created for noncommercial purposes. It was also a blatant attempt by the Met's landlord to impose something that would affect our patrons without bothering to ask what we thought of it in the first place. And it was—though I didn't know it at the time—a sign of worse "architectural" fiddling to come.

New Yorkers are world champs when it comes to rationalizing dumb decisions. Beverly and Nat outdid themselves. "I like it," Beverly told *The New York Times.* "It reminds me of one of the figures at Stonehenge."

"Which one?" I wanted to ask.

Nat said: "The idea is to have both an attractive piece of sculpture and something that would be useful to all the patrons of Lincoln Center." By that he meant that New Yorkers, who are famous for never looking at their watches, would now get into the theaters on time.

*The Movado clock and Dante*

How could you argue with such nonsense? I protested loudly enough that Movado and Johnson agreed to move the clock off the plaza and into a little public park, Dante Square, directly across Columbus Avenue. Again I complained that this would be a compromise of public space— but to no avail. The city, which owns the park, approved the new location. The Movado advertisement now stands twenty-one and a half feet tall on an ugly pedestal in another place where it looks ridiculous. The only

NO LIGHT IN THE TUNNEL

person I've ever seen looking at it is the thirteenth-century Italian poet who gave the park its name and who towers above it on a nearby pedestal. He hasn't made it on time to a performance yet. I loved what Arlene Simon, the president of Landmark West, a preservation group, said at one of the public meetings: "When I'm in a park, the last thing I want to know is the time. Nor do I want to be sold a Movado watch." Why wasn't she running Lincoln Center?

That summer I had another skirmish with the landlord when I discovered that Beverly Sills had approached Harvey Golub, the CEO of American Express and a member of the Lincoln Center board of directors, about underwriting the new summertime Lincoln Center Festival. Golub agreed, and then had his people notify my development department that American Express was cutting back its annual corporate donation to the Met from $100,000 to nearly nothing. I complained to American Express and was told that the company could not afford to support both the festival and the Met. I then called Nat Leventhal and told him that by approaching one of our sponsors, he had violated a provision in our lease that prohibited Lincoln Center, Inc., from competing with the other constituents. Nat said that he didn't see this as an issue of competition. I threatened to take the matter to arbitration and called up Martin Segal, a former president of Lincoln Center, and asked him to be the arbitrator. Marty spluttered, "Could you ask me to do something else?" But I knew he would tell Beverly and Nat about the call. I then notified American Express that unless they reinstated their funding, the Met would be forced to take "certain actions." There was no reinstatement.

American Express had been doing well by the Met. Our ticket buyers charged $20 million a year to their AmEx cards, and as payback for the company's support I had instructed the telephone operators to say, "We prefer American Express." Now I instructed them to say, "We prefer MasterCard or Visa."

American Express wasn't happy about the new phone etiquette. I met with the company's head of marketing, Thomas Schick, who said that he was prepared to give the Met ten thousand dollars for the following season. I said, "No thanks."

A few weeks later, the Met ran a big ad in the Sunday *Times* Arts and Leisure section, announcing the schedule for our next season. Previous ads had carried a line that read "the Metropolitan Opera accepts

American Express, MasterCard and Visa," with "American Express" in boldface. Now, on my orders, the name of American Express was nowhere to be seen. This made Harvey Golub really upset. He called the Met's chairman, James Kinnear. Jim called my handler, Bruce Crawford. Bruce called me.

"Harvey says you're holding a gun to his head," Bruce said.

"Really?" I said. "I don't see any other way to protect the Met's interest on this."

"I'm sure we can make up the money somewhere else," Bruce said.

"Maybe," I said. "But there's a principle here. I'm not going to back down."

Golub came up with fifty thousand dollars. I was not inclined to accept it, but Bruce said, "Take it and say it's not acceptable next year." Reluctantly, I agreed. Months later, Tom Schick and I sat down to discuss what American Express would come up with for the following season. Schick said, "Fifty-five thousand dollars."

I laughed and said, "Tom, you don't get it, do you? American Express is making plenty from twenty million dollars in Met ticket sales, and your service charge is more than what MasterCard and Visa charge. If we eliminated American Express altogether, everyone would use the other cards and we'd come out ahead. I suggest that you reimburse the Met the amount you're getting in service charges over and above what MasterCard and Visa are getting."

He looked at me in disbelief. Finally he muttered, "We'll think about it."

"I'd like your answer sooner rather than later," I said.

Before long, Shick called and said that American Express had agreed to my "suggestion." The Met would get a rebate on the service charge—a nice piece of change. I put my gun back in its holster.

By 1999, the people who worked at Lincoln Center were calling it "Leakin' Center." In the course of forty years, the campus had deteriorated badly. Much of the granite on the plaza had bellied and folded thanks to heavy vehicular traffic by caterers and other delivery services, for which the plaza had never been intended. Loose tiles were floating in the reflecting pool around Henry Moore's reclining nude. Elevators, doorways, plumbing, and electrical systems needed updating. The most visible deterioration was in the travertine. Ini-

*The falling travertine of "Leakin' Center's" garage entrance*

tially chosen for its luminescence, the porous and brittle stone had taken a beating during New York's winters, and in many places it was cracked and chipped. In the spring of 1997, a woman caught her foot in one of the cracks in the steps along the east side of Avery Fisher Hall and broke a knee and fractured a hip. She sued Lincoln Center.

Four of the constituents were in good shape. The Performing Arts Library had started its own reconstruction project. Lincoln Center Theater had done significant renovations. Jazz at Lincoln Center was waiting to move into a new hall in the Time Warner complex at Columbus Circle. The Met had taken good care of itself. In 1990, to celebrate the twenty-fifth anniversary of the "new Met," Jim Naples, our house manager, had supervised $15 million worth of capital improvements, including a new roof.

It's interesting that the initial impetus for refurbishing the campus didn't come from Lincoln Center's leadership, but from the constituents. At a meeting of the Lincoln Center Council in the spring of 1999 (the council's members were the operating heads of each constituent), the labor lawyer Martin Oppenheimer, with whom I had become friendly during the Met's labor dispute of 1980, brought the matter up, in his capacity as chairman of City Center, the landlord of the State Theater. I had stayed away from most of the council's meetings, finding them a waste of time. But I was there when Marty spoke up. This time, the meeting was productive.

It was like opening Pandora's box. Beverly and Nat's first mistake was to hire a consultant—the architectural firm of Beyer Blinder Belle—to survey Lincoln Center's capital needs. I'm not criticizing the job they did—they did the superb renovation of Grand Central Terminal—but there's something about bringing in a big fancy architectural firm with names that all begin with the same letter that encourages everyone to lose their sense of reality.

If Lincoln Center had limited the survey to improvements of existing facilities, the work would have been done by now. An initial cost estimate for basic refurbishing came to $93 million. But then somebody got the bright idea of asking the constituents for a wish list of all the things they'd like to have if money were no object. Suddenly, we were no longer dealing with capital needs; we were dealing with "redevelopment." Suddenly, the cost of the project was $1.7 billion.

Two of the major constituents had dreams of rebirth. City Opera, which had long resented its stepchild status alongside City Ballet in the State Theater, wanted a new house of its own. The New York Philharmonic, having already gone through several expensive acoustical renovations of Avery Fisher Hall, still wasn't satisfied and was talking about gutting the place and installing a new auditorium in the old shell. Smaller institutions, such as the School of American Ballet, the Chamber Music Society, and the Film Society, viewed the project as a windfall—an opportunity to cash in on Lincoln Center's greater fund-raising capacities.

The Met could have benefited from a few alterations. For example, Beverly, who was also a member of the Met's board, thought we should have a bigger lobby area on the main floor. To my mind, none of these matters was urgent. My wish list consisted mainly of a few nuts and bolts. In any case, as we entered the new millennium, it was clear, at least to me, that with the Nasdaq index in a nosedive, the easy money of the Clinton years was no more.

Everyone realized that nothing could happen without a major commitment by Lincoln Center's ultimate landlord, the City of New York. Because of my friendship with one of the Met's most enthusiastic patrons, Rudolph Giuliani, Beverly asked me to join her and her handpicked chairman of the project, the real estate developer and philanthropist Marshall Rose, in pitching Hizzoner.

The mayor and I had been buddies for years. At his request, I'd arranged for Plácido Domingo to sing "Take Me Out to the Ballgame" in Spanish at a City Hall celebration after the Yankees won the 1996 World Series. I'd made Rudy's New Year's Eve by giving him a walk-on part in *Die Fledermaus*. (He played his best role—himself.) It's my habit to show up early for appointments, and I was schmoozing outside the mayor's office with his deputies when Beverly and Marshall arrived. They were startled to discover that I was one of the boys. Rudy didn't help matters when he greeted me with "What's up, Joe?" During the meeting, he persisted in asking for my opinion rather than theirs. I could feel their annoyance rising.

Giuliani didn't need much of a pitch. He was concerned about the ballooning cost of the redevelopment and he wanted to know how the money would be divvied up among the constituents. But nobody had to remind him about the vital importance of Lincoln Center to New York. Within days, the city had committed itself to contributing $240 million toward the redevelopment, to be paid in chunks of $24 million over ten years. The contribution was based on the same formula according to which the city had supported the original construction of Lincoln Center.

The last thing I wanted was to assume a dominant role in the process. Still, I wasn't going to keep my mouth shut. At meetings with representatives of the other constituents, I seemed to be the only person who wanted to look realistically at what we were up to. I also seemed to be the only person who could read an architectural plan—and immediately grasp its practical implications. And I was the only person who asked questions.

I also seemed to be the only person who came to meetings thoroughly prepared. After one meeting, I said to Marty Oppenheimer, "How can you come to these things without having read the material?"

"I don't have to read the material, Joe," he said. "You're here. We all know that you've done your homework and will raise the right issues." While I talked and probed and challenged assumptions, the others sat there like bumps on a log.

The bumps were less charmed by my diligence than Marty. They particularly resented me because I wasn't one of them. In addition to Marshall Rose, they included Beverly, top officers of Lincoln Center, and Gordon Davis, a former parks commissioner who had replaced Nat Leventhal as president. (Nat had suddenly decided that retirement looked better than renovation.) The other participants were the board presidents or chairmen of the other main constituents involved in the redevelopment. Because the Met's president, Paul Montrone, lived in New Hampshire and was rarely in New York, it had fallen to me—the only operating manager in the group—to represent the Met.

Some people of wealth and influence in the profit-making world get involved with the nonprofit world in part because it feeds their self-esteem and enhances their social standing. They don't engage openly with one another at meetings because most of them haven't done their homework (after all, they're not getting paid to do that); because they don't want to risk looking foolish; and because they don't want to say anything that might have uncomfortable repercussions at a dinner party.

I didn't have any social standing to worry about. I wasn't there for self-esteem. What I cared about was seeing that Lincoln Center did its best by the money it was getting from the city and making sure that the Met had a say in how the redevelopment evolved, commensurate with our position in the constellation.

Marshall Rose had done a fine job building shopping malls in the Midwest. As president of the New York Public Library he had been instrumental in the successful renovation of Bryant Park. But Lincoln Center isn't a shopping mall, and the people who use the place aren't sycamores. Rose had on his rose-tinted developer's glasses. "We'll have a master plan in three months!" he promised. Six years later, and there's still no master plan.

Rose hadn't been in his pro bono job very long when he and I sat down. "Joe," he said, "I need you on this project. I'm counting on your input."

"Marshall," I said, "my cards are on the table, face up."

It seemed like a good beginning.

But the redevelopment leadership's promise of good-faith cooperation went the way of the master plan. Increasingly, the Met was kept out of the loop on all sorts of issues, ranging from governance of the project to the allocation of city funds. In January of 2001, Paul Montrone and I sent a letter to Beverly, Marshall Rose, and Gordon Davis, informing them that we could no longer take part in the redevelopment. The letter gets to the heart of what I felt was the proper and just way of going about this massive undertaking, in contrast to the evasive and high-handed approach taken by the leadership:

> The Metropolitan Opera has attempted over the past year to work with Lincoln Center, Inc. in a cooperative effort for the historic redevelopment of the complex. However, we have been consistently excluded from meaningful involvement and feel that we have reached the point at which the Met cannot continue with the operating structure that has been put in place. . . .
>
> The many problems we have encountered, as we have continually voiced to you, stem mainly from the fact that, although the Constituents are the financially responsible parties—the Met's share of the expense of the master plan is 30 percent of the total—our input has been disregarded and actions have been taken by Lincoln Center without our consent. . . . We are in favor of a campus that is both beautiful and functional for the public, but we must insist that the first order of business be the critically needed refurbishing and maintenance of the Constituents' current operating facilities, which we believe is the primary goal of the redevelopment project. . . .
>
> Therefore, the Metropolitan Opera Association, Inc., finds it necessary to resign from the Lincoln Center Constituent Development Project, Inc. . . .

The red flag in the letter, which was extensively quoted in the *Times*, was the Met's insistence that the needs of maintenance had priority over any user-friendly additions. Readers leaped to the conclusion that I was vehemently opposed to City Opera's hope of building a new house on the campus at Damrosch Park, which is immediately adjacent to the Met's south facade. The usual commentators accused me of fearing the "competition" that a new and improved City Opera would bring and of being unsympathetic to what City Opera called its "second-class citizenship" at the State Theater.

None of this was true. For one thing, Damrosch Park was a city-owned facility whose use was beyond the Met's control—though I happened to think that its open green space was a valuable amenity for the Center and should not be invaded by more stone. In the second place, although I supported City Opera's desire to work in a house that was more flattering to singers and was equipped with better administrative and rehearsal facilities, I thought that there were ways to achieve that by reconfiguring the State Theater. An addition could be built to give more backstage area. Movable walls and a movable raked floor could be put in for better sound projection. Movable seats could be installed to create a center aisle in the orchestra section. I was surprised to learn that City Opera didn't use stage monitors—as the Met does—so that the singers can adequately hear the musicians in the pit.

City Opera's finances had improved in recent years. The company had a pledge of $50 million toward a new house from one of their board members. And there was buzz around the artistic leadership of Paul Kellogg, who had made a success of the Glimmerglass Opera Festival in Cooperstown, New York, before becoming general director of City Opera in 1996. But I knew that it was still a stretch for City Opera to sustain even their current eighteen weeks of performances. Nothing I had heard or seen convinced me that the company could support a new opera house on its own at Lincoln Center. Given that the Met paid 30 percent of the Center's shared operating costs, I didn't want City Opera's debt to land on our doorstep.

As I saw it, at the heart of City Opera's predicament was the inability of Paul Kellogg, a diplomat by nature, and Peter Martins, City Ballet's undiplomatic ballet master in chief, to engage with each other. After the Damrosch Park idea fell by the wayside, I brought the two of them together for lunch one day. I pointed out that opera and ballet companies amicably shared many of the finest European houses, including La Scala and Covent Garden. "There has to be a way to work this out," I said. They both seemed to listen to me, though they also passed the buck for the acrimony between them: Kellogg said that his board was insisting on a new house. Martins said that he would make sure his staff would be "more cooperative" with City Opera in the future.

I had dreams of becoming a matchmaker. However, some months later, after the terrorist attacks of September 11, I got a call from Martins. He wanted me to know that Kellogg was refusing to pony up City Opera's share of the costs of new security measures at the State Theater, claiming that they were too much for his budget. "I screamed and told him what I thought of him," Martins said. "I pulled a Volpe."

That wasn't how I would have handled the problem, and I didn't take the compliment.

The Met's pullout from the redevelopment process began to bother members of our board, who didn't like being perceived as the bad boy on campus. I didn't mind being perceived that way, but at the urging of Paul Montrone, I went to work on an agreement with Rose and company that would allow the Met to rejoin the project and free up the city's pledge of $240 million. The agreement we arrived at in May of 2001 sharply curbed the leadership committee's role and strengthened the Met's defenses against potential idiocies that were not in our interest. In addition to clarifying many points of governance and fund-raising, it also reaffirmed the power of each of the constituents to veto any major decision. The Met agreed to participate in the project until there was a vote on the master plan, but we reserved the right to walk away after that, while retaining our 30 percent share of the city's money.

I hammered out every detail of the new terms until I was sure that the Met's position was as impregnable as it could be. But there are certain things that not even an ex–master carpenter can hammer out, and one of them is protection against grandiose schemes that arrive out of the blue. Like a hurricane, this one had been slowly gathering force.

Covered malls were invented to concentrate the mind on one activity—shopping. The builders of these artificial environments hate anything that's beyond their control. What they hate most is weather. There's no weather in a mall. Skies, cloudy or blue, are distractions from the merchandise in the windows, so banish the sky. A stiff wind makes it hard to carry a shopping bag, so banish the breeze. Rain keeps shoppers at home, so banish the rain.

You don't go to Lincoln Center to shop. You go to listen, to look, and to be surprised. Because you'll be sitting indoors with hundreds or thousands of people in the semi-dark for hours, you're grateful for the clear expanse of sky as you walk across the plaza before curtain time. At intermission, you appreciate the fresh air as you step outside on one of the terraces. When the architect Frank Gehry, who'd been hired by the mall builder Marshall Rose, unveiled his design for a glass dome that would enclose the entire plaza, part of his pitch was that it had rained during his last three visits to the Met. I said, "The Met has hundreds of umbrellas in our Lost and Found. Would you like to borrow one?"

When I first heard about the possibility of a dome, I told Rose that the Met would not look favorably on such a massive alteration of the present campus. Rose said with a smile, "You know, Joe, I'm building an entire city in the Midwest."

I smiled and said, "Are you building the people, too?"

Somehow the dome made it to the drawing board, despite my repeated objections, which ranged from the loss of the sky to the cost of air-conditioning, heating, and window cleaning. Not content with glass above, the world's hottest architect also wanted glass below. He added a transparent floor for pedestrians to cross without putting on ice skates. Gehry designs people, too—or at least imaginary ones— and he envisioned the dome as a Montmartre of "sidewalk cafés" with strolling musicians and people mingling and making animated conversation. I was beginning to feel nostalgic for that clock. The more Gehry talked, the more he earned—$1.3 million in architectural fees, some of it paid by the city.

But the dome didn't fly. I dangled the Met's veto power, and Beverly, after months of flashing a dimpled smile at Marshall every time the subject came up, finally decided that she was against the dome, too. "It gives me a feeling of claustrophobia," she said. "And what are the men in the garage under the plaza going to see when the women in skirts walk across that floor!"

Attagirl.

The "coup-de-glass" was delivered at a meeting of the Center's executive committee on October 11, 2001. I was the offstage villain. With the demise of the dome went the last shred of decorum. As I subsequently learned, I was loudly denounced for "obstructionism." My chief denunciators were Paul Guenther, the chairman of the New York Philharmonic; Linda LeRoy Janklow, chairwoman of Lincoln Center Theater; and Bruce Kovner, the chairman of Juilliard. Paul Montrone, who had backed all my positions from the beginning, stoutly denied the charge. Beverly rose to my defense. "Joe is not an easy person to deal with," she said accurately. "But Joe is a sane, rational man."

I try to be.

Two weeks later, Marshall Rose packed it in after telling Beverly, "You stabbed me in the back." How he must have looked forward to returning to that project in the Midwest he'd told me about. What was it called—the Emerald City?

. . .

Since the Met was too big for the other constituents to go head to head with, the redevelopment's leadership decided to go around us. (The point person was now the project's executive director, Rebecca Robertson, a protégée of Rose's.) After we rejoined the project, four "working groups" were formed to address the needs and dreams of the four public aspects of the campus—the main plaza, Damrosch Park, the north plaza in front of the Vivian Beaumont Theater, and the north side, along which Avery Fisher Hall and offices face the Juilliard School across Sixty-fifth Street. The leaders made Sixty-fifth Street the top priority. To keep me as isolated as possible from the process, they declared that only institutions contiguous to the street could be represented on the Sixty-fifth Street committee.

The Met has no facade along the street, but it does have a vital interest there—the Lincoln Center parking garage, which contains the principal drop-off point and parking spaces for Met patrons, as well as the entrance to the Met's backstage. Again, a famous firm—Diller and Scofidio—was hired to make architectural magic. But this time, there was some big money behind the plan: a promised gift of $20 million from Juilliard's chairman, Bruce Kovner.

Like Marshall Rose, Kovner, who runs one of the world's largest hedge funds, also had a mall on his mind—the sort of mall you find in little college towns: a coffee shop, a bookstore, and a couple of restaurants. The Upper West Side isn't exactly lacking in coffee shops, bookstores, and restaurants, but why should the Juilliard kids have to cross Broadway to go to them when they could have all that at their feet?

Diller and Scofidio came up with a plan that, from a strictly aesthetic point of view, was a considerable improvement over the bunker-like appearance of that block on Sixty-fifth Street between Amsterdam and Broadway. But from the Met's point of view, the plan had a major flaw: gone were the entrances to the Lincoln Center garage and the Met's backstage. Under the new plan, the Met's patrons would have to find their way to the house via a circuitous route that might have been designed by Rube Goldberg.

Once again, the Met disagreed. Wagner could have filled a libretto with what Lincoln Center has proposed and what the Met has counterproposed, with what their traffic expert has come up with versus what our traffic expert has come up with. As of this writing, both sides have agreed that the solution to the puzzle is an elaborate tunnel. Like everything else that flew out of that Pandora's box when the constituents were asked for their wish list, the Sixty-fifth Street plan has grown vastly more elaborate and expensive. The cost of the tunnel alone, which started out at $17 million, is likely to end up at $40 million. And it doesn't get you across the Hudson River. It only gets you across Sixty-fifth Street.

# 18

## THE CLUB

The model for the president of the Metropolitan Opera Association was Otto Kahn, who oversaw the fortunes of the company for twenty-three years, from 1908 to 1931. Kahn, a partner at the investment bank of Kuhn, Loeb, was out of a mold different from that of the Met's founders—the Vanderbilts, Morgans, Whitneys, Roosevelts, and Goulds—men who had laid the foundations and made the rules for modern American finance and industry. Kahn was an immigrant German Jew from a wealthy family in Mannheim that made featherbedding. With that background, he certainly wasn't a candidate for one of the boxes in the Diamond Horseshoe. Until 1921, he had to make do with seats in the orchestra, where he felt more at home than he did with the Old Boys upstairs.

Immediately, through generous personal donations, the astute hiring of Gatti-Casazza as the Met's first salaried general manager, and his belief that a great opera house was essential to New York's ambitions as a world capital, Kahn set about converting what had been a profit-seeking venture into a not-for-profit enterprise—one devoted to the highest international standards of artistic excellence and to dismantling the Met's image as an exclusive hangout for railroad barons and their bankers. Kahn had a number of railroad barons on his client list, too, but he believed that opera belonged to everybody.

Kahn may have been the most influential American arts patron of the last century. He not only led the Met into a Golden Age, but he also brought Nijinsky to America with Diaghilev's Ballets Russes de Monte Carlo; backed the career of the controversial African American bass Paul Robeson; was a principal investor in the Gershwin musical *Lady Be Good!* after he heard the composer play "The Man I Love"; and supported the poet Hart Crane, who dedicated his epic poem "The Bridge" to him. According to one of Kahn's biographers, Theresa M. Collins, he once told a New York mayor that "a piano in every apartment would do more to prevent crime than a policeman on every corner." Not a bad idea. Art, Kahn was fond of saying, was "the truest League of Nations." Years after his death in 1934, Tony Bliss was heard to say during one of the Met's financial crises, "Where is Otto Kahn?" I've asked the same question myself many times.

*Otto Kahn and Gatti-Casazza*

When the company ran up deficits of $363,000 in 1908–1910, Kahn and William K. Vanderbilt made up the difference out of their own pockets in return for bonds, which they later converted to stock. When Vanderbilt died in 1920, Kahn bought his stock and acquired 84 percent ownership of the Metropolitan Opera Company. With that kind of position, he could have demanded anything he wanted, but he realized that at the heart of every successful opera house is the separation of church and state—a clear division between the board and the person hired by the board to run the house.

The Met can function at its highest level only when the president and the general manager have a close working relationship and a trust in each other's judgment. A good general manager looks out for the interest of his president, and a good president looks out for the interest of his general manager. In his memoirs, Gatti writes of his desire to take the Met to Paris in 1910:

> I went to Mr. Kahn and said to him, "Will you permit me to give a season of Italian opera in Paris at the Châtelet next year in the spring with the Metropolitan company?"
> "Why, yes," he said, "with pleasure."
> "Only," I added, "we will need a guarantee fund."
> "Of course," he said, "we shall try to raise one."
> And he and his friends subscribed to one within a few days.

I wish I could say that a proposition like that would work out so easily a hundred years later. Today, it would take weeks of knocking on doors of corporate donors, each with its thick walls of bureaucracy. But the trust that Kahn obviously had in Gatti's judgment and the assurance of support that Gatti could count on from Kahn are still crucial to an effective relationship between the Met's executive and operating officers.

So, of course, is a clearly understood noninterference policy. Gatti tells the story of how, at Kahn's insistence, he revived *Rigoletto* with Caruso even though he felt that the tenor's voice was too heavy to sing the Duke at that stage of his career. Caruso gave a terrible performance—and to Gatti's astonishment, the critics loved it. The next season, Caruso sang *Rigoletto* again, this time beautifully. The critics panned him. Don't get me started on the critics.

But in general, Kahn was scrupulous about keeping hands off artistic matters. He once explained: "I know that many people believe that at the Metropolitan my views and wishes are paramount, but indeed they are not, and they must not be. A theatre or opera house must run on the principle of one-man power." Given Gatti's strong managerial style, it was not only a sound principle of theatrical management but also shrewdly self-protective, since it put limits on the generosity that could be expected from the Met's legendary patron.

When I became general director in 1990, the Met's president, officially, was the loyal Cleveland benefactress Louise Humphrey, but the real CEO was Bruce Crawford. (Bruce reclaimed his old title in 1991.) Throughout most of my tenure as general manager, I've been incredibly lucky to have Bruce as my Otto Kahn. Thanks to our long familiarity with each other's working styles, Bruce's deftness at handling the board, and the years of trust between us, I have been able to run the house with a feeling of security and stability. Because I had long since proved my ability to keep a tight rein on the company's finances and to deal with labor issues before they got out of hand, the board did not make the kind of inroads into those areas that it had done during the years when Rudolf Bing would dismiss the trustees with the comment "They pay for it. I spend it."

I can't afford to be as high-handed with my board as Bing was with his. Before coming to the Met, Bing ran the Glyndebourne Festival for a single, wealthy patron, John Christie, who was willing to pay for everything, and the Edinburgh Festival for a government that was willing to pay for everything. He expected the money to just *be* there, and it was. In those days, things were also different at the Met. When times got tough, someone on the board—as the saying went—could "invite Mrs. Rockefeller to lunch and everything would be taken care of."

That's history. Even Otto Kahn might be daunted by the democratic transformation of his beloved opera company. A few facts and figures:

The Met's budget for fiscal year 2005–2006 is $221 million. The cost of running the whole show is roughly what it takes to run the next five largest opera companies in the United States. The Met's expenses represent about 30 percent of the total spending by all American opera companies. By far the largest single item in the Met's budget is the cost of producing a thirty-three-week season in New York. That comes to approximately $143 million. The Met also spends significant sums on touring; on producing symphonic concerts at Carnegie Hall, summer concerts in New York's parks, and radio and television broadcasts; on preparing new productions; on maintaining the house; on paying the Met's share of Lincoln Center's costs; and on fund-raising activities too numerous to mention.

Where does the Met get the money to pay for all this? Box-office revenue covers 46 percent of the expenses—$101 million. The Met's endowment, which currently totals $300 million, contributes $18 million. The Met's share of the all-important Lincoln Center garage and other common revenues brings in $10 million. When it's all added up, we still come up short—to the tune of about $92 million. That's a lot of cash to raise every year, especially in light of the fact that support from federal, state, and city agencies is negligible—$375,000, or less than one-fourth of 1 percent of the Met's total expenses. (In America, we don't give government credit for supporting the arts through tax deductions.) Foundations contribute $5 million; corporate giving comes to $7 million.

This still leaves a very big hole. To fill it, the Met turns to its far-flung "family"—at last count, some 125,000 private donors, whose annual gifts range from $60 to more than $500,000, and who provide almost $80 million, or 85 percent of total contributions. The Metropolitan Opera Club, whose three hundred members keep a reserved section of Dress Circle boxes and who hobnob with one another in their private dining room, makes an annual contribution of $500,000. Two-thirds of Met donors live outside the New York metropolitan area. Somehow, the Met, in its 123-year history, has gone from being a plaything of the rich to a real grassroots organization. And we're still called "elitist"?

Every Wednesday morning at nine o'clock, I sit down with the Met's chairman and president, and the three of us go over the company's financial picture in the near and long term; the current health of the box office; labor issues; Lincoln Center issues; changes in the board's membership. I make sure that my overseers are made fully aware of everything that's vital to the Met and its foreseeable future. I inform them about what we're doing with new productions and who's going to pay for them. I don't ask their opinion about what the productions should be like.

The chairman and the president are responsible to the Met's board and executive committee, whose nine members meet once a month. I give a monthly report to the committee on the Met's operations and initiatives—on new productions, new avenues of fund-raising, and new ways of marketing what we do. There are no closed doors at the Met. Everyone with a need to know does know. I may sometimes talk as though I'm out on a limb, but there are a lot of people out there with me.

The Met's board has three functions. The first is to provide oversight of all operations for the company. The second is to raise funds to support the company through donations by the board members themselves, through collaboration with the Met's development staff to solicit contributions from other potential donors, including foundations and corporations, and through the recruitment of new board members who have the capacity to make financial contributions above and beyond the cost of buying tickets. The board's third function is to hire the general manager.

Hiring the general manager doesn't give the board the power to tell him (or her) how to run the company. It does not include advising him or her on what operas should be performed, or who should direct, design, sing, or conduct them. Those decisions are up to the general manager, working with the music director and the artistic staff. If the board is dissatisfied with the general manager, it can replace him.

As of this writing, there are 105 people on the Met's board, of whom the critical members are 37 managing directors. Each managing director is required to give an annual donation to the Met of at least $250,000. The three other tiers of board membership include honorary directors, advisory directors, and members. The board's work is divided among twelve working committees. In addition to the executive committee, these include a committee for archives and art; for artists and performers; for financial audits; for employees' compensation; for development (fund-raising); for general finances; for upkeep of the house; for investments; for the nomination of new board members; for productions; and for liaison with the Metropolitan Opera Guild, which does fund-raising among small donors, runs education programs about opera, and manages the Metropolitan Opera gift shop of opera merchandise.

A couple of seasons ago, during the intermission between the second and third acts of *La Traviata*, one of the managing directors, Mercedes Bass, buttonholed me. She wanted a new sofa.

"Joe," she said, "the pattern on that sofa is dreadful. It's wrong for the room. I'll buy you a new one. And the desk is in the wrong spot, too."

The offensive piece of furniture in question occupied a central location in the first scene of Act 2 in Verdi's opera of Parisian high life. The scene takes place in a country house where the courtesan Violetta and her lover, Alfredo, have gone to escape the fast lane. More than any other opera, *Traviata* invites directors to set it in whatever period they like. This production was by Franco Zeffirelli. The French Provincial decor of the country house scene had been Franco-fied, which is to say that it didn't have a lot to do with French restraint. "Martha Stewart on a spree," one critic cracked.

I'm very fond of Mercedes. She's one of the liveliest and most active of the Met's trustees. She and her husband, the Texas billionaire Sid Bass, give great dinner parties at their Fifth Avenue apartment. I can vouch for their impeccable taste in furniture. "Thank you, Mercedes," I said. "That's very generous of you. But, as you know, Franco Zeffirelli designed this production, and Franco Zeffirelli likes that sofa."

Mercedes flashed me one of her sharp, witty looks. A born Carmen, I thought. "Well, Joe," she said, smiling, "the offer stands." Last December, Mercedes gave the Met the best Christmas gift it has ever received, a $25 million donation from her and Sid, which is the largest unrestricted contribution in the company's history.

*Yo-Yo Ma, Mercedes and Sid Bass on opening night,*
*2005-06 season*

The Met's board members are constantly trying to give me artistic advice. I don't begrudge them. Their generosity is crucial to the company's survival. Opera is like baseball and golf—a big part of enjoying it is talking about it. These people love to talk, especially about opera. Forty percent of the Met's board directors spend at least twenty-five thousand dollars for tickets each season. They know their opera, not just the scores and the librettos, but also the current fashions in production. When they travel to Europe, their destinations are La Scala, Salzburg, Bayreuth, Munich, and Covent Garden. But the people who make the company tick aren't fans—they're professionals who've learned over many years what's possible and not possible in this most impossible of art forms.

When a board member calls me up and says, "Joe, I'm in Palm Beach and I just heard this incredible young American soprano—you must come down and hear her," I smile and say, "Thanks for the tip." I do not say that someone on the Met's artistic staff heard that incredible young American soprano three years ago. Or when a board member grabs me after the opening of a new production and says, "I loved the cast, but that production! Ugh!" I put on a sympathetic look and say, "I'm sorry—please excuse me," and walk away.

There's something about opera that gives opera lovers extraordinary powers of memory. Nothing they hear today is as good as what they heard ten, twenty, thirty, or forty years ago—or what their grandparents heard when Caruso was alive a hundred years ago. Board members seem especially blessed with long memories, and I have to tune out when they say about a wonderful, promising young Verdi soprano, "Well, she's no Callas."

For the most part, the Met's managing directors aren't the city's movers and shakers, who are generally drawn from the top rungs of Wall Street, the big real estate firms, and the media. Our leading trustees tend to be over sixty and conservative in outlook. Most of them have built successful companies or run successful companies, but they don't have the kind of national clout that marked the Met's founding directors in the nineteenth century. Forty percent of today's managing directors are women—a remarkable increase over the relatively few but distinguished women who played a prominent role on past boards, among them Eleanor Robson Belmont, Nin Ryan (the daughter of Otto Kahn), Sybil Harrington, and Louise Humphrey.

Most of today's female managing directors have inherited wealth or have wealthy husbands. Their growing presence has given the board a more sociable, less businesslike complexion than it used to have.

Well, opera is the most sociable of cultural attractions—it's more festive and communal than symphonic concerts; unlike at museum gatherings, there's no smell of commerce in the air. People go to the opera to enjoy themselves, and like everyone else, the Met's directors are there to have a good time. Because there are no term limits on Met board membership, there is less turnover among the members than on most boards. This creates the feeling of a club—which, of course, has been there from the beginning.

As with all clubs, people join the Met's board for various reasons: some because they love opera; some because they love being at the opera, which isn't quite the same thing; some because they genuinely believe, as Otto Kahn did, that opera is one of the great artistic inventions and that the world would be a better place if more people appreciated it. And some join the board because associating with other people on the board might be helpful socially or economically. As a functioning overseer of the company's fortunes, the Met's board tends to be a "good times" club—competent and engaged when things are flush; less so when the financial going gets tough, as it has after 9/11.

In keeping with the Met's expansive sense of family, the board is also a national club whose members draw their wealth from a wide variety of sources. The current chairman of the board, whose primary responsibility is fund-raising, is Christine Hunter. Chris lives outside Washington with her husband, the head of a real estate holding company. She learned to love opera from her father, J. William Fisher, who founded a company in Iowa that manufactures control valves. The valves were used in the Manhattan Project at Los Alamos—an interesting connection I have with Chris, since my uncle Joe, as chief counsel to the Atomic Energy Commission, was also involved, at least after the fact, in the making of the atomic bomb. Bill Fisher was a longtime benefactor of the Met, and he passed on his passion for opera to his daughter. Chris has a midwestern lady's natural, down-to-earth elegance. She's very difficult to say no to—just what you need in a fund-raiser.

William Morris, the Met's current president, is an investment banker and a petroleum industry executive. Bill has been in the job only since 2003. He's a fast-learning CEO, smart and sympathetic to the needs of a company that relies on human oil.

To cite just a handful of the other managing directors: Kevin Kennedy, the treasurer and secretary, is an executive vice president at Goldman Sachs. Frayda Lindemann is the vice president. Others include: the former president Paul Montrone, the chairman and CEO of Fisher Scientific, a major manufacturer of medical supplies; Jim Kinnear, the retired CEO of Texaco, which sponsored the Met's Saturday afternoon broadcasts for sixty-three years; Leonore Annenberg, the widow of the late media tycoon and encyclopedic philanthropist Walter H. Annenberg; Edgar Foster Daniels, an heir to a big newspaper family in North Carolina; Benjamin M. Rosen, the founding chairman of Compaq computers; Howard Solomon, a pharmaceuticals tycoon, who is married to Sarah Billinghurst, the Met's assistant manager for artistic affairs; Ann Ziff, the wife of a publishing executive; Leonard Coleman, a sports executive; and Cecile Zilkha, the sparkling, tireless wife of an Iraq-born investment banker, who has organized the Met's special fund-raising events for the past twenty years.

Believe it or not, when they're all at the Met, they act like a family.

In 1940, Texaco—the Met's most generous corporate donor—became the sponsor of the Saturday broadcasts, to clean up its image after it was revealed that it had sold oil to Hitler. Today, corporate support of the arts—which used to be inspired by a sense of corporate citizenship—is now largely a marketing decision. When Texaco was swallowed up by Chevron in 2001, the new oil giant had no interest in boosting its image among the opera crowd. The Met was in danger of losing the broadcasts until October 2005, when a builder of upscale new homes, Toll Brothers, agreed to take on the sponsorship for the next two years.

*Alberto Vilar*

The generosity of the most notorious of the Met's donors in recent years, Alberto Vilar, was similarly inspired. In his case, the brand was his name. Vilar was a Cuban American financier whose firm, Amerindo Investment Advisors, soared on the Nasdaq index's high-tech bubble in the 1990s, then crashed when the bubble burst in the new millennium. In 2002, *Forbes* magazine listed Vilar as the 256th richest man in America and estimated his worth at $900 million.

Vilar was addicted to going to opera, addicted to giving money to opera, and, like Kilroy, addicted to seeing his name everywhere. Before his $900 million ran out and he began reneging on his pledges to the Met and other opera houses, he gave, it is said, $225 million to classical music institutions and medical establishments throughout the world. This was a man who liked to *give*—and I wish there were more people with that impulse. Sadly, according to a criminal indictment that landed Vilar in jail in the spring of 2005, where he was unable to make bail, he also appears to have used his investors' money as a "personal piggy bank."

In the 1990s, the Met was lucky to receive substantial financial support from Cynthia Wood, a California oil heiress. Unmarried and highly cultivated about music, she came to us by way of her love of Jimmy Levine's work with the orchestra. (She was also a principal donor to the Vienna Philharmonic.) Between 1990 and 1994, she paid for four new productions—including *Parsifal* and *Elektra*. Her gifts came with no strings—on time and paid in full. She'd walk into my office and say, "Joe, I'm concerned that I'm not going to have a production next year." I'd suggest a project that we'd been thinking of, and she'd say, "Fine." The next day, she'd be back with a check for $2 million. She'd hand me the check and then say, "Could I have a look at that, Joe? I want to make sure I've written on the right account." Cynthia's death in 1993 was an immense loss to the Met and to the music world. You don't get cash on the barrel like that anymore. And the only place she wanted to see her name was on the signature line.

Vilar's gifts, on the other hand, came with a timetable. He was a shy, quiet man who talked a good game to the press, but he always seemed to be harboring secrets. I'm not intrigued by secrets, and he and I had little personal contact. But he was very clear about how the payout would go—strictly on his terms. A pledge by Vilar was doled out in small sums. He was giving away so much money to so many different institutions—and traveling the globe to make sure that his generosity was being sufficiently recognized—that I wondered when all this would go up in smoke. But the Met's board, on which he became a managing director, had its job to do, and I had mine.

Vilar, who liked to see his money on the stage, paid for Zeffirelli's *La Traviata*, including the sofa in Act 2. He also paid for the Met's current productions of *Così Fan Tutte*, *The Marriage of Figaro*, and *La Cenerentola*, as well as half the costs for *Fidelio*. He gave contributions to the Young Artists Development Fund. In all, the Met benefited from $12 million of Vilar's generosity. At his insistence, we renamed the Grand Tier after him and emblazoned his name on its wood-paneled entranceway.

Vilar insisted that the booking operator say the whole name "Vilargrandtier," to patrons when they called for a reservation in the Grand Tier Restaurant. When he failed to come up with more than 50 percent of what he had pledged for the new *Fidelio*, I began to get nervous. The Met covered that shortfall, as well as the $3 million he failed to deliver in support of *War and Peace*. His last pledge to the Met—$20 million toward the company's endowment—yielded not a penny when Amerindo's stock plummeted. The well had dried up.

The first thing I did was to instruct the operator who took the reservations to say only "Grand Tier." The Met's executive committee decided to take Vilar's name off the wall. Some board members thought we were being both cruel and foolhardy. After all, if Vilar's stock had once climbed so high, who was to say it wouldn't get back up there again? That argument reminded me of Madame Butterfly waiting for Pinkerton.

The Met can't live on wishful thinking. Based on Vilar's promises, the company had made its own promises to productions and leading artists. When Vilar's pledges went out the window, so did our balance sheet. It was clear that the board needed to apply better oversight to the terms of major donations and the motives of the donor. Since then, the board's executive committee has been working on the issue, spurred by the fallout from the Enron and other corporate scandals. This, in turn, has forced nonprofit corporations like the Met to be more scrupulous about their financial dealings.

Still, I felt a twinge of sorrow as I saw the name of this genuine opera lover come down—it was like watching the man's personality stripped bare. Alberto Vilar's crash wasn't only financial, it was personal—a tragedy in keeping with this age of big spenders and under-developed egos.

Call it "The Man Who Gave Too Much." Now *there's* a title for an opera, and I know just the fellow to back it. . . .

# 19

## THE NEW CLASS

Opera lovers, for the most part, are supposed to be serious people. But sometimes the barbarians take over. For example, at a performance of *La Gioconda* in 1982, Plácido Domingo, who had a bad cold, was forced to cancel after Act 1. When his replacement, a tenor nobody had ever heard of named Carlo Bini, was announced, you could feel the storm coming. Bini was booed on his first entrance. Somehow, to nobody's satisfaction, he got through one of the most beautiful of all tenor arias, "Cielo e mar." He was booed every time he reappeared. Halfway through the act, the conductor, Giuseppe Patanè, became so upset that he put down his baton and lectured the audience about their behavior. The boos got louder. An argument broke out in the balcony, and a fistfight ensued. One man left with a bloody nose, and a small woman standing in an aisle was heard to shout, "Who's next?" Patanè and the singers plowed ahead, but when the catcalls continued during Act 3, the maestro's blood pressure hit the ceiling and he had to be carried to his dressing room. The incident made national news, but the best account of the incident appeared—fittingly—in *Sports Illustrated:*

"When other audience members tried to quiet the boo birds, fist fights broke out and some patrons slapped one another. . . . Meanwhile, at Madison Square Garden, the New York Rangers were beating the Philadelphia Flyers 5–2. There were no fights in the game. To round out a perfect evening, most hockey fans managed to get home without running into any of that rowdy opera crowd."

The people who come regularly to the Met are every bit as zealous in their attachment to the art form as the people who have a season ticket to the Rangers, the Yankees, or the Knicks. Like the sports fan, the opera fan tends to have acquired the taste early on in life—and, some would say, has never outgrown it. But going to the opera is expensive and time-consuming, and even the most avid fans find they cannot always support their habit.

A case in point is William Rollnick, one of the Met's managing directors. As a boy, Bill learned to love opera by singing in a children's chorus in Cleveland. He avidly followed the Met's broadcasts and collected opera recordings during his teenage and undergraduate years. Whenever he could, he bought himself a ticket to a Met matinee—generally for standing room. But beginning in his midtwenties and continuing into his midforties, he had to abandon the pastime. He was raising a family and making his way in the business world as a venture capitalist in Silicon Valley. Only when he was secure financially and his children had begun to leave home was he able to indulge his love of opera again. When Bill reached his midforties, he took up his old passion with more enthusiasm than ever. The Met's audience is filled with people like Bill Rollnick.

I thought of my friend Bill when I met recently with a group of young people who were on the brink of their professional lives. For some time, I've been teaching an evening course in managing the performing arts at the Stern School of Business at NYU. At the beginning of each school year, I invite the new class to the Met for a tour of the house. The students attend a stage rehearsal. Afterward, we all sit down for a Q&A intended to help the students get acquainted with me and help me get acquainted with them. One of the questions I asked at the last session was how many of them had ever come to the Met for a performance. Out of the approximately 450 graduate students in the room, very few raised their hands. When I asked, "What about the rest of you?" I was told that, between the demands of schoolwork and, in many cases, the demands of after-school jobs,

*Board member William Rollnick*

most of them simply had no time for anything like the Met. One of the kids said, "By Friday night, I'm so exhausted that all I'm good for is going to a bar to chill out."

There's no doubt that the Met, like all the other American opera companies, ballet companies, symphony orchestras, and concert halls, is audience-challenged. Many people are fond of calling the situation a "crisis," but I'll stick with challenge. The situation is serious, but I don't believe it's beyond fixing. Still, it's not going to be a quick fix.

In stark terms, the Met is attracting fewer patrons today than it did before the terrorist attacks of 9/11. Before then, the Met's box office had been selling at a rate of slightly more than 90 percent each season since 1990. The 2001–2002 season's box office plummeted to 82 percent. Since then, the drop has been less dramatic. The 2004–2005 box office sold at a level of 79 percent.

One of the chief reasons for the decline in ticket sales, of course, is the decline in tourism in New York, post-9/11—a trend that's been encouraged by the incessant drumbeat about terrorism coming out of Washington and by ongoing anxieties about the American economy. People just aren't going out as much as they used to. Before 9/11, 8 percent of the Met's patrons were Japanese tourists. After 9/11, the Japanese stayed home—as did the Italians, the French, the Germans, the Dutch, the Scandinavians, the Spanish, the British, the Australians, the South Americans, and many North Americans who live beyond the Boston–New York–Washington corridor. But the problem didn't start with the destruction of the Twin Towers. And it won't end when tourists return to the Big Apple.

Attendance at the Met is changing—not just numerically but habitually. In Rudolf Bing's time, 75 percent of the Met's patrons were subscribers—that is, they bought a prepaid bloc of tickets, year in and year out, which guaranteed them seats at a dozen or more operas throughout the season. Bing used to go on the radio at the start of every season and announce how many seats were left for nonsubscription ticket buyers. The days when the Met, or any arts organization, could rely on that level of support have vanished. In recent years, Met subscribers have accounted for roughly 50 percent of all ticket buyers. But their number is also in decline. Today, the bulk of the tickets go to the people we call single-sales buyers. This phenomenon, along with our own audience surveys, tells us that something is happening out there. Not only are people going out less than they used to, but they're doing less advance planning before they do go out.

Today, there is both more last-minute ticket buying and less-predictable ticket buying. A few seasons ago, our perennial block-busters—*Aida*, *La Bohème*, *Carmen*, etc.—were losing ground to less-familiar works in the repertory. This was a sign, we thought, that people were finally getting tired of the old warhorses. In the fall of 2005, a run of *Carmen*s with a less-than-sterling cast outsold the run of *Manon*, even though that French chestnut had Renée Fleming in the title role. Our best guess is that this was a sign of renewed tourism, but who knows and for how long?

The Met has developed a customer database that tells us something about almost every Met patron—from pattern of residency to pattern of ticket-buying, history of charitable contributions to, as far as we can determine, spending habits. There are 1.5 million names in the database, of which somewhere between 300,000 and 400,000 are active. For Stewart Pearce, the Met's assistant manager for operations, and his staff, the database is an indispensable tool for finding out who our vast audience really is: the moment the Met's telephone order-taker hears your name or phone number, we know who you are. The database system, which is called Tessitura (the term for the median pitch of a musical range), has been so effective that the Met makes a nice chunk of extra income by licensing the software to more than 150 arts institutions throughout the world, including the Sydney Opera House, Royal Albert Hall, the Lyric Opera of Chicago, the San Francisco Opera, and the Kennedy Center.

But at a time when many of the old certainties are gone, we're still whistling in the dark. Today, the Met's competition for audiences comes not only from the theater, the ballet, the symphony, and the concert halls but also from all the smaller opera companies throughout America that have taken root since the Met's spring tours first brought opera to the hinterlands. Time and again, I've run into patrons from St. Louis or Dallas or smaller towns who used to come for their Met fix five or six times a season. Now they limit their visits to one or two. When I ask why, they mention the discomfort of air travel and also the fact that they now have an opera company at home to support. For a supposedly endangered art form, there's an awful lot of opera around. Has supply, I wonder, outstripped demand?

Some of the audience problem is beyond the Met's control. The average price for a ticket is $110, with the cheapest being $25 for a student discount ticket and the most expensive exceeding $320 for a seat in one of the boxes, depending on the night. There are plenty of people around who can afford those prices, but for the most part they're not the same people who used to come to the Met regularly. Today's affluent spenders are apt to be a family with two wage earners who work at their high-paying jobs until seven or later in the evening, race home for an hour or two with the kids, have a couple of drinks and dinner in front of the TV, and then fall into bed at eleven so they can be up at dawn to do the same thing all over again.

Nowadays, the wife, who used to drag her husband to the opera so she could get dressed up and clear her mind of household chores, often gets home later and more exhausted than her husband. On Friday and Saturday evenings, the wiped-out couple is more inclined to drop two hundred dollars in one of New York's noisy new restaurants than raise their spirits with four hours of *Figaro*.

The Met used to draw potential operagoers from the rising, upper-middle level of management at the big financial, manufacturing, and media firms. (The CEOs and their wives always came to the opera, and they still do.) These days, the Met has found that level to be increasingly occupied by hardworking Asians who have no cultural grounding in Western opera. Getting them into the house requires a substantial education process, beginning with an eagerness on their part to be educated in a field that isn't likely to advance their careers, unless their boss happens to love *Carmen*.

Another obstacle, of course, is the general abandonment of music education, not just in the schools but also in the media. Opera, the most worldly of entertainments, has become an otherworldly activity to people obsessed with the "news" and blips of pop culture at the expense of knowing anything about their roots in an older, deeper culture. Today's grandmothers aren't apt to ask their grandchildren to join them in listening to an opera like *Cavalleria Rusticana* that evokes life in the Old Country. And there just aren't many opportunities to learn about opera on the job, as I did.

The Met spotted this problem as long ago as 1935, when the company was in desperate financial straits at the height of the Depression. That year, one of the company's legendary benefactors, Mrs. August Belmont, came up with the idea of the Metropolitan Opera Guild—she called it an association of "opera-minded men and

*Mrs. August Belmont*

women"—to rescue the Met from impending ruin. Before her marriage to the scion of one of America's oldest banking fortunes, Mrs.
Belmont had been the actress Eleanor Robson, for whom Shaw wrote
*Major Barbara*. She took on the better role of saving the Met by making radio appeals and curtain-call speeches. In no time, the Guild had
signed on 2,239 members, whose contributions paid for a new cyclorama. "Small gifts from large numbers" was Mrs. Belmont's fund-
raising philosophy. Today the Guild has 40,000 members who
contribute more than $4 million a year.

From the beginning, Mrs. Belmont also envisioned the Guild as the
Met's educational arm for both children and adults. Her belief that
children who are exposed to opera at an early age will be hooked on it
for life was, as the story of Bill Rollnick shows, right on the money.
She laid the groundwork for many of the Met's current educational
initiatives. Six years ago we started an opera program for teacher
training and for children in kindergarten through second grade. This
complemented the student-discount program we began in the mid-
nineties and expanded a few years ago. During the 2004–2005 season,
forty thousand student tickets were sold.

Mrs. Belmont believed that loving opera made you a better person.
I'll have to think about that. In any case, I'm convinced that she was
right about opera's strange powers of immersion: the more you go, the
more you want to know.

The bulk of the Met's audience comprises some of the world's best-
educated opera lovers, thanks in good part to the Guild's publication
*Opera News* and its series of public lectures, which takes place throughout the season. When I last looked, the topics ranged from *"Aida: A
New Perspective: What If Verdi Had Entitled This Opera Amneris?"* to
"Creating Character with Makeup"—a demonstration by one of the
company's assistant makeup artists, Steven Horak, of techniques that
transform beautiful singers into hideous monsters. In opera, the possibilities are endless.

When I point out to people that the average age of the Met sub-
scriber is sixty-six, the reaction I generally get is a look of horror. The
implication is that if opera caters primarily to people of such
advanced years it must be on its last legs.

Nonsense.

There are two photographs of Met audiences in my office—one
taken in the old house in the 1890s, the other of the first-nighters who

opened the new house in 1966. As I scan the faces and figures, the average age seems to be the *equivalent* of what it is today. Today, as people routinely live well into the eighties, the age of sixty-six is no longer "old." It's also fair to say that people aren't just living longer, they're going to opera longer.

It's futile for people to wring their hands over the relative absence of "young people" at the Met, if by "young people" they mean people in their twenties, thirties, and forties. Trying to reach that group in any significant numbers just won't work. After all, when you're in your twenties, thirties, and forties, you're putting in long hours, raising children, and setting aside money for your children's college education.

In any case, it's not their fault. Opera requires discretionary money for expensive tickets. Opera also requires the time to sit through it. Unlike watching a football game, a movie, a television show, or a computer screen, sitting at an opera is not a passive experience. You can't get up and get yourself a beer or a bag of popcorn. You have to engage with opera—with your heart as well as your head.

By and large, the opera crowd has always been an older crowd. At last they've reached an age where they're ready for it. I did.

# 20

## AT HOME

During a recent Saturday matinee of *The Marriage of Figaro*, I spent most of the performance in my office, catching up on work. Occasionally I glanced at the in-house television monitor across from my desk to see what was happening in the frantic Almaviva household. The monitor is on all day. It keeps me informed about what's going on during scenery set-ups, rehearsals, and performances. It also reminds me that the Met never sleeps—that it's a place where someone is always up to something, night and day.

At the end of the fourth act, when the Count (the Swedish baritone Peter Mattei) went down on one knee to beg the Countess (the Korean American soprano Hei-Kyung Hong) to forgive him, I made my way backstage to congratulate the cast. For me, this is when it all comes together. I love being with the soloists, the chorus, the stagehands, and the musicians as they take in the applause for a great show. No matter how many times they've performed a particular opera, the elation is written on everyone's face. As I stood to one side behind the parted curtain, I heard the audience cheering with the enthusiasm that's typical at a Saturday matinee performance, which generally gets the best crowd of the week. I could almost feel the heat of the singers' glow as they stepped forward to take a bow. I glanced at the stage-hands watching from the wings. They were grinning as though they were the ones who'd been out there singing.

Cherubino, sung by the young American mezzo Joyce DiDonato, got the biggest ovation. After the last curtain call, I went up to Joyce, gave her a hug, and said, "You were great. You've got a real claque!"

She laughed. "Oh, just a couple of high school friends."

I laughed. "It must have been the whole school!"

I went to my favorite spot in the wings—the stool where Joe Green, who opens and closes the curtain, sits. I often perch there and banter with the crew and the technicians, all of whom I've known for years. I watched as forty carpenters dismantled the enormous, peeling Almaviva mansion, which was lying at a tilt to suggest that the Age of Enlightenment was sliding into the Age of Revolution. The top sections were pulled up into the flies. The terrace was taken apart piece by piece. Eventually, the main shell would be moved on a rolling wagon to a spot behind the main stage.

The crew was divided into two teams—one for stage left, the other for stage right. They worked silently, without stopping. This is a young man's job: bending, kneeling, pulling, lifting, stacking. Each

*Stagehands striking* The Magic Flute

man had his assigned task—he does the same thing after every *Figaro*. But it isn't the sort of job you can do in your sleep.

In the middle of everything, holding a clipboard, was the assistant master carpenter, Lou Pavon. I'd hired Lou as an apprentice in 1969, when I was master carpenter. He was still here, smoothly running his umpteenth show. I thought, "One secret to what makes this place tick is continuity."

A few days ago, I was taking a visitor on a tour of backstage when we ran into Lou's boss, the current master carpenter Steve Diaz. "Either you love this place or you leave it," Steve said with a laugh. For Steve, a typical day begins at eight in the morning and ends after the evening performance—around midnight. The crew is given time off for meals, but Steve and his assistants eat on the run. "Usually standing," he told the visitor. "Four minutes max."

He added, "I've been here thirty-three years. Lou's been here thirty-six years. And Bobby [Bobby Carlson, the other assistant master carpenter] has been here thirty years. That's ninety-nine years between us, and we're all still in our fifties." What Steve didn't have to remind me was that his dad, Steve, Sr., had been my assistant before he suc-

*Moving* Aida

ceeded me as master carpenter in 1975. When he retired in 1997, his son inherited the title. It wasn't a case of nepotism; it was know-how. the Met's stage was in the Diaz blood.

Steve explained why he and so many others backstage have made the Met their life. "For a stagehand, the Met is Harvard—the top of the heap," he said. "You're learning something all the time. No two weeks are the same because no two weeks have the same combination of shows. It's not just putting up another *Bohème* or *Aida*. It's putting them up and taking them down in the context of what's happening *around* them. Each show has its own technical requirements, its moving requirements, its storage requirements. With *The Magic Flute*, everything is about the timing—making sure that everything turns and flies and gets onstage and off at precisely the right moment. A lot of *Tristan* arrives through trapdoors—that's tricky. With *Turandot*, there's just an incredible amount of scenery to move. You're always working three or four shows at a time. You're constantly shuffling the deck. I couldn't work on Broadway where *Phantom of the Opera* is playing every night. I'd get bored out of my skull."

I glanced at my watch. It was 6:00 p.m. and most of *Figaro* was history, for now. The evening show, a little affair called *Aida*, was waiting in the wings to be hauled in and set up by seven thirty—from eighteenth-century Seville to ancient Egypt in an hour and a half.

I often stroll through the Met's backstage maze to see what's going on. While *Figaro* was lumbering out and *Aida* was lumbering in, I took an elevator to the third floor to check out an antique luxury convertible. The car, which was made entirely in the Met's shops, was to make its appearance in the new Tobias Picker opera, *An American Tragedy*, opening in a few weeks. It was ready to roll—a sleek, red symbol of class and wealth, circa 1906. Bob Nelson, one of the shop men, proudly pointed out to me that he'd salvaged the steering wheel from a real Model T.

I went up to the fourth floor and into one of the carpenter shops. There was no one around at this hour, but the smell of recently cut plywood was fresh and so were the ghosts of Tex Lawrence's crew, with whom I'd set the place up forty years ago. There were the lumber racks I'd cut and mounted, the tool bins, and, in the same spot where I installed it, the big Oliver bandsaw. I remembered a day in 1968 when the blade broke and I nearly lost my thumb.

Up a floor I entered a rehearsal room. Several young singers—covers for the principals—were going through a scene in *Roméo et Juliette* with an assistant director. They stopped what they were doing to say hello, and then got right back into character.

I went down two floors and stepped onto a catwalk that bridges the stage. I looked down. Thirty-five feet below, ancient Egypt was coming together on the main stage. Midway along a higher catwalk was a little cage. In *War and Peace,* it provided access to an upstairs room that looked into the garden of Count Rostov's estate. Anna Netrebko, as Natasha, and Ekaterina Semenchuk, as her cousin Sonya, had perched there to sing the opening scene behind a window. They had both worn safety cables, but not many singers would have been as brave. When I mentioned my concerns to Joe Clark, he shrugged and said, "Russians will do anything."

I took the elevator to the second floor. In one of the coaching rooms, a pretty young voice was singing something that sounded like Handel. I opened the door: the prompter and assistant conductor, Joan Dornemann, was finishing a voice lesson. "Sorry to barge in," I said. "Not at all," Joan said. The young soprano looked as though she couldn't decide whether to hide under the piano or sing the whole first act of *Julius Caesar.*

I walked through one of the costume shops: rows of mannequins draped in patchwork; bins crammed with rolls of velvet and silk in every pattern and color. I admired a grenadier's costume that had more gold braid than you see in front of Buckingham Palace. Seated at a nearby sewing machine, all alone in the shop, was a seamstress. She looked up and said, "Good evening, Mr. Volpe." I returned the greeting, and she went back to another grenadier's outfit. Saturday night at the Met.

I was curious to see how the newly renovated lounge for members of the chorus had turned out. It was on the first floor, one level above the main stage. To get to it, I had to go through the men's dressing room. Each chorister has a tiny cubicle in which to get out of his street clothes and into the garb of a soldier, a sailor, a peasant, a courtier, a gypsy, a monk. The place had the feeling of an athletes' locker room, with everyone on top of one another, no privacy. The women's dressing room is just the same. I'd recently had a conversation with two choristers about their life at the Met. One of them, Gloria Watson, a mezzo, said jokingly, "Living with the chorus all day gets pretty earthy and familial. And you don't get to pick your brothers and sisters." Talking about life in the men's dressing room, Rob Maher, a baritone, said, "It's like Attica—with lots of jokes."

Working at the Met may be hardest on the chorus. Many members once aspired to a solo career. They trained in a conservatory, studied extensively with a voice teacher, and had a promising start in a regional or a European opera house. But at some point, they had to swallow their pride and look at reality. Perhaps they realized that they'd never cut it as a soloist; perhaps they had a family to support and needed the security of a full-time job. But they wanted a life in opera. And so they joined an immensely talented group of 150 singers (eighty full-time, seventy part-time) and concealed their personality behind costumes, wigs, and makeup that make everyone look like everyone else.

Not every opera has a big part for the chorus, but many do. What with four or five different operas a week and long rehearsal hours, the Met's choristers have more than a full-time job. "It's a difficult life when you have a nine-year-old daughter and a fifteen-year-old son and you're living in New Jersey," Gloria Watson said. "Sometimes you're here from ten thirty in the morning until midnight. You feel like a factory worker doing two jobs. Many mornings I cut across the plaza instead of entering through the garage, just to remind myself what an incredible place this is."

Rob Maher said, "It's like perpetual third grade. You sit or stand where you're assigned. Some people fight for the front positions, some fight for the back positions. *Lohengrin* is the toughest production. The men's chorus is onstage most of the time and we have three makeup changes. The production [by Robert Wilson] is really tough on the knees because it's got all those extreme postures. Everybody's in the chiropractor's office the next day. We call it 'Long and Grim.' But you forget about all that when Jimmy's in the pit and you're riding the Wagner wave."

Rob pointed out something I'd never realized before: the chorus, which spends more time on its feet than anyone else, has a special perspective on life at the Met. "We see things that nobody else sees," he said. "Because we're standing so much of the time, we notice it when there are empty red seats in the auditorium. We feel terrible. No matter what we gave up when we joined the Met chorus, we feel lucky to belong to a wonderful, extended family. This is home."

*The Met's chorus in Verdi's* Nabucco

I entered the refurbished lounge. It had worked out fine—a sooth-ing place for R&R from the rigors of life in the chorus.

I headed to the lowest floor of the theater—C level. It was only 6:20—an hour and forty minutes before curtain time. Already a dozen dancers in the corps for *Aida* had arrived in the ballet rehearsal room. As I watched them sitting motionless on the floor in splits or stretch-ing themselves in various contortions, I realized that I couldn't get a leg anywhere near one of those bars. I also thought, "These are some of the hardest-working people at the Met." Of course, they have to be, because a dancer's career is relatively short.

Diana Levy, the Met's dance director, was in her tiny office. The light was dim, and the air—what there was of it—was chilly. "Isn't there any heat around here?" I said.

Diana, who has kept her trim dancer's figure after thirty years at the Met, said, "We're always negotiating with the singers about the tem-perature. They're always too warm. We're small and thin, and we're always too cold."

Back on stage level, I walked past the soloists' dressing rooms. There are fourteen rooms along both sides of the corridor. Tradition-ally, the two rooms in the middle are reserved for the leading soprano and the leading tenor of the evening. I remember the day when Kathy Battle threw Carol Vaness's clothes out of the soprano's room. It's exactly like the one next door, but for some singers, position is every-thing. Pavarotti always used the tenor's room. Domingo prefers one at

*Julia Welch as a dancing bird and Rodion Pogossov*
*as Papageno in* The Magic Flute

the end of the hall. It's slightly larger and a little bit farther away from the potential voice pollutants on Amsterdam Avenue.

The stage was now set with the enormous columns and masonry of *Aida's* second scene in the Temple of Vulcan. (The Vulcan set is put up first so that it can be pre-lit. It will then be taken down and replaced by the simpler set in which Radames sings "Celeste Aida" and Aida returns the compliment with "Ritorna vincitor!") The set is made of fiberglass, but the columns looked as authentically ancient as anything you'd see in the Egyptian wing at the Metropolitan Museum. The spritzer system I had installed at the urging of Teresa Stratas was spraying mist to keep the dust down.

As the lighting men set up lamps to hit the right spots on the Egyptian hieroglyphs, Joe Green, the curtain man, came over.

"Giuseppe Verdi!" I said, translating Joe's name into Italian.

Joe grinned and pointed out that he was not the only Met employee with the name of a famous composer. "Don't forget about the two Richard Wagners!" he said.

We reminisced about the several old-timers in the crew—men in their forties—who can somehow still keep up with the younger guys.

(The stage crew's average age is about thirty.) Joe said, "Were you around when Steve Diaz [Steve the Elder] came out of the elevator and saw one of our great European directors making eyes at the young guys while they were changing a scene?"

"No."

"Steve said, 'Move along now. This ain't a supermarket!' "

By now it was after seven, and members of the orchestra had begun filing into the pit. I waved hello, and they waved back. Then they turned on their music-stand lamps and began tuning up and peering at their *Aida* scores.

One of the biggest changes during my time at the Met has been the change of attitude among the members of what was once the company's most disgruntled union. Gone is any feeling of defensiveness about being a "pit band" and any sense that they're merely hired hands. Sure, the Met musicians will tell you how much more demanding their rehearsal and performance schedule is than it is for symphony players; how many of their days begin with an hour of practice at home to keep in top condition before getting to the Met at ten thirty for the morning rehearsal; how they sometimes don't arrive home until 1:00 a.m. or later. But then I'll hear a player—such as the first violinist Sandy Balint, who came to the Met in 1956—talk about how good relations between the orchestra and management have become since the 1980 labor lockout and about how his pride as a player has taken a big leap since Jimmy Levine made the Met Orchestra a top concert attraction in its own right.

I recently heard Michael Parloff, one of two principal flutists, singing the Met's praises for committing to a player's "growth over time"—a process that begins when the orchestra members themselves audition an applicant who's playing behind a screen, sight unseen.

I've developed a friendship with Sylvia Danburg, the associate principal second violinist, whose bow was broken by the jumper in *War and Peace*. We met after that performance, when I went into the orchestra lounge to see if everyone was okay. She was still shaken, but the incident hadn't dampened her enthusiasm for playing at the Met. "I don't want to make music anywhere else, even when I feel like my right arm is going to fall off after five hours of *Meistersinger*," she recently told me. "The Met Orchestra attracts people who don't have to be in the limelight."

As the lighting of the Vulcan set began, my second son, Philip,

*Levine rehearsing with his orchestra*

came over. Philip has followed in my footsteps—though entirely in his own way. He was eighteen when he first started working at the Met as a member of Steve Diaz, Jr.'s, crew. Today, he's the Met's sound man—the fellow who runs the system that allows the singers to hear the orchestra clearly no matter where they are onstage, and who enables offstage singers to be audible in the auditorium. He's also in charge of special sound effects, such as the computerized tolling of the bell in *Tosca.*

Philip loves opera and he knows the scores better than I do. He calls the Met his "second home." The other day he said to me, "You know, if everyone weren't so supportive of each other, you just couldn't work here." Like most people who work at the Met, Philip doesn't think twice about contributing to the collection plate that's passed around when someone gets sick, or has a baby, or dies. At such moments, more money gets raised backstage than during a full-blown mass at St. Patrick's.

Now, as I watched the lighting of *Aida,* he said, "How does it look, Dad?"

"Good," I said.

# 21

# THE ANGEL

Peter F. Drucker, the management guru, writes in his book *The CEO in the Next Millennium*, "Increasingly, a CEO's job will be much more like the most complex job I know, which is running an opera. You have your stars and you can't give them orders; you have the supporting cast and the orchestra; you have the people who work behind the scenes; and you have your audience. Each group is completely different."

Rudy Giuliani put it more succinctly when he was running the city: "You know, Joe," he said, "you have the toughest job in New York, including mine."

I recently glanced through my diary for the 2004–2005 season. Here's how the week of April 10 began:

*Sunday evening*
Go with my wife Jean to a "Limited Editions" dinner for the Met's top donors given by one of the managing directors, Emily Fisher Landau, at her private museum of art in Long Island City. Listen to Debbie Voigt sing in the company of

paintings by Picasso, Mondrian, and O'Keeffe. Return home at 11 p.m.

*Monday morning*

Review minutes of meetings I've been having with representatives of the stagehands' union, Local One, whose contract is expiring on July 31.

11:00 a.m.—Drop in on rehearsal of Andrei Serban's new production of *Faust*, which is opening the following Monday. Appalled to see that, despite my demands for an uncluttered production, which I'd made clear from the beginning, the opening scene in Faust's study is teeming with distracting little devils, and the carnival scene is so busy with prostitutes and dancing bears that you can hardly spot the principals—Roberto Alagna as Faust, René Pape as Mephistopheles, Dmitri Hvorostovsky as Valentin, and Soile Isokoski as Marguerite. I make my displeasure known to Serban and to Joe Clark. They assure me that they're still in the "shakedown phase." I kick myself for having taken a sailing cruise in the British Virgin Islands during my daughter Anna's spring vacation. If I hadn't been away from the Met for a week, I would have caught a lot of the *Faust* nonsense earlier. And I wouldn't have caught food poisoning from some Caribbean conch.

11:30 a.m.—Meet with Marty Oppenheimer, the Met's lawyer for Local One negotiations.

Noon to 3:00 p.m.—Meet with Local One representatives.

4:00 p.m.—Meet with Stephen Rayne, the intendant of the Salzburg Easter Festival, to discuss a new production of *Peter Grimes*, which the Met is co-producing in 2007–2008.

6:00 p.m.—Meet with Peter Gelb, the president of Sony Classical recordings, who was a Met usher as a teenager and who later became the executive producer of Met broadcasts and television programs. Peter has just been named to succeed me as general manager, effective August 1, 2006. We discuss how much time he'll be able to spend looking over my shoulder before I leave.

6:45—Meet with Bruce Simon, the lawyer for AGMA (American Guild of Musical Artists) about a collective bargaining agreement.

7:55 p.m.—Meet Jean at the general manager's box for the opening performance of a revival of *The Masked Ball*.

11:45 p.m.—Go to buffet dinner in the Belmont Room on the Grand Tier for members of the cast, a popular ritual I instituted to help everybody wind down after opening nights.

1:30 a.m.—Arrive home.

My phone log indicates that starting at eight in the morning, I fielded twenty calls about everything from fund-raising to the imperiled sponsorship of the Saturday broadcasts to Lincoln Center's proposal for that tunnel under Sixty-fifth Street.

So it goes throughout the week: more fights with Serban about the devilettes and dancing bears; more negotiations with Local One; meetings with the Japanese promoter who's presenting the Met on tour in the summer of 2006, with the Lincoln Center redevelopers, with the Met's European talent scout, Eva Wagner-Pasquier, with Chris Hunter, the chairman, and Bill Morris, the president, for our weekly catch-up; with the executive committee, with the Met's strategic planning committee, and the finance committee to discuss the budget for the 2005–2006 season. I also have a psychoanalytic session with Roberto Alagna after he walks out of a rehearsal, frustrated by my fights with Serban over the devilettes.

In between, I've had 163 phone conversations with callers ranging from Andrea Bocelli, who wants tickets to *Don Giovanni*, to my son Michael who wants to know when I'm free for lunch.

Evenings—three or four hours in the general manager's box: *Don Giovanni* on Tuesday, *The Magic Flute* on Wednesday, *Tosca* on Friday. On Saturday afternoon—*The Magic Flute*. After every performance, I congratulate the cast backstage, then crawl into bed no earlier than one in the morning, wondering how on earth I've managed in the past twelve hours to give more performances than anyone else at the Met.

It's a rich, exciting life, and for many years I couldn't get enough of it. I felt I was on a great adventure, constantly measuring myself against new problems and new possibilities. Unlike Parsifal, I wasn't looking for the Holy Grail, but the quest was exhilarating. Then, at some point, the exhilaration started to become exhausting.

Rudolf Bing called his memoirs 5000 *Nights at the Opera*. The title is catchy but exaggerated, since the Met wasn't presenting enough operas in those days (nor is it now) for him to have sat through that many performances during his twenty-two years running the company. By my math, during my sixteen years on the job I've put in something like 2,500 nights at the opera—the majority of them at the Met, but also at City Opera and at most of the major houses in Europe and elsewhere.

There's a lot of mental activity involved in attending an opera, especially when you're sitting in the general manager's box and listening for a crack in the soprano's or tenor's vocal armor or hoping that a chunk of scenery won't fall on somebody's head. But on most nights, the experience is entirely sedentary. I don't want to blame the Met, but the two operations I've had for a bad back and the two I've had for bad knees must say something about the occupational hazards of running an opera house. Maybe I should have taken the phone number of Pavarotti's yoga teacher.

The exhaustion I'm talking about, however, isn't physical. As I look back on that week of April 10, I realize that all the business clamoring for my attention had become variations on familiar themes. They were no longer challenges to work out; they were problems I already knew how to fix. After I turned sixty, I began thinking about the next chapter of my life. I still had my energy, my health (most of it), and my enthusiasm. I didn't want to stop. I wanted to tackle things I'd never done before.

My great escape from the Met has been sailing. When I'm out in a stiff wind on my forty-seven-foot Benetau sloop *Jean Louise*, the only person who can get to me is myself. It's not me against agents, singers, directors, and a sagging box office; it's me against the elements. When I'm out on the water, I'm free. I wanted that feeling in my working life. I wanted to see how much I still have in me.

In February of 2004, I announced that I was retiring from the Met in August of 2006. I was giving the trustees more than two years' notice because I wanted them to have as much time as possible to find

*With Jean and Anna on the* Jean Louise

a suitable successor and to give him or her ample time to get acquainted with the workings of the company while I was still around to help out. I also wanted to give myself time to put on a new skin in which I would no longer be Joe Volpe of the Metropolitan Opera, but just Joe Volpe. As of this writing, the new skin is beginning to feel good.

Of course, I had more to consider than just myself. I had my wife, Jean, my eight children, and my eleven grandchildren. From the time I started out as a stagehand on Broadway forty-five years ago, I've been accustomed to putting in long hours. My rise at the Met took a toll on my personal life. During my first two marriages I lived more at the Met than at home. I wasn't there for my children when they needed help with homework or when they just needed help. To get to the Met on time, I'd leave Glen Cove at five thirty in the morning. The only other person awake at that hour was my daughter Beth. She'd stand behind one of the windows in the front door and wave as I headed to my car. I had a hard time looking back. I recently reminded her of those mornings, and she told me that when I was out of sight, she'd cry.

I thought I was resilient, but my kids sometimes took a different

*The real boss and me*

view. Until fifteen years ago, I smoked more than a pack of cigarettes a day. One day, Beth made me sit down with her in my living room. Jean joined us.

Beth said, "Dad, you're overweight and you're smoking too much. I'm so afraid that you're going to die." Then she and Jean burst into tears.

I heard what they were saying and I stopped the cigarettes. I still can't give up the occasional Cohiba, though.

My first two marriages fell apart because my wives and I grew apart. I was on a demanding, exciting learning curve that didn't leave much time for marriage. Now I'm married to a woman who's growing faster than I am. Jean reads more than I do. She takes in more art, dance, and music and more information about the world than I do. I have trouble keeping up with her, and I like it.

All my kids, thank God, have turned out well. Among my four sons, Michael, the firstborn, was my first mate during my early sailing days and other life trials. He's a labor lawyer in New York. Philip, as I've said, is the head technician in the Met's sound department. John does social work, counseling young people. Jason sets up shows on Broadway and in Las Vegas—but not with his hands. When you see the roof going up in the current revival of *Fiddler on the Roof*, it's going up because of something Jason figured out on his computer. Don't ask me what.

Among my daughters, Beth is a housewife and a librarian in Glen Cove. Tara is a housewife in Southold, Long Island. Cassandra is a housewife with her own landscaping business on Fire Island. And my fourteen-year-old daughter, Anna, is in the eighth grade in a private girls' school in Manhattan.

Anna, who's a chip off the old block, was concerned about my retirement. She recently asked me, "What will you do, Daddy?"

I replied, "Help you with your homework."

She said, "I don't think so. You better get a job."

Just as opera embraces the entire range of human experience, so has my life at the Met. I've tried to erase from memory certain events. In August of 1968, I promoted a stagehand named Jack Csollany to assistant master carpenter. Jack, who was in his early thirties, had had a drinking problem, but he'd recently married, and his wife was expecting a child. He'd turned his life around. During a technical rehearsal, he warned the crew to be careful about the trapdoors that were open onstage. As he was talking, he pulled some plywood off one of the traps, stepped backward, and not realizing that someone had opened a trap behind him, fell twenty-eight feet to his death. I immediately drove out to Jack's parents' house in Queens to inform them about the accident. I arrived too late—the police had already been there.

During the summer of 1980, when the Berlin Ballet was in residence at the Met, a violinist in the orchestra, Helen Hagnes, disappeared during the intermission. The following morning, her nude body was found at the bottom of an airshaft. An autopsy revealed that she had died after being hurled from the Met's roof. A twenty-two-year-old stagehand, Craig Crimmins, with no previous criminal record, was arrested and later convicted for attempted rape and murder.

In January of 1988, a Bulgarian-born, eighty-two-year-old singing coach, Bantcho Bantchevsky, who was renowned among friends for doing Cossack dances at parties, jumped from the top balcony to his death in the orchestra section during an intermission at a matinee performance of *Macbeth*. One of his voice students, Ludmilla Ilieva, later said of the suicide, "The opera was his house of worship, and I think he felt it was the natural place he should die."

In January of 1996, a sixty-three-year-old tenor, Richard Versalle, died onstage after suffering a heart attack during the Met premiere of *The Makropoulos Case*. Versalle, who had been a member of the company since 1978, was singing the role of Vitek, an elderly clerk in a law firm. In the opening scene, he sang about a case that was nearly a hundred years old. He climbed a ladder to put the file back in its drawer and sang the words "Too bad you can only live so long." With that, his voice faltered and he fell ten feet to the floor, landing on his back with outstretched arms. This time, I instructed everyone not to tell the police about the death; giving Richard's wife the terrible news was *my* responsibility.

Is the Met a haunted house?

I suppose it is.

But for me, it's a house haunted mainly by people struggling to get the best out of life. What I'll really miss when I retire is being the head of such a wonderfully diverse family. My door has always been open to any member who wants career advice, financial advice, medical advice, legal advice, real estate advice, or just plain personal advice. I'm the maestro of referrals. Need an investment counselor? A doctor? A lawyer? An agent? I've got the best names in town.

The other day, I ran into the bass Paul Plishka at a *Figaro* rehearsal. Paul had recently been dating Sharon Thomas, a staff stage director. "Sharon needs to talk to you, Joe," he said. "Nothing difficult."

I called Sharon, and she came to my office.

Sharon said, "Paul and I are going to get married. We'd love to have the ceremony on the Met's grand staircase."

I said, "Congratulations—great news! When?"

"Either Sunday, November the thirteenth, or Sunday, the twentieth."

"Do you have anyone to marry you?" I asked.

"No."

I picked up the phone and called my old friend Judge Michael Pesce at the Appellate Court in Brooklyn. Michael's a longtime opera fan. "Are you free on November thirteenth or November twentieth?" I said.

Michael said, "I'm busy on the twentieth, but I have some time on the thirteenth. What do you need?"

I said, "The great Paul Plishka is marrying one of our stage directors. Can you do it?"

Michael said, "Plishka! Two o'clock on the thirteenth."

I said, "On the grand staircase."

"I'll be there," he said and he was, along with thirty or so "family" witnesses.

Lately, I've been hearing people ask, "How can a place like the Met survive?" The question should be reframed: "In what form will the Met survive?" Can an institution that's been dedicated to presenting the grandest visions of musical theater continue to do so? Will the Met have to adapt to a leaner, meaner time in such a way that it will no longer be the Met as we've known it?

I have no ready answers to those questions. I'll leave them for my successor, Peter Gelb, to wrestle with. Change is inevitable. Change is healthy. But I'm sure about one thing: the Met *will* survive. It survived a devastating fire before it was ten years old. It survived the Great Depression and two world wars. It has survived countless civil wars. The Met is tough.

The Met is also, I believe, unusually blessed. I've never been religious, but I'm convinced that there has always been an angel watching over it. How else, with all that it's gone through, could the company still be so vibrant?

A few years ago, the Met was embroiled in a lawsuit involving a major benefactor's endowment. One of the trustees didn't like how we were spending the benefactor's money. Bill Morris, who had recently been named president, expressed his fear that we would lose a considerable source of income. Bill is a great businessman, but he comes from a world where everything's for sale.

The Met is not for sale. It never will be. Since it's not in the business of making a profit, it can never show a loss. It's a company in the true sense—a collective of singers, musicians, dancers, directors, designers, and backstage and front-of-the-house people of many callings. They all work at the Met because making opera is a job for the human spirit. Who would even think about acquiring a firm like this in a leveraged buyout?

"Don't worry, Bill," I said, "the Met has an angel up there somewhere. We'll pull through."

In my new life I'll no longer be at the Met every night, but that doesn't mean I won't be out in the audience. I don't want to lose the emotional rush that only opera can give you, whether its rooting for Papageno to get himself a girl or feeling Desdemona's terror as Otello comes closer with his goodnight kiss. God help me, but I still get a lump in the throat when Mimi breathes her last breath before the curtain falls. I can see my Sicilian grandmother smiling.

# BIBLIOGRAPHY

Bing, Sir Rudolf. 5000 *Nights at the Opera*. New York: Doubleday, 1972.

Collins, Theresa M. *Otto Kahn: Art, Money, & Modern Time*. Chapel Hill: University of North Carolina Press, 2002.

Dexter, John. *The Honourable Beast: A Posthumous Autobiography*. New York: Routledge/Theatre Arts, 1993.

Eaton, Quaintance. *The Miracle of the Met: An Informal History of the Metropolitan Opera, 1883–1967 (Hypnosis and Altered States of Consciousness)*. New York: Da Capo Press, 1984.

Gatti-Casazza, Giulio, *Memories of the Opera*. New York: Vienna House, 1973.

Gilbert, Susie, and Jay Shir. *A Tale of Four Houses: Opera at Covent Garden, La Scala, Vienna and the Met Since 1945*. London: HarperCollins, 2003.

Harewood, the Earl of, and Antony Peattie. *The New Kobbe's Opera Book*. New York: G.P. Putnam's Sons, 1997.

Mayer, Martin. *The Met: One Hundred Years of Grand Opera*. New York: Simon and Schuster, 1983.

Ponselle, Rosa, and James A. Drake. *Ponselle: A Singer's Life*. New York: Doubleday, 1982.

Wecter, Dixon. *The Saga of American Society: A Record of Social Aspiration, 1607–1937*. New York: Charles Scribner's Sons, 1970.

Zeffirelli, Franco. *Zeffirelli: An Autobiography*. New York: Weidenfeld and Nicolson, 1986.

# INDEX

Page numbers in *italics* refer to illustrations.

# ILLUSTRATION CREDITS

| | |
|---|---|
| 1, 9, 10, 11, 12, 15, 21, 281, 282 | Collection of Joseph Volpe |
| 24, 78, 98, 108 | Henry Grossman |
| 31, 32, 35, 37, 41, 53, 56, 72, 133, 156, 210, 248 | Metropolitan Opera Archives |
| 43, 48, 49, 69, 191 | Metropolitan Opera Archives/Louis Mélançon |
| 64, 71, 192 | Metropolitan Opera Archives/James Hefferman |
| 76 | Metropolitan Opera Archives/Jack Mitchell |
| 86 | Joyce Balint |
| 93 | Tommy Leonardi |
| 111, 135, 180, 216, 224, 228, 256 | Metropolitan Opera Archives/Winnie Klotz |
| 117 | Michael Avedon |
| 119 | *Connoisseur* magazine/Carter Goodrich 12/89 |
| 124 | Robert Messick |
| 128 | Metropolitan Opera Press Department/ Jörg Reichardt |
| 137, 196, 203, 207, 217, 227, 261, 268, 269, 273, 274, 276 | Nancy Ellison |
| 146, 175 | Metropolitan Opera Press Department |
| 152 | Metropolitan Opera Archives/ Caricature by G. Viafora |
| 159 | Metropolitan Opera Archives/Erika Davidson |
| 162 | Metropolitan Opera Archives/Beth Bergman |
| 171 | Metropolitan Opera Archives/Clive Barda |

A NOTE ABOUT THE AUTHORS


JOSEPH VOLPE was born in Brooklyn and lives
in New York with his wife and daughter.

CHARLES MICHENER is the coauthor of two
previous books and has written cultural profiles
and criticism for many leading publications.

A NOTE ON THE TYPE

The text of this book was set in Weiss, a typeface designed in Germany by Emil Rudolf Weiss (1875–1942). The design of the roman was completed in 1928 and that of the italic in 1931. Both are well balanced and even in color, and both reflect the subtle skill of a fine calligrapher.

COMPOSED BY

*North Market Street Graphics, Lancaster, Pennsylvania*

PRINTED AND BOUND BY

*Berryville Graphics, Berryville, Virginia*

DESIGNED BY

*Iris Weinstein*